When Black

MW01201816

This book draws from the successes of award-winning schools, teachers, students, and parents to help leaders understand how they can positively change the educational experience of Black students.

When Black Students Excel offers real-life examples of outstanding elementary, middle, and high schools where teachers and school leaders have rejected policies and practices built upon deficit perceptions about the capacity of Black students. Chapters highlight leadership implications and offer specific suggestions for educators who are seeking to transform their schools in ways that advance the success of Black students. This practical guide includes questions to ask students and their parents, self-assessment tools, and an array of leadership and teaching practices that are effective to empower Black students, elevate school attendance and academic engagement, and improve other important outcomes.

Unpacking important themes that influence the success of Black students, this book is a useful tool for educators who are seeking to understand how they can change programs, procedures, and practices in ways that engage and empower Black students.

Joseph F. Johnson, Jr. is Founding Executive Director of the National Center for Urban School Transformation, Dean Emeritus of the College of Education, and Professor Emeritus of Educational Leadership at San Diego State University, USA.

Cynthia L. Uline is former Director of the National Center for the 21st Century Schoolhouse and Professor Emeritus of Educational Leadership at San Diego State University, USA.

Stanley J. Munro, Jr. is Executive Coach and Superintendent in Residence with the National Center for Urban School Transformation (NCUST) at San Diego State University, USA.

Praise for this Book

"*When Black Students Excel* is the book I have been waiting on for over 30 years. Finally, a book that sheds the deficit narrative about Black children and provides a blueprint for schools who serve these students. Black children are brilliant, and this book provides the type of insight that will allow any sincere educator to bring this brilliance to the surface. Bravo!"

– Anthony Muhammad, *author of* Transforming School Culture *and* Overcoming the Achievement Gap Trap, *among others*

"At long last, a timely book from Joe Johnson and his NCUST colleagues on what works, not only in moving the needle on Black student performance, but also in getting results for all historically underserved students. Examples of urban schools in different parts of the country that are beating the odds in measurable ways are the meat and potatoes of this long-overdue volume, which celebrates Black student excellence throughout. As someone who has served as superintendent of two large urban systems, a state board of education member, and a founding executive director of a state educational agency, I could have used this practical guide to improving student performance many years ago, but I now celebrate the fact that it's finally here! Thank you, NCUST!"

– Carl Cohn, *Former Superintendent of Long Beach Unified School District, Former Director of the California Commission on Educational Excellence*

"This deeply important work transcends commonly held narratives and popular notions about Black student 'underachievement.' The writing gives those of us who toil on behalf of closing the opportunity gap more than a glimmer of hope, so to speak, as the book inspires innovation while challenging education leaders to dig deeper. In my work on the California Association of Black School Educator's Blueprint for Education Equity, and having activated strategies on behalf of Black students in Compton Unified

School District, I can say with certainty that the exemplars called out offer great promise for our work."

"*When Black Students Excel* is a powerful volume that demonstrates the role that schools and educators have in fostering environments that are conducive to Black student success. The book represents a meld of research, insights from practitioners, and powerful case studies from six schools that show that a culture of love is central to empowering Black students, their families, and their communities. The book highlights schools where Black students succeed because of district leaders, school leaders, and teachers who implemented anti-racist practices that begin with an authentic belief that Black students can and will succeed! I believe this volume is a must-read for every educator who is committed to demonstrating that Black minds matter in education."

"The authors of this book have been successfully doing the best urban school transformation work I have seen. In this book, which is focused on successful schools for Black students, they first detail what six urban schools each did to create supportive, successful learning environments for Black students. They then discuss the three major themes that emerged from close study of the six schools. If you want to learn about these schools from some scholars you can totally trust, read this book now."

"Many years ago, Ron Edmunds challenged us to effectively educate African American children. He was emphatic that we had the tools and resources that were needed to educate our children. What was missing in many cases was the will to do what was best for our children. In *When Black Students Excel: How Schools Can Engage and Empower Black Students*, Johnson and his colleagues at San Diego State University's National Center for Urban School Transformation answer Edmunds's call. Working with various stakeholders in several urban school districts, they produced results which confirm and validate the dictum that all children can, indeed, learn.

Backing up their bold opening statement, in which they express their belief that *Black children are born brilliant*, they present evidence and case studies which are replicable. Doing so provides other educators with a guide which they may employ as they endeavor to improve the education outcomes of their students."

— **Fadhilika Atiba-Weza**, *Executive Director, National Alliance of Black School Educators*

"When Black Students Excel is a must-read for every educator and policy maker. The educators in this book clearly understand that if our schools are not successful, it is not the fault of the students but the adults. The foundation of this democratic nation is based on the promise that all citizens have an inalienable right to life, liberty, and the pursuit of happiness. The caste system in education makes mockery of this promise to Black students. *When Black Students Excel* illustrates the possibility of excellence for all regardless of their life circumstances."

— **Shirley N. Weber**, *PhD, California Secretary of State*

Other Eye On Education Books
Available from Routledge
(www.routledge.com/eyeoneducation)

When Black Students Excel

How Schools Can Engage and Empower Black Students

Joseph F. Johnson, Jr.,
Cynthia L. Uline, and
Stanley J. Munro, Jr.

Routledge
Taylor & Francis Group

NEW YORK AND LONDON

Cover image: © Getty Images

First published 2023
by Routledge
605 Third Avenue, New York, NY 10158

and by Routledge
4 Park Square, Milton Park, Abingdon, Oxon, OX14 4RN

Routledge is an imprint of the Taylor & Francis Group, an informa business

Library of Congress Cataloging-in-Publication Data
Names: Johnson, Joseph F., Jr., author.
Title: When Black students excel : how schools can engage and empower Black students / Joseph F. Johnson, Cynthia L. Uline, and Stanley Munro.
Description: First Edition. | New York : Routledge, 2023. | Includes bibliographical references.
Identifiers: LCCN 2022021631 (print) | LCCN 2022021632 (ebook) | ISBN 9781032234328 (Hardback) | ISBN 9781032234854 (Paperback) | ISBN 9781003277910 (eBook)
Subjects: LCSH: African American children—Education—Case studies. | Public schools—United States—Citizen participation—Case studies. | Charter schools—United States—Case studies. | School improvement programs—United States.
Classification: LCC LC2717 .J65 2023 (print) | LCC LC2717 (ebook) | DDC 371.829/96073—dc23/eng/20220727
LC record available at https://lccn.loc.gov/2022021631
LC ebook record available at https://lccn.loc.gov/2022021632

ISBN: 978-1-032-23432-8 (hbk)
ISBN: 978-1-032-23485-4 (pbk)
ISBN: 978-1-003-27791-0 (ebk)

DOI: 10.4324/9781003277910

Typeset in Optima
by Apex CoVantage, LLC

Contents

Part II: How Schools Can Engage and Empower Black Students 125

Preface

We believe Black children are born brilliant. Their family trees are planted in deep, rich soils of intellectual curiosity, creativity, and wisdom. Black children have inherited abundant persistence, determination, and resilience. They possess tremendous capacity to excel academically.

Simultaneously, we acknowledge that on almost all indicators of academic performance, Black children in the United States perform at lower levels than children from all other racial/ethnic groups. From preschool through graduate school, Black students are less likely to attend school regularly; be enrolled in challenging courses or programs; earn high grade point averages; demonstrate essential skills related to literacy and numeracy; perform well on local, state, or national assessments; graduate; and persist to higher levels of educational attainment. They are more likely to be punished for minor infractions of school rules, receive failing grades, receive suspensions or expulsions, receive referrals to special education, be retained to repeat a grade or a course, and end their formal education prematurely.

Social psychologist Leon Festinger suggested that when our beliefs conflict with our experiences, the discomfort is powerful, causing us to try to reduce the dissonance. In response, we either 1) change our beliefs based on the evidence we experience, 2) seek new/additional evidence that confirms what we believe, or 3) discount the importance of the contradictory evidence so that it is easier to cling to our beliefs (Festinger, 1957).

For those of us who sincerely believe that Black students possess tremendous capacity to excel, dismal results across so many indicators generate anguish, distress, and dissonance. We, who fervently believe that Black children can be among our nation's highest-achieving students, ache when we see the wasted human potential reflected in low reading levels, high suspension rates, alarming course failure rates, and overrepresentations in special education. We acknowledge the many factors that contribute to opportunity gaps, urgency gaps, and ultimately, achievement gaps among various racial/ethnic groups in our country; however, we refuse to discount the power of schools to create learning environments in which Black students excel.

We acknowledge the horrible impact of poverty on children across our nation, and we deplore our nation's insistence upon policies that perpetuate poverty and homelessness while vigorously promoting opportunities for multimillionaires to become multibillionaires. This book, however, is about schools that lead Black children who live in low-income communities to achieve remarkable indicators of academic success. This book is about schools where Black children learn to see their humble economic circumstances as springboards for their future successes. This book is about schools that offer Black children real hope that, as adults, they will escape poverty and raise families that may never experience poverty.

Similarly, we do not excuse the inadequate and inequitable funding of public education and public education facilities throughout America. Although the US Constitution assigns states the responsibility of establishing systems for financing public education, most states perpetuate systems that provide far fewer resources to schools serving predominantly Black students than provided to schools serving predominantly White students. Often, states choose to fund districts substantially through property tax revenues, even though poorer communities could never generate comparable per-student revenues because of their limited tax bases. Nonetheless, this book is about schools where Black students achieve comparable or even better learning outcomes than schools in more affluent communities in their states. Generally, the schools featured in this book do not have more or better resources than other schools within their neighborhoods or districts; however, they have teams of educators who are committed to making every resource matter in a way that advances the success of the students they serve.

While we are excited to see some colleges and universities reduce their reliance on standardized tests to determine admission eligibility, we recognize that our public education system continues to suffer from an overreliance on standardized assessments that claim to be focused on objective academic criteria, even though they retain features of discriminatory norm-referenced assessments. This book, however, is about schools where Black students outperform statewide averages on standardized assessments, as well as many other academic indicators. In the schools that are the focus of this book, educators focus less on the imperfections of the scales used to measure what their students have learned and focus more on ensuring that Black students are fed abundant quantities of intellectually nutritious content, especially content that students perceive as relevant to their lives.

We do not excuse the inadequate number of qualified teachers and school administrators in this country. As well, we do not excuse the inadequate number of qualified teachers and school administrators of color. We recognize that our nation can and should do much more to ensure that all children have access to teachers, counselors, support personnel, and administrators who reflect our children's rich racial/ethnic diversity. This book, however, is about schools that recruited, hired, trained, and retained teams of talented, caring, and committed educators despite the limitations of the systems that surround them.

Similarly, we do not excuse publishers who continue to produce educational materials that Black children are likely to perceive as alien to their experience, backgrounds, and interests. Neither the occasionally colored-in pictures of Dick and Jane nor the ad nauseum chapters about slavery in America are likely to inspire a strong sense of personal efficacy among Black students. However, this book is about schools where educators create lessons that resonate with Black students. Often, without much or any help from textbooks, workbooks, or educational software products, educators in these schools create lessons that help Black students see mathematics as a tool for promoting their success in life, explore science as leverage for improving the lives of their families and their communities, experience literacy and social science as windows for understanding themselves and others with whom they share the world, and enjoy art, music, drama, and dance as expression of their beautiful humanity as well as the humanity of others throughout the world.

We do not excuse teacher unions who promote policies that decrease the likelihood that Black students will access experienced and qualified teachers, nor do we excuse school boards that agree to such policies as they negotiate away the rights of Black children to receive a high-quality education. We do not excuse Black parents who shirk their responsibility to do their utmost to support their children's education, nor do we excuse teachers and school administrators who establish school environments that are hostile to Black parents who seek to engage constructively to promote their children's school success. Especially, we do not excuse politicians (regardless of party affiliation) who persistently blame teachers, parents, school administrators, and students and assume no accountability for developing systems that enhance the likelihood that all students (and, particularly, all Black students) will excel. Instead, this book is about schools where administrators and teachers have reached out and collaborated with parents, students, community organizations, and businesses to build a powerful sense of collective efficacy, despite the many challenges that confront their efforts to lead Black children to academic success.

This book is a response to the dissonance many of us experience as we hold tightly to our belief in the capacity of Black children to excel academically. Wave after wave of disappointing academic indicators suggest we should be satisfied with tiny incremental improvements, considering the poverty Black students experience, or the unfair funding systems plaguing our schools, or the imperfections of state assessments, or other indicators of educational success, or the lack of well-trained teachers and school administrators who are committed to the success of Black students, or the paucity of curricular resources designed to promote the success of Black students, or the lack of political will to change systems in ways that address any of these issues. We recognize that the educational outcomes achieved by Black children are the result of systems that were not designed to promote the success of Black children. Yet we are inspired by the accomplishments of a small number of elementary, middle, and high schools that provide compelling evidence that educational success for Black students is attainable now. By sharing their stories and describing their common practices and approaches, we hope to inform and inspire teachers, principals, school support personnel, district leaders, parents, and policy makers who still believe that Black children are born brilliant. We hope that the examples provided by these schools will guide school administrators, teachers, parents, and policy makers in implementing practical changes that generate meaningful improvements in educational outcomes for Black children throughout our nation. We hope to provoke state and federal policy makers, mayors, school board members, superintendents, central office administrators, principals, counselors, school social workers and psychologists, teachers from every race and ethnicity, parents, and students to take constructive, immediate, substantial, and sustained action based on the lessons learned from the outstanding practices that have led Black students to outstanding successes in the schools we describe in this book. If it has been done, it can be done again, even better!

Over 40 years ago, Ronald Edmonds wrote:

> We can, whenever and wherever we choose, successfully teach all children whose schooling is of interest to us. We already know more than we need to do that. Whether or not we do it must finally depend on how we feel about the fact that we haven't so far.
>
> (Edmonds, 1979, p. 23)

Since 2005, the National Center for Urban School Transformation (NCUST) has been identifying, awarding, and studying remarkable elementary, middle, and high schools that 1) served predominantly low-income students, 2) did not use selective admissions criteria, and 3) achieved outstanding results for every racial/ethnic group served. This book is based on what we learned from educators in these typical schools that achieved very atypical results. More specifically, however, this book is about what we learned from six of those outstanding schools where Black students achieved outstanding evidence of academic success.

Intended Audience

This book is written for everyone who can and should play a role in improving public education for Black students in America. The book provides many examples that teachers, principals, and other school personnel will find immediately applicable. Additionally, however, the book explains concrete implications for district-level administrators and policy makers at all levels. As well, parents will find this book useful as they endeavor to work with school and district-level leaders and policy makers to generate changes that better serve students of color.

We are particularly hopeful that institutions that prepare educators will choose to use this book in their efforts to prepare teachers, principals, and other school professionals. It would be wonderful if colleges and universities chose to lead transformational efforts by preparing educators and educational leaders to understand how they can become equity champions by emulating the practices described in this book.

About the Schools Studied, Awarded, and Featured in This Book

Each year since 2005, NCUST publishes and disseminates a set of award criteria (see https://ncust.com/americas-best-urban-schools-award-eligibility-criteria/); solicits nominations from state superintendents, local urban superintendents, and leaders of schools that won various national and state-level distinctions; and begins a rigorous process of identifying schools for the America's Best Urban Schools Award (previously called the National Excellence in Urban Education Award). The six schools featured in this book are among the 167 schools that have won the America's Best Urban Schools Award. The award criteria and process described below have also been described in *Teaching Practices from America's Best Urban Schools* (Johnson et al., 2019).

From the beginning, the award program was designed to identify schools that achieved both excellent and equitable learning results. We looked for urban schools with learning results (e.g., student success rates, graduation rates, state assessment scores, attendance rates, etc.) that were comparable to the results achieved in respected suburban schools. At the same time, we insisted that award winners demonstrate considerable evidence of high rates of academic success for all demographic groups they served, specifically students of color and students from families who met low-income criteria. Some of the schools awarded might be considered turnaround schools because they improved dramatically over a short period of time. Other award-winning schools had a long history of impressive academic successes.

Schools could not earn the America's Best Urban Schools Award simply by achieving strong overall learning results. Instead, schools were also required to provide evidence that every racial/ethnic/income group served was achieving at rates that exceeded state averages for all students. We sought to identify, award, and study schools that evidenced both excellence and equity in learning results. This focus on both equity and excellence makes the America's Best Urban Schools Award different from many other award programs. For example, some programs focus solely on measures of excellence without attention to the levels of attainment of the diverse groups of students served. As well, some award programs focus solely on schools that demonstrate impressive progress for diverse populations of students. Also, some award programs (like the National Blue Ribbon Schools Program) include two separate and distinct programs, one focused on excellence (high rates of academic attainment), and one focused on equity (growth for diverse populations of students). In contrast, NCUST has sought to award and study urban schools with evidence of both excellence and equity in student learning outcomes.

To apply for the award, schools had to demonstrate that they served large percentages of students who typically were not served well in public schools. Minimally, the school had to be in an area designated by the US Census Bureau as a metropolitan statistical area. These areas have populations of at least 50,000 residents. This broad definition allowed us to consider schools that were in inner-ring suburbs, such as Maplewood, Missouri (bordering St. Louis). As well, award winners have included many schools in typical big-city urban districts, such as the New York City Public Schools, Miami-Dade County Schools, and the Los Angeles Unified School District.

Some might think that this book does not apply to their school or district because they are not located within an "urban" area. While the schools discussed in this book all met the urban criteria described prior, this book is about schools that overcame a variety of challenges to achieve outstanding learning results for every demographic group of students they serve.

To ensure that applicant schools were grappling with and overcoming the real challenges associated with educating typical urban students, applicants were required to guarantee they did not use admission policies that allowed them to select students with better academic records or potential or to reject students with fewer academic qualifications. NCUST disqualified schools that required students to take entrance tests or maintain certain grade point averages. Magnet schools or charter schools could apply only if they accepted students on a first-come, first-served basis or if they used lotteries and/or attendance areas to determine which students would be enrolled. Of course, this restriction eliminated many outstanding schools from our consideration. However, by excluding schools with selective admission policies, NCUST helped ensure that the schools we identified were achieving atypical learning results for typical urban students. The majority of schools awarded have been typical public schools that serve students who live in the neighborhood surrounding the school; however, approximately 11% of the schools awarded have been charter schools.

It is also important to note that applicants had to serve predominantly low-income communities. In elementary schools, at least 60% of the students had to qualify for the federal free- or reduced-price meal program. Often, students in secondary schools are reluctant to apply for free-meal programs (even though they may not be more affluent than their siblings in elementary school). Consequently, we considered middle schools if at least 50% of the students met the low-income criteria, and we considered high schools if at least 40% of the students met low-income criteria. Even with these lenient criteria, in most of the schools NCUST awarded, over 75% of the students served met the family income criteria for the federal free- or reduced-price meal program.

School Effectiveness Criteria

Applicants for the America's Best Urban Schools Award were required to meet multiple criteria related to excellence and equity (not just good test scores). For example, NCUST looked carefully at attendance rates, graduation rates, participation in advanced courses of study, suspension/expulsion rates, college entrance exam scores, and a variety of other indicators. For many indicators, applicants had to present data for the entire school population served, as well as data for each demographic group served. Applicants had to show that they maintained average daily attendance rates of at least 92%. They had to demonstrate very low suspension rates for all students and for every demographic group they served. High schools had to demonstrate strong graduation rates for all students and for every demographic group they served.

Results from state standardized tests were a critical determinant for many schools. Applicants were required to demonstrate that a higher percentage of their students achieved proficient or advanced academic levels than the statewide percentage of students who achieved proficient or advanced levels. On at least half of the tests administered for state accountability purposes, the school had to perform at or above the state average for two consecutive years.

Additionally, schools were required to show evidence of strong academic accomplishment for every racial/ethnic group of students they served. For each demographic group served, the school was required to demonstrate that the percentage of students performing at the proficient or advanced level was equal to or higher than the statewide percentage of all students who performed at those levels. Schools were required to demonstrate this high level of achievement on at least two state assessments. Please note that NCUST compared each demographic group to the statewide performance of all students, not simply the statewide performance of students in the same demographic group. This requirement eliminated many schools from consideration. For example, in some schools, Black students performed very well compared to the average for other Black students in the state; however, these schools would be considered for the America's Best Urban School Award only if Black students (and every other racial/ethnic group served) achieved at a level equal to or higher than the average for *all* students in the state.

NCUST also required applicants to present strong evidence of academic success for students with emerging bilingualism and students with disabilities. Applicants had to demonstrate that students with emerging bilingualism were developing greater proficiency in the use of the English language, as well as greater proficiency in academic areas. Schools also had to show data related to the academic progress of students with disabilities. In sum, to qualify for the America's Best Urban School Award, schools were required to demonstrate evidence of academic excellence for every demographic group they served.

The Selection Process

Each year, many schools make inquiry about the America's Best Urban Schools Award. School and district personnel call with questions regarding the award criteria or attend the center's free webinars regarding the application process. Often, these interactions result in school leaders determining that they do not qualify for the award program. Typically, applicants include 50 to 80 elementary, middle, and high schools. Applicants have included many National Blue Ribbon Schools, National Title I Distinguished Schools, schools recognized on *US News and World Report's Best High Schools in America*, and schools that earned a wide array of statewide distinctions.

To apply, schools completed an application. Most of the application information focused upon quantitative data related to the award criteria (e.g., percentages of students meeting low-income criteria, average daily attendance percentages, percentages of students who performed at the proficient or advanced levels on state assessments, graduation rates, suspension rates, numbers of students in advanced classes). The applications provided schools limited opportunities to write narrative descriptions of their schools. By limiting the writing required, NCUST hoped to minimize the time school leaders had to spend preparing the application. As well, NCUST hoped to focus eligibility primarily on results achieved for all demographic groups of students.

In addition to submitting an application, schools submitted a DVD with video recordings of two lessons. Schools were required to send video clips (between 10 and 30 minutes in length) featuring some of their best examples of instruction. The video recordings provided additional perspective on curricular rigor, instructional effectiveness, and the climate and culture of the school.

After reviewing the applications, NCUST selected, as finalists, the schools that presented the strongest evidence of academic success for all demographic groups of students. Schools that met all eligibility criteria but were not selected as finalists were listed on the center's website as honor roll schools.

We conducted on-site visits to every finalist school. Teams of researchers, teachers, and administrators (including educators from previous winning schools) visited each finalist. Team members spent considerable amounts of time observing classrooms; interviewing teachers, administrators, counselors, students, and parents; and reviewing student work. With the permission of the interviewees, team members made audio recordings of the interviews and video recordings of some of the administrator interviews. Additionally, the teams observed teacher planning meetings, parent meetings, and staff meetings. They talked with district administrators and neighborhood leaders.

During our site visits, we noted evidence of the pursuit of excellent and equitable learning results beyond the impressive application data the schools submitted. For example, we observed teacher collaboration teams pushing themselves to design lessons that would intrigue and engage Black, Latinx, and low-income students. We watched special education personnel work in general education classrooms to help ensure that students with disabilities progressed toward mastering the same academic standards all other students learned. We heard students from low-income families describe the many ways that teachers and administrators had helped them feel accepted, respected, and valued. As well, students shared how their relationships with school personnel positively influenced their motivation to work hard and excel.

By visiting and observing all classrooms in each finalist school, we affirmed that all students (regardless of demographic groups) were receiving access to challenging academic standards. By interviewing students and parents, we learned that the schools had developed cultures that helped all students believe that they had the opportunity to graduate, pursue postsecondary education, and succeed in meaningful careers. By interviewing large samples of teachers and administrators, we acquired evidence that educators were relentlessly striving to create learning conditions that ensured the success of all students and every demographic group of students they served. Equity and excellence were not merely slogans, random workshop topics, or bullet points buried within planning documents. Instead, the pursuit of excellent and equitable learning results was the underlying purpose for practically every activity, program, routine, and policy.

Since 2006, NCUST refined observation and interview protocols so that the center might learn more about the practices that influenced excellent and equitable learning results in high-performing urban schools. We endeavored to probe deeper to understand how leaders initiated changes, generated stakeholder commitment, managed setbacks, and sustained momentum.

Each year, after all site visits were completed, team leaders met to compare detailed notes from visits. The schools selected as award winners were those where team members found the most evidence of curricular rigor, instructional effectiveness, positive relationships, and focus on continuous improvement.

Additionally, apart from our award program, we conducted phone interviews and face-to-face interviews with selected teachers and administrators from these impressive schools. Our doctoral students engaged in in-depth case studies of several of the winning schools. And we continue to examine data, identify themes, discuss conclusions, seek additional evidence, and deepen our understandings. These efforts continue to focus on developing deeper understandings of the factors that contribute to excellence and equity in these schools.

This book focuses on six of the America's Best Urban Schools Award winners. We selected these schools because 1) they served large numbers of Black students and 2) the Black students they served were achieving phenomenal academic results. Additionally, we selected these schools because they continued to generate outstanding successes for Black students in the years after they won the America's Best Urban Schools Award.

Cautions

Schools change. Just as we have been thrilled to see urban schools achieve dramatic improvements in learning results over four or five years, we have been stunned to see precipitous declines in performance over a similar amount of time. Success comes from practices that are implemented each day and systems that promote the refinement of those practices over time. When educators stop implementing the practices that promote great learning results, and when systems fail to promote continuous improvement, growth diminishes and stops. Sometimes, the schools we once celebrated fade into mediocrity.

Leadership matters. We have seen both positive and negative swings in learning results accompany changes in school leadership. In some cases, new leaders reinforce and strengthen the systems that promoted outstanding teaching practices. In other cases, new leaders fail to understand and sustain what educators need to keep improving outcomes for students.

We would love to be able to guarantee that the schools described in this book continue to achieve excellent and equitable learning results for their students, but we can't. However, we can guarantee that Black students will continue to learn, grow, and excel as long as systems continue to promote, refine, and sustain the practices we describe in this book.

Contents of the Book

Part I of this book, including Chapters 1 through 6, profiles each of the six schools featured. By providing some of the background, history, and demographics of each school, we seek to help readers understand that some of these schools were (and others could easily have been) places where Black students floundered. We expect that many readers will see depictions that resemble their schools currently or schools in their districts or states.

Each of these first six chapters also describes key aspects of the changes that transformed these schools. Through the words of principals and teachers, we share how these schools became places where Black students are likely to excel. We have endeavored to describe the key leadership moves that placed these schools on the road to success. As well, we provide examples of the evidence that continues to demonstrate that these schools are making a powerful, positive difference for Black students.

In Part II of this book, including Chapters 7 through 9, we describe three major themes that emerged through our close investigation of these impressive schools: Black students need to benefit from committed school leadership; Black students need to experience belonging, love, and joy at school; and Black students need clear pathways to success. Each theme targets a pivotal issue that influenced the success of Black students in all six schools. Each theme targets a pivotal issue in the lives of Black students and articulates the specific way(s) in which all six schools addressed this important concern. We believe every school must address these three issues well in order to engage and empower Black students to succeed academically.

In addition, each chapter in Part II includes a set of Empathy Interview questions that teachers, support personnel, and school and district leaders might ask Black students and their parents. If a school's or district's transformational efforts do not respond to the perceived needs of the students served, the likelihood of success is diminished. We encourage every school and district to interview Black students and their parents regularly to ensure that their efforts will resonate with the students they serve.

Finally, each chapter in Part II includes sections that articulate the implications of our findings for various stakeholder groups. For each chapter, we include implications for school leaders, teachers and other school personnel, district leaders, parents, policy makers, and institutions of higher education.

We believe this book will have the greatest impact when teams of educators read, study, and use this book collaboratively. We hope that teachers, instructional coaches, department chairs, school administrators, and their district-level supervisors come together to read and discuss the practices described in this book. Certainly, we believe that the practices described can be useful in elevating the academic success of Black students; however, we also believe that the practices will help schools maximize their effectiveness in ensuring that all students experience academic success. Please remember that the schools upon which this book is based achieved outstanding results for Black students; however, they also achieved outstanding results for every other racial/ethnic group they served. To the degree we work together honestly, examining existing conditions in our schools and transforming policies, routines, practices, and programs in ways that respond to the strengths and needs of Black students, we ensure many more schools become places where Black students excel.

References

Edmonds, R. (1979). Effective schools for the urban poor. *Educational Leadership, 37*(1), 15–18, 20–24.

Festinger, L. (1957). *A theory of cognitive dissonance.* Stanford University Press.

Johnson, J. F., Uline, C. L., & Perez, L. G. (2019). *Teaching practices from America's best urban schools: A guide for school and classroom leaders* (2nd ed.). Routledge.

Acknowledgments

Sharing the stories of dedicated educators is both an honor and a responsibility. It is difficult to place words on pages that adequately and accurately convey the heart, energy, thoughtful action, and conviction of teachers, administrators, and support staff who model the pursuit of equity so well. Educators at the schools featured in this book, including Concourse Village Elementary in New York City's South Bronx; Maplewood Richmond Heights High School in St. Louis, Missouri; O'Farrell Charter High School in San Diego, California; Patrick Henry Preparatory School in New York City's East Harlem; Paul Laurence Dunbar Young Men's Leadership Academy in Fort Worth, Texas; and Wynnebrook Elementary in West Palm Beach, Florida, are improving the trajectory of Black students' lives in ways that are far too rare in our country. We appreciate their willingness to open their schools to us (especially during an all-consuming pandemic). We have learned so much from them. Because of them, we have a deeper faith in our collective power to improve schools in ways that lead Black students to excel. We hope this book offers a glimpse into their powerful efforts to engage and empower Black students. This book is a celebration of these schools, the efforts of their outstanding teachers, administrators, parents, and support personnel, and the accomplishment of their brilliant students.

We also acknowledge the thousands of educators around the nation who strive to improve the education of Black students each day. So many teachers, administrators, counselors, support staff, professors, superintendents, policy makers, and other school personnel dedicate their careers to improving the education of Black students. We have endeavored to convey the stories of these six schools clearly and accurately so all of us can learn from their successes, emulate their accomplishments, and contribute to an educational renaissance for Black students in the United States. This book is designed to be useful to dedicated educators as they consider how they might refine their practices in ways that lead many more Black students to attain ambitious academic, personal, and professional goals.

This book did not begin with us. Our work builds upon a tradition of scholarship and inquiry started by heroic educators, such as James A. Banks, Wilbur Brookover, Ron Edmonds, and Larry Lezotte, and extended through the work of others, such as Karin Chenoweth, Lisa Delpit, Ron Ferguson, Geneva Gay, Zaretta Hammond, John Hattie, Kati Haycock, Tyrone Howard, Gloria Ladson-Billings, Ellen Moir, Anthony Muhammad, Gholdy Muhammad, Pedro Noguera, Doug Reeves, James Scheurich, and Linda Skrla. These leaders constructed the foundation upon which this effort stands.

We especially acknowledge the strong support of our colleagues at San Diego State University and the National Center for Urban School Transformation. A former SDSU president, Stephen Weber, and a former dean of SDSU's College of Education, Lionel "Skip" Meno, envisioned a national center that would identify, study, and promote excellence and equity in urban schools. They secured initial funding support from the Qualcomm Corporation, and they creatively provided other support that helped us start the National Center for Urban School Transformation (NCUST). The current SDSU president, Adela De la Torre; the current SDSU College of Education dean, Y. Barry Chung; the chair of the Department of Educational Leadership, Douglas Fisher; and the new NCUST executive director, Francisco Escobedo, continue to provide remarkable support for our efforts. San Diego State University has been a great home for NCUST, in part, because of the outstanding faculty, staff, and students who have been important collaborators in our efforts. We have been enriched by opportunities to work with, and learn from, our colleagues in the Educational Leadership Department at San Diego State University, including Doug Fisher, Nancy Frey, Cheryl James-Ward, Vicki Park, Ian Pumpian, and James Wright. Their efforts to study and promote equity-driven leadership have influenced our thinking about schools that generate outstanding learning results for all students. As well, we have learned from our collaboration with brilliant scholars, including Cristina Alfaro, J. Luke Wood, and Frank Harris III.

Finally, we acknowledge the time, wisdom, and commitment of our colleagues and staff at NCUST. We are honored to work with and learn from a team of executive coaches who have experience leading and/or supporting high-performing urban schools. NCUST was initiated and shaped through the work of former executive coaches, superintendents-in-residence, and leaders Barbra Balser, Tony Burks, Gina Gianzero, Debbie Costa-Hernandez, Lynne Perez, Hazel Rojas, and Christina Theokas. Today, the center flourishes through the work of current executive coaches and superintendents-in-residence Angela Bass, Rupi Boyd, Jose Iniguez, Karen Janney, Shirley Peterson, Cara Riggs, Sid Salazar, Jeff Thiel, and Granger Ward. Also, our work has been supported superbly by Karen Jones, Rachel Ricker, and Mark Wilson. These talented individuals have committed themselves to identifying, studying, and promoting the best practices of America's best urban schools. This book would not exist without their efforts.

Meet the Authors

Joseph F. Johnson, Jr. is the founding executive director of the National Center for Urban School Transformation at San Diego State University. He has served as a teacher, school administrator, district administrator, state-level administrator in Texas and Ohio, and as the director of the federal Title I program for the US Department of Education. In higher education, Dr. Johnson has served as a professor of educational leadership, as the dean of the college of education, and as the interim provost and senior vice president at San Diego State University. His research focuses upon schools that achieve remarkable academic results for diverse populations of students. He is also an author of *Leadership in America's Best Urban Schools* and *Five Practices for Improving the Success of Latino Students: A Practical Guide for Secondary School Leaders*.

Cynthia L. Uline is Professor Emeritus of Educational Leadership at San Diego State University. Dr. Uline served as Director of SDSU's *National Center for the 21st Century Schoolhouse* from 2005 to 2017. She has also served as a teacher, teacher leader, and state education agency administrator. Cynthia's research explores the influence of built learning environments on students' learning, as well as the roles leaders, teachers, students, and the public play in shaping learning spaces. Her current research considers the potential of green schools as student-centered, ecologically responsive, and economically viable places for learning. She has also published journal articles, books, and book chapters related to leadership for learning, leadership preparation, and schools that achieve remarkable academic results for diverse populations of students. Her latest book, coauthored with Lisa A. W. Kensler, is entitled *A Practical Guide for Leading Green Schools: Partnering with Nature to Create Vibrant,*

Flourishing Sustainable Schools. She is also an author of *Leadership in America's Best Urban Schools*.

Stanley J. Munro, Jr. is an executive coach with the National Center for Urban School Transformation at San Diego State University. He has served as a curriculum writer, teacher, job-embedded mathematics professional developer, principal, executive director, and superintendent. During his career, Dr. Munro's most important work has been that of a student advocate. All children have the right to maximize their greatest potential and every person on a campus has the responsibility to ensure that scholars know that they are valued in the school community and in the world at large. Dr. Munro is committed to equipping each student with the twenty-first-century job skills that higher education requires and the global workforce will demand in order to prepare our students for jobs that don't exist yet with technology that has not been invented yet, to solve problems that have not occurred yet.

Case Studies of Schools Where Black Students Excel

Sometimes, the headlines obscure the real news. For example, headlines often describe how Black students score dramatically lower than all other racial/ethnic groups in both mathematics and literacy at fourth, eighth, and twelfth grade on the National Assessment of Educational Progress. Often, the headlines point to the disproportionate numbers of Black students who are suspended and expelled from high schools, middle schools, elementary schools, and even preschools, suggesting that the school-to-prison pipeline starts flowing before Black children enter kindergarten. Often, the headlines focus on the deplorable dropout rates among Black students starting at middle school and moving through high school. Other headlines emphasize the absence of Black students in many Advanced Placement programs, International Baccalaureate programs, and programs for gifted and talented students.

Often, the headlines suggest that poor academic performance among Black students is monolithic and consistent; however, the real news is the variation in the academic performance of Black students in certain states, school districts, and schools. For example, while it is true that only 14% of Black eighth-grade students scored at the proficient or advanced level on the mathematics section of the National Assessment of Educational Progress (compared to 20% of Hispanic eighth-grade students, 44% of White eighth-grade students, and 64% of Asian eighth-grade students), Black eighth-grade students in Massachusetts, Washington, New Hampshire, and Arizona were more than twice as likely to score proficient or advanced in mathematics than Black students in Alabama, Alaska, California, Iowa, Louisiana, Michigan, Mississippi, Nebraska, North Dakota, Oklahoma, or South Carolina (The Nation's Report Card, 2019).

Similarly, there is substantial variation across states in the percentage of Black fourth-grade students who demonstrate proficient or advanced performance on the NAEP reading assessment (The Nation's Report Card,

DOI: 10.4324/9781003277910-1

2019). Ramanathan (2022) argued that Black parents in California who want their young children to become strong readers should consider moving to Colorado, Massachusetts, New Jersey, Florida, or Mississippi because greater percentages of Black fourth-grade students in those states are reading at proficient or advanced levels.

Whether one is examining NAEP data, state assessment scores, drop-out rates, graduation rates, suspension rates, attendance rates, or any other important measure of academic progress, there is substantial variation in the performance of Black students across states, school districts, and schools. The variation tells us that the depressing headlines miss a critical part of the story. The variation pushes us to acknowledge that the performance of Black students is not about an inherent inability to succeed academically. Instead, the variation begs us to ask, "If we can successfully educate some Black children, what must be done to educate more?" The variation prods us to examine the systems in which Black children learn. Clearly, some systems have been structured in ways that increase the likelihood that Black students succeed academically and other systems have not.

"There is nothing wrong with Black students," as Kunjufu (2012, p. vi) emphatically stated. The headlines hide the academic successes of Black students across states, school districts, and schools. In particular, many scholars have noted huge variations among schools, in the attendance rates, grades, dropout rates, graduation rates, course-taking patterns, course success rates, suspension rates, expulsion rates, state assessment results, and other indicators of academic success for Black students (Chenoweth, 2017; Johnson & Asera, 1999; Johnson et al., 1997; Johnson et al., 2019; Kunjufu, 2012; Szachowicz, 2015).

The first six chapters of this book highlight the real news about the performance of Black students in schools where educators have established systems in which Black students excel. By exploring the practices, procedures, programs, and policies of these impressive schools, we can begin to understand what is needed to ensure the success of Black students in elementary and secondary schools throughout our nation.

References

Chenoweth, K. (2017). *Schools that succeed: How educators marshal the power of systems for improvement.* Harvard Education Press.

Johnson, J. F., & Asera, R. (1999). *Hope for urban education: A study of nine high-performing, high-poverty, urban elementary schools.* U.S. Department of Education.

Johnson, J. F., Ragland, M., & Lein, L. (1997). *Successful Texas schoolwide programs.* Retrievable from ERIC database. (ED 406084)

Johnson, J. F., Uline, C. L., & Perez, L. G. (2019). *Teaching practices from America's best urban schools: A guide for school and classroom leaders* (2nd ed.). Routledge.

Kunjufu, J. (2012). *There is nothing wrong with Black students.* African American Images.

The Nation's Report Card. (2019). *NAEP data explorer.* www.nations-reportcard.gov/ndecore/xplore/NDE

Ramanathan, A. (2022). To fix our education crisis, let's focus on educating. *EdSource.* https://edsource.org/2022/to-fix-our-education-crisis-lets-focus-on-educating/667763.

Szachowicz, S. (2015). Brockton high school, Brockton, Massachusetts. In A. M. Blankstein & P. Noguera (Eds.), *Excellence through equity: Five principles of courageous leadership to guide achievement for every student.* Corwin.

Patrick Henry Preparatory School (PS/IS 171)

New York City Department of Education, District 4 East Harlem, New York City, New York

My teacher is very nice and she makes sure I learn what I'm supposed to learn. When I make a mistake, she makes sure I learn from it. She always helps me with my needs.

– Melissa, Patrick Henry primary-grade student

It is all about respect and consistency. That's why I rerouted my kids here. It's because of the traditions, the consistency, and the respect the principal has shown. The teachers are the same. It's home. It feels safe. You can see it in how the principal carries himself. You can see it in the way he shows leadership to his staff. And then the staff shows that same respect to kids and parents. It hasn't failed.

– parent of a Patrick Henry student

The expectation at PS 171 is that every child can learn. Mr. Pantelidis and the staff recognize, however, that children will excel at different rates. It doesn't mean that all students get to the same place at the same time, but there's a lot of support helping kids succeed. There is an expectation that with love, support, structure, and a rigorous curriculum, every kid can excel at this school.

– parent of a Patrick Henry student

DOI: 10.4324/9781003277910-2

This past year we took a critical look at our curriculum to ensure it included multicultural and diverse characters, histories, and themes reflected in our scholars. While our curriculum was already diverse, we found many opportunities for enhancement to expose our scholars to even more diverse individuals, ideas, and issues. Using the work of Dr. Gholdy Muhammad (Muhammad, 2020) as a guide, we looked at the novels, activities, and lessons taking place in the classroom to make learning relevant, relatable, and real. By taking this approach, our hope is that our scholars will be able to learn about people all over the world while connecting to their identities, and the stories, similarities, and differences of the characters.

A few actions that resulted from our curriculum audit:

- *Revised read-alouds and chapter book selections to include more diverse characters and families (3K-3).*
- *Revised novel study selections (grades 4–8) to ensure inclusion of BIPOC and differently abled characters.*
- *Refined instructional practice (collaborative work, small group supports, independent-led inquiry) to promote more voices and engagement of diverse learners.*
- *SEL [Social Emotional Learning] blocks have evolved to be student-led and teacher-facilitated; share topics and activities are more reflective of current issues and student experiences.*
- *Teacher surveys / teacher team meetings focused on the creation of student-centered, culturally sustaining libraries in each classroom.*
- *Please look at the attached documents to see the edits we have made to our curriculum for this year. Thank you for believing in our school.*

Kreshna Billings and Dimitres Pantelidis
– email message to Patrick Henry parents on 9/28/21

The comments above from Patrick Henry students and parents and this email message to parents offer perspective on the reasons Patrick Henry Preparatory School in East Harlem, New York, generates outstanding learning results for Black students, as well as all other racial/ethnic groups of students. Educators relentlessly aim to ensure their students learn challenging academic standards (at least as challenging as the academic standards learned at schools that serve the most affluent families in New York). However, Patrick Henry educators also understand that students of color are more likely to master challenging standards if they ensure students can "see themselves" in the learning materials, relate concepts and ideas to their backgrounds and experiences, and become actively involved in learning. Furthermore, educators at the school recognize they are more likely to educate Black students successfully if they establish and maintain a climate and a culture that makes students and their families feel like they are the primary reason for the school's existence.

Accomplishments and Achievements

Black students at Patrick Henry maintain high daily attendance rates, low suspension rates, high course passage rates, and many other indicators of success. Patrick Henry's Black students perform at impressive levels on New York State's Student Achievement Assessment. The results in Figure 1.1 show that only 35.3% of Black students in New York State (grades 3–8) achieved proficient or advanced levels of performance in English language

Figure 1.1 Comparison of English Language Arts Performance in New York State

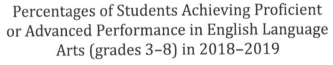

Percentages of Students Achieving Proficient or Advanced Performance in English Language Arts (grades 3–8) in 2018–2019

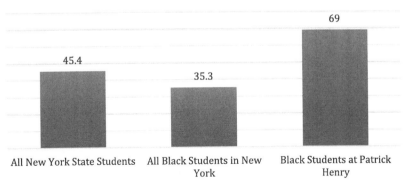

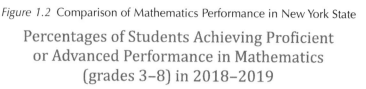

Figure 1.2 Comparison of Mathematics Performance in New York State

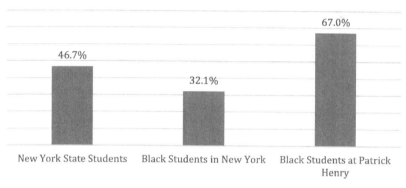

Percentages of Students Achieving Proficient
or Advanced Performance in Mathematics
(grades 3–8) in 2018–2019

arts in 2018–2019. In contrast, 69% of Black students at Patrick Henry achieved proficient or advanced levels in English language arts. Black students at Patrick Henry were almost twice as likely to achieve grade-level proficiency than Black students elsewhere in New York State. Furthermore, only 45.4% of all students (grades 3–8) in the state of New York achieved proficient or advanced levels in English language arts. So Black students at Patrick Henry were much more likely to achieve proficiency in English language arts than students, in general, in the state of New York. These successes are the result of deliberate, persistent, and coordinated efforts.

Similarly, Black students at Patrick Henry outperformed the average of all New York students in mathematics. As shown in Figure 1.2, Black students at Patrick Henry were more than twice as likely to achieve proficiency in mathematics than Black students elsewhere in New York. Also, Black students at Patrick Henry were far more likely to achieve mathematical proficiency than students, in general, in the state of New York.

History, Background, and Demographics

Housed in a nineteenth-century building it shares with Central Park East II school, Patrick Henry Preparatory, also known as PS/IS 171, is a combined elementary and middle school known for its nurturing, supportive, caring, loving, calm, and orderly environment. Located on East 103rd Street in East Harlem, the school is part of New York City's Department of Education, District 4. Though students wear uniforms and walk in straight lines in the hallways, the atmosphere is neither rigid nor harsh. The school's classrooms are cheery spaces, with students' creative works lining the walls.

The school was constructed in 1899, but renovations over the years have kept it well-maintained. Exterior work, waterproofing, and electrical upgrades to support air-conditioning and Wi-Fi ensure both comfortable learning spaces and excellent access to the internet and instructional technology.

Patrick Henry serves approximately 800 students, 53% of whom are female and 47% are male. Nearly 60% of students identify as Latinx or Hispanic. Just over 27% are Black or African American. Seventy percent of Patrick Henry's students qualify for free- or reduced-price meals. The student-teacher ratio is 16:1. Multiple public charter schools and private schools can be found in the blocks surrounding Patrick Henry. While the charter and private schools endeavor to convince families they can offer superior educational services, independent sites such as schooldigger.com (see www.schooldigger.com/go/NY/schoolrank.aspx) and greatschools.org (see www.greatschools.org/new-york/new-york/schools/?page=2) rank Patrick Henry among the best schools in the state, even though Patrick Henry does not utilize selective admissions criteria.

Schooldigger.com produced the graphic in Figure 1.3 to illustrate the growth of Patrick Henry Preparatory School over the past 15 years

Figure 1.3 Percentile Ranking of Patrick Henry Preparatory School vs. Other NY Schools (as reported by Schooldigger.com)

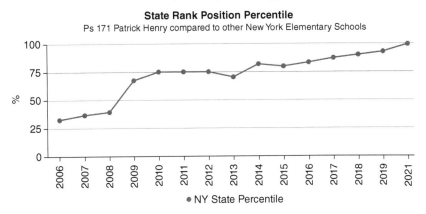

compared to schools throughout the state of New York. The chart shows that this East Harlem school, serving predominantly Latinx and Black students, has become one of the state's highest-performing schools. The chart provides evidence that Patrick Henry has traveled far beyond a journey to mediocrity and far past a brief episode of glory. Instead, the graphic provides strong quantitative evidence that a team of committed teachers, support staff, and leaders, working in collaboration with parents and a wide array of community agencies, can elevate and sustain the success of Black and Brown students in ways that can alter their opportunities for decades to come.

Distinguishing Values, Goals, and Strategies

Dimitres Pantelidis, known as "Mr. P," has been the school's principal since 1999. For more than two decades, he has endeavored to guide Patrick Henry toward becoming a school that prepares all students with the essential skills, attitudes, and motivation to achieve success in high school, college, and careers.

To meet the learning needs of all its students, Patrick Henry provides thematic and project-based instruction that encourages collaboration, inquiry-based discussions, and authentic learning experiences. This means that everyday classroom instruction at Patrick Henry looks and sounds different from those in thousands of classrooms around the country that serve large numbers of students of color. For example, at Patrick Henry, teachers frequently engage students of color in conversation about ideas and concepts. In our observations of classrooms, we heard student voices more than we heard the voices of teachers. Students were not sitting passively, waiting to be informed. Instead, they were asking questions about phenomena and working in small groups to solve problems. We heard groups of second-grade students organize and present reports on the physical characteristics of a praying mantis. In an online lesson, we saw middle school students extrapolate data from a line graph to determine how much money they would earn when their candy bar sales reached certain heights. In many classrooms, we heard teachers ask students, "How do you know? What evidence supports your claim?" At Patrick Henry, the goal is to help all students become "independent learners of the future."

PS 171's values are reflected in its "3 Rs to Student Achievement," based on the Bill Dagget Rigor/Relevance Framework (Nussbaum & Daggett, 2008):

1. **Rigor** focuses on degrees of acquisition, assimilation, application, and adaptation.

2. **Relevance** promotes connections, purposefulness, and cultural diversity and utilizes empathy maps.

3. **Relationships** speak to student achievements and reflect their social and emotional intelligence in areas like expressing, regulating, understanding, trust, and more.

One can find thousands of schools where leaders talk about Daggett's conceptualization of rigor, relevance, and relationship. However, at Patrick Henry, these concepts have influenced the scrutiny of multiple data sources, including state assessment results, student performances on challenging academic tasks, and acceptance rates for Patrick Henry graduates in New York City's elite high schools. Discussions about rigor have changed how teachers and administrators plan what is taught, when it is taught, and how it is taught so all students are more likely to achieve deep levels of understanding. At Patrick Henry, we saw second-grade students who were eager to explain how they were studying entomology, fourth-grade students who were comfortable discussing the inferences they were making as they read a novel, and middle school students who were writing detailed essays about strategies for ending gender stereotypes. At Patrick Henry, rigor is not simply defining what students need to learn to score well on state assessments. Rigor is about ensuring that students learn what they need to learn to succeed after they leave Patrick Henry and move into high school, college, and careers. For example, during eighth grade, many Patrick Henry students take New York High School Regents courses. "This way they are ahead of their peers when they get into ninth grade," Mr. P explained. Throughout the past two decades, Principal Pantelidis and his colleagues have pushed themselves to elevate the rigor of what they teach, because they believe they can change students' lives by leading them to master concepts and skills that many students of color are never given the opportunity to access.

At some schools, educators believe they are providing students rigor simply by allowing students to take difficult courses or by presenting challenging concepts. At Patrick Henry, however, teachers have learned that rigor must mean more than setting students up to fail. Collaborative planning has focused deliberately and consistently on identifying the supports students will need so they can successfully master the rigorous concepts and skills they need to succeed in school, in careers, and in life. Patrick Henry teachers raised the bar, by asking, "Shouldn't our second-grade students be able to use the various features of an article about insects to answer questions about insect anatomy?" However, the teachers also worked together to consider how they could organize learning activities so their second graders would have a high likelihood of successfully using an article in such a manner. They considered what students would need to know, how they might group students, and how they could support groups when the groups needed help. Principal Pantelidis explained that teacher collaboration fuels excitement at Patrick Henry. He shared, "The euphoria of professional development is in making sure that the teachers are collaborating. That's how they learn from one another. It keeps them invigorated. It keeps them excited. I have veterans who have been teaching over 20 years, and they still want to improve and they want to still push all of us to improve teaching and learning."

At some schools, students are left to fail before they have opportunities to access the support they need to learn. Unfortunately, many students are reluctant to try again after they experience failure. In contrast, at Patrick Henry, educators have learned that the most powerful supports are often provided during initial instruction of a concept or skill. Providing rigor means more than challenging students: it means providing students the support they need to learn the rigorous concept or skill well.

Similarly, educators at Patrick Henry have realized that their students are far less likely to master rigorous academic content if the students perceive the content has little relevance to their lives. Teachers have rejected or minimized the use of uninteresting, repetitive worksheets and dull basal readers. At Patrick Henry, educators have spent thousands of hours identifying curricular materials, planning instructional strategies, and trying various approaches to help Patrick Henry students see how rigorous academic concepts are important in their lives. Patrick Henry teachers have demonstrated that their students will master challenging algebraic standards when teachers help their students see how the concepts relate to issues the students have experienced or are likely to experience. As well, Patrick Henry students have proven they can master rigorous English language arts standards related to issues such as the analysis of text structures, the citation of textual evidence, or the variations in character point of view. They demonstrate mastery of these standards, in part, because their teachers utilize literature that resonates with their backgrounds and experiences (see Figure 1.4).

Also, our observations and interviews helped us recognize that Patrick Henry teachers and administrators understand how relationships influence efforts to ensure that students of color learn rigorous academic content. Meticulous planning has led to the development of classroom environments where students know they are respected as intelligent scholars who will make a difference in their community. Unfortunately, in many schools across our nation, Black students are not sure their teachers want them to succeed academically. In contrast, several Patrick Henry students described how school personnel were committed to their success. For example, one child explained, "So what makes me happy going to school is that the people in the school support us and everyone in the school wants us to learn. They try their best to teach us and make us understand."

Walking past one Patrick Henry classroom, we saw a teacher sitting by herself in front of her computer screen. She was teaching a group of fourth- or fifth-grade students. She interacted with her students in a sincere, genuine, caring manner. She seemed to draw the students through cyberspace so they were sitting next to her, watching her listen appreciatively to their explanations, hearing her laugh when they said something amusing, and feeling her support as they tried to make sense of difficult concepts. Even though her students might have been dealing with numerous distractions in their at-home learning environments, it was clear that this teacher had the full attention of her students. The students would engage, try, think, struggle, and do whatever they could to accomplish what they thought their teacher wanted. When students believe their teachers are committed to helping them succeed, students are much more likely to maximize their efforts.

Educators at Patrick Henry acknowledge that many students are enduring emotional and social difficulties. At Patrick Henry, teachers take the time to listen to students. Regular morning meetings provide students opportunities to talk about issues that may have little to do with reading, mathematics, or science but may prevent students from focusing on any academic topic. Teachers and support staff offer a variety of supports, such as "Finding Your Zen" or "Respect for All," as well as connections to mental

Figure 1.4 Grade 4–8 Novel Study Scope and Sequence

P.S. 171
Patrick Henry Preparatory School
Grades 4–8 Novel Study Scope and Sequence
2021–2022

Grade	September	October	November	December	January	February	March	April	May	June
Grade 4	*Number the Stars* by Lois Lowry and *Resist: 40 Profiles of Ordinary People Who Rose Up Against Tyranny and Injustice* by Veronica Chambers			*Sadako and the Thousand Paper Cranes* by Eleanor Coerr and *They Called Us Enemy* by George Takei			ELA 4-Week Plan	*I Survived The Destruction of Pompeii* by Lauren Tarshis and Natural Disaster Project		
Grade 5	*Among the Hidden* by Margaret Peterson Haddix and *Resist: 40 Profiles of Ordinary People Who Rose Up Against Tyranny and Injustice* by Veronica Chambers			*Hidden Figures* by Margot Shetterly and *Resist: 40 Profiles of Ordinary People Who Rose Up Against Tyranny and Injustice* by Veronica Chambers			ELA 4-Week Plan	*Hidden Figures* by Margot Shetterly	*Heroes of the Environment* by Harriet Rohmer and Environmental Activism Project	
Grade 6	*Children of Blood and Bone* by Tomi Adeyemi and African Diasporic Myths, Folktales, Legends, and Fables					World Myths, Legends, Folktales, and Fables	ELA 4-Week Plan	Dis/ability Literature Circles (*The World Ends in April, Mascot, Out of My Mind, Harbor Me, Song for a Whale*) and Social Activism Project		
Grade 7	*The Absolutely True Diary of a Part-Time Indian* by Sherman Alexi			*The Barren Grounds* by David Robertson		*The Crossover* by Kwame Alexander	ELA 4-Week Plan	Intersectional Poetry Literature Circles and Social Activism Project		

	ELA 4-Week Plan				
Grade 8	Primary Source Analysis: Declaration of Independence and Constitution	Immigration and Refugees: *Refugee* by Alan Gratz and *The Night Diary* by Veera Hiranandani	Civil Rights: *The Hate U Give* by Angie Thomas and *Just Mercy* by Bryan Stevenson	Women's Rights and LGBTQ+ Rights: *George* by Alex Gino, *I Am Malala* by Malala Yousafzai, *Yes She Can* by Molly Dillon	Social Activism Project

health resources throughout New York City. Patrick Henry educators do more than provide social-emotional learning lessons; they create socially, emotionally healthy environments in which Black students (and all other students) know they are valued, respected, and appreciated.

As the email message at the start of this chapter suggests, the quest to strengthen academic rigor, relevance, and relationships is ongoing. Principal Pantelidis continues to push his team (and himself) to scrutinize the rigor of their curricula, the relevance of educational approaches and materials to the lives of their students, and the quality of the school relationships experienced by each their students.

Challenges

Before Mr. P became principal, the district placed Patrick Henry under corrective action because student achievement in reading and mathematics had not improved for three consecutive years. Like many principals assigned to schools where students of color are not achieving well, Principal Pantelidis was eager to lead the school toward better learning outcomes. Even though the school had a generally positive reputation (especially for its early childhood education programs), he knew that students could achieve more if they were taught more challenging academic content in ways that students would find meaningful and relevant. Nonetheless, there were many factors that made improvement difficult.

Principal Pantelidis focused considerable effort on sustaining and building upon the strengths of Patrick Henry's early childhood program. He explained:

> Our little three-year-old students in our 3K program, they're not even 1,000 days old, and they're coming here, building a good foundation. I can tell you, they want to be here. The parents have a choice not to enroll them. They can ask themselves, "Do I want my child to come here in pre-K? Do I want my child to come here in kindergarten?" And unanimously, the answer is, "Yes, yes, and yes."

The early-childhood efforts were a critical foundation for the school's success, because they are designed to ensure that children will succeed as they proceed into kindergarten, first grade, and all the way into high school. The early-childhood program helps children and families see that Patrick Henry is a place where they will succeed.

Still, Mr. P realized that the school was losing students to nearby charter and private schools. Often, charter schools and private schools endeavored to attract the most academically successful students away from Patrick Henry and other traditional public schools in the neighborhood. If Patrick Henry was to succeed, the school had to convince students and their families that they would achieve strong, positive learning outcomes by resisting the advertisements and promises of competitor schools and staying at PS 171.

Principal Pantelidis recognized that parents needed to hear more than promises. Parents needed to see concrete evidence that the school was building the capacity to ensure their children's academic success. For example, Mr. P knew that over 80% of Patrick Henry students were visual learners. Students were more likely to understand concepts and develop skills if they could see those concepts and skills represented visually (instead of just hearing the teachers' words). He knew that instruction could be enhanced if every classroom had a "smart board" that allowed teachers to engage students through the visual representation and manipulation of ideas. But he also knew that his budget was not sufficient to purchase smart boards for all classrooms.

In response to this challenge, Principal Pantelidis learned how to pursue competitive grant proposals and network with district officials and other community leaders. The school won a grant that enabled them to purchase smart boards. Subsequent grants enabled further technology upgrades and other curricular enhancements. These enhancements provided parents and students concrete evidence that educators at Patrick Henry were willing to do what was necessary to provide their children a high-quality, twenty-first-century education. Also, the enhancements made it easier for teachers to help students learn challenging academic concepts. Each year, Patrick Henry averages approximately $1 million in grant awards.

Parents appreciated the changes they saw at Patrick Henry. Many did not want to see their children leave the school after elementary school. A strong group of parents approached the district and insisted that the school expand to serve middle school grades. As a result, Patrick Henry now serves children from age three through the eighth grade.

Principal Pantelidis also recognized that he needed to play a key role in building a strong professional team at Patrick Henry. He wanted to make sure that educators understood that children in East Harlem could achieve at high levels if teachers worked together to ensure that all students benefitted from excellent instruction. Principal Pantelidis used data to motivate and inspire Patrick Henry educators to work together in support of their students. He helped teachers see how Black students, Latinx students, and all other demographic groups of students could excel if they were taught rigorous content, in ways that resonated with their backgrounds, experiences, and interests, and in an environment where they felt adults valued them and believed in their ability to succeed academically.

Principal Pantelidis wanted to ensure that all Patrick Henry students would be guaranteed the opportunity to learn challenging academic skills. Marzano (2003) emphasized the importance of schools providing a guarantee that all students would access a rigorous academic curriculum. Marzano suggested that students should access the same challenging content whether they are assigned to Ms. Fatima's algebra class or Mr. Henry's algebra class. He contended that every student should be guaranteed the learning experiences that prepare them for algebra, and every student should be guaranteed the learning experiences that allow them to learn the same challenging algebraic concepts and skills when they are assigned to an algebra class.

Even in the absence of a guaranteed curriculum, middle-class, affluent parents have managed to ensure their children learn rigorous academic standards. Typically, affluent parents will know which teachers provide the strongest academic curricula, and they lobby the principal, school counselors, or other administrators to ensure their children are placed in the classes where their children will learn the content needed to succeed at the next level. Often, however, parents in low-income communities lack the information or the lobbying power to ensure their children access strong academic curricula. So Principal Pantelidis sought to engage teachers in developing and teaching a guaranteed curriculum (referred to as the instructional core at Patrick Henry) that would provide students at every grade level, in every classroom, a solid curriculum built on advanced literacy concepts and skills. Patrick Henry educators determined that they wanted all their students to be able to think critically about concepts, construct logical arguments based on evidence, and apply the concepts they were learning to real-life situations. As part of Patrick Henry's instructional core, teachers developed engaging, thematic units of study that focus on key academic concepts and skills. Teachers planned in a manner that helped ensure that when students exited one grade level, they would be prepared to succeed at the next. "The number one thing that describes our school," explained Principal Pantelidis, "is consistency. Consistency with leadership, consistency with staff, consistency with our instructional core."

Also, Patrick Henry educators developed their instructional core to elevate learning outcomes for all students, including students who were already performing at high levels and students who were performing at low academic levels. In some struggling schools, educators assume that students who have experienced persistent failure do not have the ability to succeed academically. In contrast, at Patrick Henry, educators worked to identify the supports that could be powerful in helping students succeed, even if they were behind two grade levels in reading or even if they had a special education diagnosis.

As well, in some struggling schools, educators tend to spend less time and energy in support of students who have already demonstrated mastery of grade-level skills. In contrast, Patrick Henry educators recognized how they could help Black and Brown students advance beyond grade-level skills to even greater academic accomplishments. At Patrick Henry, state standards came to be perceived as the floor, not the ceiling, for the educational expectations for all students.

When the COVID-19 pandemic emerged early in 2020, New York City was hit hard. Unfortunately, the school's zip code, 10029, had the highest number of COVID cases in New York City. When the district closed school buildings and initiated remote learning, Patrick Henry teachers (like many teachers across the nation) had not been trained to teach via distance learning technology. To meet these challenges, the school's instructional technology team and teachers joined together to train and support one another. Teachers supported one another in adapting elements of their instructional core for online instruction. The instructional technology team worked with families and students to ensure that every child had access to working hardware, software, and internet connectivity. While teachers worked to maintain a strong instructional program, they also redoubled efforts to support students and families with the multiple crises they were enduring. Patrick Henry became an important hub of support for students and families. While schools have reopened, the challenges of the pandemic continue. Teachers, support staff, and school administrators continue to focus on building the school's academic strengths while also supporting students and families to the extent they can.

Recognitions

During Mr. P's first year as principal, Patrick Henry was recognized as a statewide early-childhood exemplary site, memorializing PS 171 as a special place where students had limitless opportunities to achieve and progress. Also, during the same year, Patrick Henry was one of the schools selected to represent the district at the signing of a bill providing the mayor with control of the city schools. Since that first year of Principal Pantelidis's tenure, Patrick Henry has received many other accolades.

Over the years, PS/IS 171 has earned many awards and distinctions, including recognition from the city and the state for the school's early-childhood education programs. These awards have acknowledged the quality of the school's early-childhood team, the impressive progress of students, and the school's socially and emotionally supportive culture.

Additionally, the school has received multiple recognitions from New York State Department of Education, *The New York Times*, US News and World Report, GreatSchools.com, and SchoolDigger.com for the school's strong academic performance. In 2018, Patrick Henry won NCUST's America's Best Urban Schools Gold Award.

In 2018, talk show host Ellen DeGeneres partnered with Verizon and surprised the Harlem-based school with a check for $50,000 to be used in improving the students' education experience (see https://education.hunter.cuny.edu/news/ellen-degeneres-surprises-school-of-education-partner-school-in-harlem-with-50000/). Verizon also provided the school a high-tech, on-site laboratory.

Mr. P is particularly proud of the fact Patrick Henry consistently performs among the top schools in the city and has done so for the past 15 to 20 years. For him, it's perhaps the greatest award the school could receive, as it recognizes the consistency of leadership, teachers, staff, and students.

For Mr. P, Patrick Henry will, in many ways, always be a "first home" for its students. He believes all Patrick Henry students have something meaningful to contribute. He wants students to know they are central to the school's decision-making. Looking ahead, he plans to keep the school a vital part of the community and the students' lives. "We're going to continue this legacy of supporting our Black kids, our Latinx kids, all our kids, to achieve greatness," says Mr. P. "We're going to make it possible, because this is what we live for."

What It Is and What It Isn't: Factors That Have Influenced Success at Patrick Henry Preparatory School

What It Is: Classrooms in Which Students Are Actively Engaged in Learning

At Patrick Henry students were actively engaged in Socratic seminars, project-based learning, and a wide array of learning activities. In elementary, intermediate, and middle grades, students were active participants in learning activities. Teachers deliberately structured classes so students engaged with one another to discuss important concepts and complete interesting projects.

What It Isn't: Classrooms in Which Students Sit Quietly and Passively

In some schools that serve large numbers of Black students, students are expected to sit quietly and listen to their teachers for large percentages of the class day. Even though classrooms were orderly, often students at Patrick Henry were not sitting quietly in their seats, working independently. In fact, we heard students' voices more than we heard teachers' voices.

What It Is: Ensuring All Students Have the Support They Need to Learn Rigorous Academic Content Successfully

Patrick Henry teachers worked together to identify the supports students might need in order to learn challenging content well. Teachers identified the most challenging concepts and skills students needed to master. They worked together to plan strategies to help ensure their students would learn those concepts well.

What It Isn't: Providing All Students Opportunities to Learn Rigorous Academic Standards, Even If Some Are Not Likely to Succeed

In some schools, Black students are placed in rigorous courses and are given the opportunity to "sink or swim." In such situations, Black students often learn that it is safer to avoid tackling challenging academic courses or tasks. Patrick Henry students were not placed in situations where they were likely to fail. Teachers created challenging tasks and kept learning expectations high; however, teachers also provided a high level of support so that Patrick Henry students had a high likelihood of academic success.

What It Is: Supporting Students in Learning More Advanced Concepts/Skills, Even When They've Already Mastered State Standards

When students demonstrated they had mastered state standards for their grade levels, Patrick Henry teachers continued to support students in developing deeper, richer understanding of concepts. Teachers found interesting ways to enrich instruction so students had opportunities to apply the concepts they learned to real-life situations.

What It Isn't: Focusing Almost Exclusively on Students Who Have Not Yet Achieved State Standards

In some schools, Black students who demonstrate early success with state standards are given "busy work" while teachers help other students catch up. In contrast, at Patrick Henry, teachers provided support for students who needed additional help to master standards and simultaneously provided enrichment that helped students build upon what they had already learned.

What It Is: Identifying Examples, Literature, and Teaching Tools Likely to Resonate with Students

At Patrick Henry, teachers worked collaboratively to identify literature and other resources that can help students see how important learning standards are relevant to their backgrounds, cultures, experiences, and interests. Specifically, Patrick Henry educators have utilized Muhammad's equity framework (Muhammad, 2020) to support their efforts to develop lessons that will engage and inspire the school's students.

What It Isn't: Exclusively Utilizing Adopted Textbooks and Supplemental Materials to Teach Rigorous Concepts and Skills

In some schools that serve large numbers of students of color, teachers are told that they must use adopted textbooks, workbooks, and other supplemental materials, even when those materials are not likely to resonate with the backgrounds, cultures, and experiences of the students served. This did not happen at Patrick Henry Preparatory School.

What It Is: Taking Instructional Time to Listen to Students Discuss Issues Influencing Their Social-Emotional Well-Being

At Patrick Henry, teachers prioritized the social and emotional well-being of students. During observations, we saw teachers "checking in" with students to identify issues that might need to be addressed. Additionally, teachers conducted morning meetings to provide opportunities for students to share concerns that may need to be addressed before attention can be focused on core academic issues.

What It Isn't: Ensuring That School Time Is Focused Exclusively on Academic Content

In some schools where large numbers of students are not achieving state standards, administrators insist that teachers use every available minute to focus on core academic subjects. In these schools, there isn't time to address social-emotional concerns. In contrast, leaders at Patrick Henry have helped teachers understand that, in some cases, taking time to promptly and thoroughly address social-emotional issues may remove impediments to learning.

References

Marzano, R. J. (2003). *What works in schools: Translating research into action*. ASCD.

Muhammad, G. (2020). *Cultivating genius: An equity framework for culturally and historically responsive literacy*. Scholastic, Inc.

Nussbaum, P. D., & Daggett, W. R. (2008). *What brain research teaches about rigor, relevance, and relationships and what it teaches about keeping your own brain healthy*. International Center for Leadership in Education.

Maplewood Richmond Heights High School

Maplewood Richmond Heights School District, St. Louis, Missouri

In other schools, a lot of Black students feel like, when you're in a classroom, you're taking up space just by being in the room, like your presence is already too much when you're one of the only Black people in class. But I think that, at this school, a lot of teachers go out of their way to make us feel comfortable. Like when we're talking about social justice issues and current events, they make sure we feel comfortable putting in our two cents. And they make sure no one else in the classroom badgers us.

*   – Nola, a senior at Maplewood Richmond Heights High*

We feel embraced by the teachers and this community we're in. You're accepted here; you feel like you can be yourself more. Society is abnormal. This place is our normal.

*   – Kim, a senior at Maplewood Richmond Heights High*

If I'm not doing my work or something like that, a teacher or someone will try to reach out to my parents. They're close or something like that. So whenever I'm down or having problems, teachers will make sure I'm okay at home.

*   – Adam, a junior at Maplewood Richmond Heights High*

My teachers are really understanding. They try to have a relationship with you as a student. They'll check in on you, or

DOI: 10.4324/9781003277910-3

they'll try to find something that you can connect with, so then you look forward to coming to their class.

– Ola, a junior at Maplewood Richmond Heights High

I try to get to know all my students well. I try to engage them. I try to make my classroom a fun place and a welcoming place so their anxieties around science loosen up. I want to make my students think they can do this. I want my students to know they can do science. I want to help my students improve their self-confidence. Of course, I want to teach science literacy. I want them to improve their reading and writing skills and their critical thinking skills. I want them to get interested in science. But I also want them to develop a sense of empathy and see things from multiple points of view.

– a science teacher at Maplewood Richmond Heights High

When a student does misbehave (because they still do), we don't get all worked up and bent out of shape about it. We keep things rolling, and we reflect, we repair it, and we restore the relationship. That's what it's about. And we move on. We don't stay stuck in it by saying, "Remember that time you did that a month ago?" That's not what it's about. We need to be able to teach and restore the relationship. . . . We know in the long run it makes us more trustworthy, we build stronger relationships, and the kids feel known, valued, and inspired.

– Dr. Kevin Grawer, principal, Maplewood Richmond Heights High School

As the preceding statements suggest, Black students at Maplewood Richmond Heights High School (MRH) are convinced that the teachers and administrators at their school (most of whom are White) are committed to their success in school and their success in life. They see evidence of this commitment in daily interactions they experience with educators at MRH. Black students at MRH believe they are perched on a springboard to success in life. They know they are well prepared to compete, succeed, and pursue their dreams.

Accomplishments and Achievements

As one Black student explained, "There's not nearly as much drama here [at MRH] as you find in other high schools. We feel accepted for who we are, regardless of race, academics, or sexual orientation. Teachers accept us, and we accept each other." Perhaps, this helps explain why suspensions at MRH are rare. As Principal Grawer explained, students still experience all the issues and challenges associated with adolescence; however, MRH educators work hard to teach students how to resolve relational problems and restore relationships.

The school culture allows students to stay focused on learning and persist to graduation. The four-year high school graduation rate at MRH hovers at or near 100% each year. Almost every Black student at MRH graduates within four years. Openly, Black students explained how they liked coming to school at MRH. High attendance rates were common. As well, Black students were highly engaged in their classes. These factors contribute to strong performances on state assessments.

As shown in Figure 2.1, on the Missouri Department of Elementary and Secondary Education's algebra I assessment, MRH students outperform averages for all students in Missouri. Black students at MRH perform approximately as well as the average for all students in the state and are

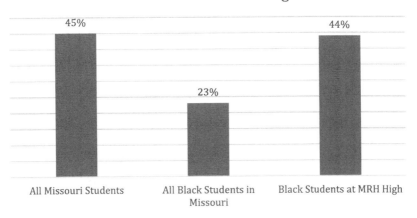

Figure 2.1 Comparison of Algebra I Performance

Percentages of Students Achieving Proficient or Advanced Performance in Algebra I

45% — All Missouri Students

23% — All Black Students in Missouri

44% — Black Students at MRH High

Figure 2.2 Comparison of English II Performance

Percentages of Students Achieving Proficient or Advanced Performance on English II Assessment (2018–19)

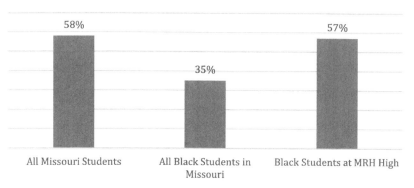

58%   35%   57%

All Missouri Students   All Black Students in Missouri   Black Students at MRH High

twice as likely to achieve proficiency or advanced levels as other Black students in Missouri.

Similarly, on the state's English II assessment, MRH students outperform averages for all students in Missouri. Black students at MRH perform approximately as well as the average for all students in the state and are almost twice as likely to achieve proficiency or advanced levels as other Black students in Missouri (see Figure 2.2).

Educators at MRH contend that they aim beyond state assessments. They design their courses so their students will be well-prepared to enroll and succeed in postsecondary education. According to GreatSchools.com, more than 75% of the school's graduates proceed to study at four-year or two-year colleges or in vocational programs (retrieved from www.great-schools.org/missouri/maplewood/1166-Maplewood-Richmond-Heights-High-School/). Most of the Black students interviewed at MRH reported they were planning to pursue four-year degrees in health professions, engineering, business, or teaching. One indication of the graduates' preparedness for postsecondary study is their performance on the ACT college entrance exam. When Principal Grawer began as principal, the average ACT score for MRH students was 14. Today, almost all MRH students take the ACT, and the average ACT score is 21. Today, many Maplewood Richmond Heights High School graduates attend highly esteemed colleges and universities, including Butler University, Columbia College, Cornell

University, Georgetown University, Howard University, and the University of Missouri.

History, Background, and Demographics

Built in 1909, Maplewood Richmond Heights High School was designed by famed architect William B. Ittner. Today, the century-old building does not resemble most urban high schools. In fact, the facility has changed dramatically over the decades, just as the school has changed.

Maplewood Richmond Heights High was initially designed to serve White middle-class students. Originally, the building's classrooms featured attractive, built-in wooden bookcases, ornate pillars, and stately brick fireplaces. As demographics changed, with White families moving farther out of the city, MRH became a "Black" school. In accordance with societal expectations for the Black student body, the fireplaces and bookcases were covered with drywall. Many aspects of the building fell into disrepair. Broken windows, graffiti, and deferred maintenance of the building structure and systems resulted in MRH devolving to resemble many typical inner-city high schools.

In the mid-2000s, MRH began changing once again. A new superintendent was hired, and she brought a new vision to the district. An MRH teacher explained how the new superintendent helped the community pass three substantial bond issues in a dozen years. In 2010, the district then hired Dr. Kevin Grawer to serve as MRH's principal. Together, the new school and district-level leaders repaired the broken windows, eliminated the graffiti, and removed the drywall to reveal the remarkably well-preserved woodwork from a prior era. A teacher explained how these new administrators believed "if kids are surrounded by beautiful things, they themselves will feel beautiful and feel appreciated and valued."

Black students talked about the school facility with pride. One student shared, "I've been to other schools that aren't far from here. The classrooms are dingy, and the grounds are trashy. Nobody wants to be in a place like that. Here, we feel special."

A teacher emphasized the impact of the renovated facility on students:

> When we finished all those renovations, students wouldn't leave. They didn't want to go home. The school day was over,

and students just hung out because they really liked being here. For some students it was nicer here than it was in their homes. So I don't have any vandalized desks in my classroom. Kids take care of this school and everything in the building.

As Principal Grawer and MRH teachers implemented many other curricular, instructional, and cultural changes, outcomes for the school's predominantly Black population improved substantially. More recently, White families have begun to return to MRH. They recognize that MRH students receive educational experiences equal to, or better than, those provided at affluent public, and even some private, schools. It is important to note, however, that the achievement of Black students at MRH remains impressively high.

Maplewood Richmond Heights High School remains comparatively small, serving approximately 405 students in grades 9 through 12. Approximately 58% of the students at MRH identify as White, 24% identify as Black, 10% identify with two or more racial/ethnic backgrounds, 6% are Latinx or Hispanic, and 2% identify as Asian. Approximately 39% of the students qualify for free- or reduced-price meals.

Distinguishing Values, Goals, and Strategies

"Literacy is the backbone of a human's intellectual life," explained Principal Grawer. "That means reading, writing, speaking, and reasoning. If we can't do one of those well, our life's going to be a lot harder than it should be." To change life at MRH High School, and to change the trajectory of the lives of MRH students, MRH educators adopted a laser focus on literacy. Principal Grawer underscored that all content areas, "English, mathematics, social studies, art, Spanish, physical education, etc.," played a role in building students' capacity to read, write, speak, and reason.

The focus on reading, writing, speaking, and reasoning was evident in almost every class session at MRH High School. For example, in a human anatomy class, the learning outcome projected on the screen explained, "I will describe how glucose is an example of negative (or balancing) feedback in the body." Early in the class session, students utilized small cutout paper representations of a liver, a muscle, a blood vessel, and glucose to model and explain (to each other) what too much blood glucose means within the context of human bodily functions, how too little blood glucose effects vital feedback mechanisms within the body, and what represented Type 1 and Type 2 diabetes. Students were not simply expected to listen to a lecture or answer multiple-choice question; they had to read, write, speak, and reason.

In an English classroom, bulletin boards reminded students, "You can't just argue," and "Your claims have to be robust and well-supported with evidence." Students were being trained to build strong, powerful arguments supported with rich evidence.

Similarly, in a government classroom, a bulletin board was covered with questions that had served as the focus for various classroom discussions. Questions such as, "Who has power?" "To what extent is government a necessity?" "What should be the goals of government?" "How is power divided?" were available to students as prompts to deepen and extend substantive conversations about the whys and hows of government and the various ways power dynamics influence governmental decisions and actions.

It is important to understand that the focus on literacy yielded positive outcomes, at least in part, because it was paired with a focus on relationships. Teachers at MRH deliberately worked to build positive, supportive relationships with students. One teacher confessed, "I think sometimes, as teachers, we are very superficial. We say to students, 'How are you? How was your day?' but we don't really take the time to ask them for real." While sincere relationships are important to all students, the teacher specified that sincere relationships are particularly important when working with Black students.

An MRH business teacher declared, "Relationship building has been the biggest thing. We know all our students. We know their strengths. We know the areas where they need a little push. We work really hard to build relationships with our students."

A social studies teacher cautioned that building relationships means more at MRH than it might mean at some schools. He explained:

> Some people think that when you say "building relationships," that means just be polite. Right? Well, you can do that with the grocery store clerk. When we talk about building relationships, it's more than just, "Hey, how are you doing?

Good to see you." It's about building a level of trust and breaking down some of those cultural barriers. The fact of the matter is, most of our staff is White, and it takes time to break down those barriers and build trust.

Teachers explained that building relationships meant taking time to listen to the challenges students were experiencing. It meant acting in a respectful manner in every situation, and especially in the most difficult situations. It meant demonstrating a commitment to helping every student experience growth, regardless of their reading level or their grade point average.

Again, the social studies teacher asserted:

> You teach the kid who comes through the door. You don't teach the kid you want to come through the door. So if Student A comes through the door reading at a third-grade level and Student B comes in at a twelfth-grade level, you better figure a way to move Student A to fourth-grade level and you better move Student B to the next level as well. You've got to build academic confidence in a kid who maybe hasn't had a lot of academic confidence. You have a kid who has been in school for ten years and has had no success. None. And for us to expect them to come in and work hard, we've got to show them, "Look, you can have success here. Even if it's a little success. Then, we can build on that."

Further, an English teacher explained that building relationships and building trust takes time and consistency. The English teacher believed that MRH is successful, in part, because students are likely to take courses from teachers multiple times during their high school career. The English teacher specifically described one of his Black students:

> When I had him as a freshman, he hated me. There was nothing I could do. I have a delightful sense of humor. He didn't appreciate it. He didn't appreciate me. I couldn't get that kid to smile. I couldn't get that kid to do anything. And then I had him his sophomore year as part of a small group of kids that I would help with homework. By the end of the year,

I had nominated him as student of the month. By that point, we had developed this relationship where he trusted me.

The connection between the focus on relationships and the focus on literacy might have best been summarized by another English teacher, who explained, "There's an ethic here of teaching the whole child. It's not an initiative or slogan or anything. It's really just an underlying philosophy." The teachers suggested that the work of building students' ability to read, write, speak, and reason could not be separated from the work of understanding each individual student and the factors that might be influencing each student's ability to focus and learn.

This focus on the whole child connects with another distinguishing value at MRH High School that might best be described as a "whatever it takes" attitude. Over the years, as teachers, support staff, and administrators came to know the MRH students, they identified a wide array of needs that extend far beyond academics. "Some need food, some have parents who are splitting up, some are experiencing homelessness," a teacher explained. At MRH, teachers, administrators, and school staff worked creatively and persistently to find all appropriate means to support their students and their families. In some cases, the MRH staff members connected students and families to useful community services. In other cases, staff members worked together to build new partnerships. For example, the school established the MRH Career Connections Program that offers students opportunities to connect with professionals in a variety of fields (e.g., nursing, engineering, architecture, media technology), shadow professionals in their work in the community, and participate in internships during their junior and senior year. A substantial amount of time and effort is devoted to building partnerships with companies and individuals so MRH students continue to benefit from these opportunities now and into the future.

Another example of the MRH "whatever it takes" attitude was the establishment of Joe's Place. MRH educators recognized that there were at least 30 students each night who found themselves without a home, due to serious family-related challenges. Joe's Place offers MRH teens a safe place to sleep, regular meals, and adult guidance and support when they are experiencing homelessness. Educators worked with local churches, volunteers, and district officials to establish Joe's Place as a successful nonprofit entity.

33

Through this laser focus on literacy and relationships, combined with a relentless, "whatever it takes" attitude, MRH High School has given life to the district's mission to inspire and prepare students to become leaders, stewards, scholars, and involved citizens in a diverse and changing world. Students at MRH are learning they can influence change in their personal lives, in their community, and across their world.

Challenges

Dr. Grawer recalled his early tenure at MRH, when the school was "struggling to get to the next level." Most days, persistent discipline issues overshadowed academic concerns. Teachers struggled to relate to the students and effectively manage classroom behavior.

A veteran teacher affirmed the principal's comments by explaining, "Twenty-five years ago, this was a different place. We had lots of fights and lots of crazy things happening here." Educators reported that, in the past, MRH was known for its athletic, rather than its academic, prowess. Well-known discipline issues further damaged the school's reputation. Community members stopped believing the school had the capacity to educate their children. Parents perceived MRH as a school that lacked rigor, lacked high expectations for either student behavior or student academic performance, and lacked a commitment to ensuring their children's success in school and in life. Further substantiating their concerns, Maplewood Richmond Heights High, like many urban schools, appeared to have a revolving door on the principal's office. One veteran teacher reported that in his first six years at MRH, the school had six different principals.

Dr. Grawer quickly endeavored to simultaneously improve student behavior and student academic success. He moved to create an orderly and supportive learning environment where teachers could teach and students could learn. Although the approach seemed logical to the new principal, the changes weren't universally appreciated. Principal Grawer recalled a Black student telling him, "Dr. Grawer, this is a predominantly Black school. We are not supposed to be good students, and it's supposed to be wild here." When asked how he, as the new principal, reacted, Grawer reflected, "[It] infuriated me, and I was determined to change the narrative."

Given the extent of the skepticism on the part of community members, parents, and students, Principal Grawer determined, "We have to start when we're undefeated. That means we start before the school year begins officially." He committed to building a new foundation by dedicating time to visit students' homes to get to know students and their families. "We get in the students' homes and we ask them, 'What does a good year look like for you?'"

Principal Grawer decided building trust required presence. Students and parents would not trust his commitment if they did not see his presence in the community. He explained, "So I'm in the neighborhood. I ride my bike, and they all know me. It's a tight urban neighborhood, three square miles. So they're used to seeing me around, at the grocery store, at the train stops, or wherever."

While presence was important, it was not sufficient. According to Principal Grawer, expectations that students would behave well and achieve well were necessary antecedents to changing the narrative and transforming the educational experience at Maplewood Richmond Heights High School. He explained, "We expect our students to be really good. I know that sounds simple, but it wouldn't work if we expected them to come in here and be crazy and disrespectful." Irvine and Fraser (1998), Bondy and Ross (2008), and Ladson-Billing (2002) described educators who cared in this manner as "warm demanders." Just as the MRH principal and teachers wanted to get to know students and families, they also wanted students to feel valued, respected, and loved. They recognized that students would feel *truly* loved, to the degree educators established and maintained high expectations for their effort and their success.

Grawer emphasized:

> We tell them, "We love you," every day. And that's a loaded statement. It means we expect more from you. And you've got to come here, and you've got to behave, and you've got to perform. And we've got to do the same as adults. We didn't create the school to give adults random jobs, and we didn't create the school to give you a rec center where you could hang out. This is a place of work, and we're going to help you and love you. We're going to have fun, too, but we're going to take our work seriously and ourselves lightly, and we're going to get after it every day.

Small steps were critical in making MRH students feel that educators at the school loved them enough to expect the best from them. One small step involved helping teachers maximize the use of every minute of class time to help students learn. Previously, it had been customary for students to begin lining up to exit the classroom door ten minutes prior to the end of each period. Even before students were lining up to exit, their engagement in class activities was minimal. Dr. Grawer insisted that students get the most out of each 50-minute class. Dr. Grawer, the school leadership team, and the teachers worked together to establish new expectations regarding the use of class time, along with corresponding routines and protocols.

Beyond filling each class period with activity, Principal Grawer and many teacher leaders at MRH knew that students would not feel truly cared for and loved unless teaching led them to learn important concepts each day, grow academically over time, and succeed throughout and beyond high school. "It's not about covering the content," one social studies teacher explained. "What good is covering? We're not making blankets here. We're building students' confidence in themselves." Teachers worked in teams to figure out how they could break down challenging content in ways that would help MRH students develop deep understandings. By "chunking" the curriculum, teachers identified the subtle concepts, vocabulary, and subskills that might have been overlooked in textbooks or traditional teaching approaches. Teachers kept their students in mind as they designed instruction together.

Also, teachers strived to show students representations of outstanding academic work. One Black student explained:

> Our teachers show us what an outstanding project looks like, and we talk about what makes the project outstanding. So after we've spent time looking at it, picking it apart, and studying it, we know what we need to do.

Principal Grawer explained that sharing examples of exemplary work with students became a standard practice at MRH. Before students begin working on a task, teachers engage students in looking carefully at a work sample that might have been produced by a student or a group of students during the prior semester. Teachers lead students in substantive discussions about *why* the work is exemplary and what students need to do to produce work that represents similar quality.

Principal Grawer expected teachers to provide MRH students nothing less than what they wanted for their own children. He contended:

> When we expect less from our students behaviorally, academically, or socially, they tend to think we don't care about them. At times teachers do that with students who don't look like them, and we make the mistake of thinking, "Well, this student cannot do that." We've got to get in front of that. We can't allow that.

It should be noted that several of the current staff members and the principal have children who attend or graduated from MRH High School. To make the expectations real, the principal kept a spotlight on data regarding attendance, student behavior, reading scores, and other major areas of focus. By the end of his first year as principal, the school's culture and learning environment had improved visibly.

While Principal Grawer expected much from MRH teachers, it is important to note that he relied heavily on teachers to lead change efforts. Many teachers commented on Dr. Grawer's leadership with statements such as, "He treats us like professionals," "We have incredible latitude as instructors," "He asks, 'What do you need? What can I get you? What do you need to get the job done?'" Dr. Grawer pushed teachers to see how attendance data, suspension data, and multiple sources of achievement data revealed the need for substantial changes in climate and culture, as well as in teaching and learning. He then enlisted teachers to lead the way in designing and executing solutions that were responsive to the individual needs of MRH students. For example, a "Lit Team," composed of teachers from multiple academic disciplines, was created to analyze student writing in each teacher's class. To realize a consistent, school-wide focus on literacy, all teachers established regular writing requirements for their students (often open-response paragraphs). The Lit Team then reviewed student writing samples and identified strengths and challenges. Teachers organized workshops to help one another build upon students' strengths and address writing needs. Writing samples gradually improved as multiple exposures to the writing process enhanced students' progress.

Today, MRH is a very different place than it was in 2010. For the most part, frequent student arguments, fights, and disruptions have been eliminated. The school is calm and civil, with a homelike atmosphere. The students know they belong, and they take care of the place and one another. One MRH parent shared that the school has adopted the philosophy of "one size fits each," as educators constantly adapt to meet the needs of every single student. Students are challenged intellectually and excited about the progress they see in themselves and their school. The new environment makes it easier for teachers to teach effectively and students to learn at high levels.

Recognitions

Maplewood Richmond Heights High School has received recognition from multiple local, state, and national sources for a variety of successes. Early in Dr. Grawer's tenure at MRH, the school received several acknowledgments based on the impressive growth of the school and the school's various efforts to respond to student needs. For example, in 2010–2011, MRH was one of only four St. Louis area high schools recognized for a perfect adequate yearly progress (AYP) score. In 2011, the Missouri Department of Elementary and Secondary Education recognized MRH for "Distinction in Performance" based on impressive academic growth. In 2012, MRH was designated as a National Model High School by the International Center for Leadership in Education because of the school's academic growth.

The school has continued to grow, excel, and receive accolades. Between 2012 and 2015, MRH was recognized as an Apple Distinguished High School. In 2014, MRH was designated as a Met-Life National Association of Secondary School Principals (NASSP) Breakthrough High School for sustained academic growth for all students. In 2015, the National Center for Urban School Transformation (NCUST) awarded MRH their America's Best Urban School Gold Award because of the school's impressive achievements for every demographic group. As well, in 2015, US News and World Report recognized MRH as Bronze Award winner in their America's Best High School Program.

More recently, in 2017, ACT recognized MRH as an exemplary high school because of their continued growth in ACT performance. In 2018, NASSP recognized MRH again as a Breakthrough High School because of sustained growth over time for all student groups. Additionally, in 2021, US News and World Report granted MRH their Gold Star High School Award, the 19th best high school in Missouri.

Recognition for MRH has come for many accomplishments beyond traditional academics. In 2012, the American School Board Journal and the National School Board Association recognized MRH as one of three national grand-prize winners of their Magna Award for the establishment of Joe's Place. Also, the school's Student Group on Race Relations (SGORR) has been featured on National Public Radio. The school's talented musicians have earned a "Best School Band" award, and in 2015, the school's science research team placed first in Missouri.

The benefits of these awards and recognitions are far-reaching. Dr. Grawer believes the awards have cemented the high school's place as a respected school in both the community and the metropolitan area. As the school garnered more respect, it was easier to hire talented staff, more students (who had been attending school outside the district) chose to return to MRH, more families moved into the district, property values rose, and more businesses came into the community.

Dr. Grawer says that he believes MRH High students are performing well because the students believe the adults at the school have deliberately tried to create an environment where the students have an excellent chance of succeeding. The students know they must work hard, but they put forth the effort, because "they perceive that the whole game has been transformed into something where they have a chance to win."

What It Is and What It Isn't: Factors That Have Influenced Success at Maplewood Richmond Heights High School

What It Is: The Development of Trust Requires Persistent Efforts

MRH educators recognized that they would not achieve the outcomes they sought unless they built positive relationships with students and families, especially students and families who had not been served well previously. Educators understood that the development of meaningful, strong, healthy relationships would require multiple, persistent efforts that built trust. As well, they recognized that the development of trust with many Black students and Black families would not happen easily or quickly. As a result, home visits became an important strategy at MRH. Also, teachers made deliberate efforts to take the time needed to get to know their students. Educators tried to listen intently to students and learn about their strengths, needs, hopes, and concerns. Wherever they could, MRH educators tried to adapt in ways to increase the likelihood that each MRH student would succeed.

What It Isn't: Superficial Politeness and Easy, Quick Fixes

At many schools that serve significant numbers of Black students, educators assume that they are doing all that is necessary or appropriate to build positive relationships with Black students and Black families by simply being polite and demonstrating good intentions. When educators do not take the necessary time to listen, and when they do not commit to sustained efforts to build trust, educators do not learn about the deeper issues that may lead students to feel educators do not want them to succeed.

What It Is: Using Almost Every Class in Every Discipline to Build Literacy Skills

At MRH, almost every class became a literacy class. Teachers worked together to consider how reading, writing, speaking, and reasoning could be key foci of their courses. As well, the school's Lit Team worked together to review student writing and develop strategies to help teachers advance the literacy of MRH students.

What It Isn't: Assuming That Literacy Is the Responsibility of Only One Department or One Set of Teachers

In many American schools, teachers build artificial walls around their courses, as if students can develop deep knowledge of one subject without understanding how the content is influenced by other disciplines. In some states and school districts, narrow-minded accountability policies contribute to a mindset that is counterproductive to the needs of students. In contrast, MRH educators recognized that their students would not achieve their potential in life if they did not develop strong literacy skills. As well, MRH educators recognized their chances of helping students succeed would be greatly enhanced if they committed to working together to build each student's literacy skills.

What It Is: Insisting Upon High Behavioral and Academic Expectations, While Recognizing That Students Might Need Different Supports to Reach Those Expectations

At MRH, educators decided to expect the best from their students, even when student behavior and student academic success were far from the best. Teachers and administrators expected students to interact with one another respectfully. They expected students to learn how to resolve conflicts maturely. As well, they expected students to perform at high levels in every academic discipline. Teachers helped students understand what constituted excellent work, and the teachers helped students know that they were expected to generate excellent work. At the same time, MRH educators understood that each student might need different support to achieve the high expectations. Teachers adopted the "one size fits each" approach to tailor strategies in ways that advanced each student's progress toward the high expectations.

What It Isn't: Lowering Behavioral and Academic Expectations so Students Feel Comfortable with Low Levels of Success

In many schools, educators believe that "it isn't fair" to have high expectations for Black students, especially when they have endured difficult situations or are performing substantially below grade level. Educators' satisfaction with students achieving only the most modest expectations allows them to be comfortable with the programs, processes, procedures, and practices that have held Black students behind for years.

What It Is: Engaging School Personnel in Designing Routes to School Success

At MRH, school and district leaders empowered teachers to work together to determine how they would generate substantial improvements in student learning. Teachers felt that their administrators trusted and respected them. As a result, they were even more committed to doing their best to grapple with difficult issues and help one another pursue growth.

What It Isn't: Making Top-Down Decisions about How Teachers and Other Staff Will Pursue Important School Goals

In many schools, well-intentioned leaders dictate to teachers and other school personnel detailed rules and procedures about how they will work to improve student achievement. Often, these dictates leave educators feeling like unskilled workers who are expected to leave their professional knowledge, commitment, and wisdom at home. Top-down leaders rarely achieve success in realizing the changes they envision, because it is almost impossible to generate quality implementation without the commitment of those responsible for implementing.

References

Bondy, E., & Ross, D. D. (2008). The teacher as warm demander. *Educational Leadership, 66*(1), 54–58.

Irvine, J. J., & Fraser, J. W. (1998). Warm demanders. *Education Week, 17*(35), 56.

Ladson-Billings, G. (2002). I ain't writin' nuttin': Permissions to fail and demands to succeed in urban classrooms. In L. Delpit & J. K. Dowdy (Eds.), *The skin that we speak: Thoughts on language and culture in the classroom* (pp. 107–120). The New Press.

Wynnebrook Elementary School

School District of Palm Beach County, West Palm Beach, Florida

"I am respectful. I am responsible. I am a peacemaker. I am prepared."

This is the code of conduct at Wynnebrook. This is it. There are not school rules, classroom rules, or cafeteria rules. This is school-wide. It applies to every student. It applies to all teachers and everyone who works here. It applies to me. We all say it every day, and we take time to talk about what it means and how it applies to everything we do. It started with the former principal, Mr. Jeff Pegg, back in 2000, and it continues to influence everything we do.

— Suzanne Berry, principal, Wynnebrook Elementary

It's amazing. I heard grown adults saying, "I'm afraid to walk out in a hallway," This is an elementary school, right? I couldn't fathom that they were afraid to walk in the hallway, but I was listening. And we had 70 great kids who were bused all the way from a very poor area. . . . Anyhow, the staff let the kids run the school because they were afraid of the kids. There just weren't good systems in place, so we put systems in place to hold everyone accountable, adults and students. And it's just about giving kids love and respect. Nobody respected the kids. Sometimes, we've got to give respect first. Not just sometimes, all the time. I can be a disciplinarian, but I also respect people, and I respect students. And when people saw the administration respecting

DOI: 10.4324/9781003277910-4

students, everybody knew I was serious about it, and they all started doing it.

– Jeff Pegg, former principal, Wynnebrook Elementary

I think one of the best things about our Professional Learning Communities (PLCs) was when we started breaking down the standards in the grade-level meetings. So we would have these discussions and say, "Okay, here is your standard, but what does that actually mean?" And it was so eye-opening to see one standard, one sentence, and see how many ways teachers at the same grade level viewed what the standard meant. So we'd look at a standard and say, "Okay, what does this verb mean in this standard?" We talked about how we had to make sure the kids knew how to do whatever was required. And to this day, I think that's what continues to make us successful. Our teachers don't have to rely on a script. They don't need that. They know this is the standard. This is what we need to teach. Everything else is just a resource we use to get to that standard.

– Suzanne Berry, principal, Wynnebrook Elementary

Almost 400 of the 900 students who attend Wynnebrook are Black, and almost all the students qualify for free- or reduced-price meals. Wynnebrook's Black students perceive themselves as avid and proficient readers. "I'm hooked on Nancy Drew books," one fifth-grade student confessed, "but I also like reading historical nonfiction." Another fifth grader shared, "I really liked reading *The Watsons Go to Birmingham* [by Christopher Paul Curtis]. It is historical fiction, but it is based on real things that happened to Black people in the 1960s." "Yeah, I liked it when we were trying to figure out each character's motivations for the things they said or did," another student added. A fourth-grade girl shared that she liked reading about the civil rights activist Claudette Colvin. "She was one brave woman! I want to be like her!" she explained.

Wynnebrook's Black students also described themselves as skillful mathematicians. For example, a third-grade student explained, "Multiplication is a little bit challenging, but when I do it right, it's actually really easy." Another student explained, "In my class, we're learning how to do statistics, like mean and median. I'm learning stuff here that my cousins in high school haven't learned yet."

Mostly, Wynnebrook students described their school as a place where they were comfortable. One Black boy shared, "I like Wynnebrook because all the teachers are patient and they never scream at you." A Black girl confirmed, "Wynnebrook is a good school because the teachers are kind. They don't yell at you for everything. They're patient, and they're kind." Students explained that their teachers cared about them and wanted them to like school.

When asked about the other students at Wynnebrook, one Black boy explained, "Tension among students is rare." Another child explained, "Everybody here is friendly." Another added, "Yes, because teachers are more in control, and the kids care for the teachers."

When asked to explain more about student behavior at Wynnebrook, one student attempted to make the situation very clear by stating:

> Here, the teachers make us learn the Code of Conduct early. You know, "I am respectful. I am responsible. I am a peace-maker. I am prepared." And you've got to follow those words. You've got to follow those words all the time. You have to be an example of the Code of Conduct. That's just what we learn here. That's what we do.

Accomplishments and Achievements

Engaging and effective instruction within a positive, accepting culture has resulted in impressive academic achievements for students at Wynnebrook. Each year, for the past 18 years, the school has earned an "A" grade from the Florida Department of Education, resulting from high levels of student performance and high levels of growth on state assessments. While Wynnebrook students, in general, perform at high levels, the school's Black students perform at higher levels than elementary students throughout Florida.

As shown in Figure 3.1, 55% of students in Florida elementary schools perform at the proficient or advanced level in English. Unfortunately, only 38% of Florida's Black elementary students perform at the proficient or advanced level. In contrast, 70% of Wynnebrook's Black students perform at the proficient or advanced level in English. If all Black students in Florida performed as well as Black students at Wynnebrook, Florida's achievement gap would vanish and perhaps would be reversed, with Black students outperforming White students.

Figure 3.1 Comparison of English Performance

Percentages of Students Achieving Proficient or Advanced Performance in English (2018–2019)

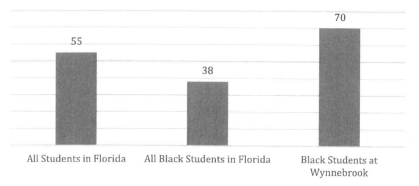

Figure 3.2 Comparison of Mathematics Performance

Percentages of Students Achieving Proficient or Advanced Performance in Math (2018–2019)

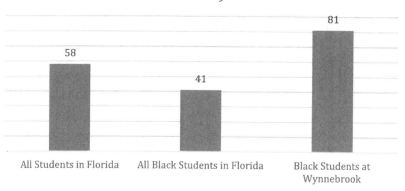

The academic performance of Wynnebrook's Black students in mathematics is similarly impressive. As illustrated in Figure 3.2, 58% of Florida's elementary-grade students perform at the proficient or advanced level in mathematics. In contrast, only 41% of Florida's Black elementary students perform at the proficient or advanced level. Impressively, 81% of Wynnebrook's Black students perform at the proficient or advanced level in mathematics. Wynnebrook's Black students are almost twice as likely to perform at the proficient or advanced level in mathematics than other Black students in Florida.

The Florida Standards Assessment (FSA) also includes an assessment of academic proficiency in science. On the science assessment, Wynnebrook's Black students outperformed Black students in Florida, as well as the state's general elementary school population. As shown in Figure 3.3, 51% of all Florida elementary students demonstrated proficient or advanced science performance in 2018–2019, compared to only 31% of Florida's Black elementary students. However, 63% of Wynnebrook's Black students demonstrated proficient or advanced performance on the same assessment.

In addition to demonstrating outstanding performance on state assessments, Wynnebrook's Black students are rarely suspended. Fewer than 1% of Black students are suspended each year (compared to 9% of Black students statewide and compared to 5% of all students statewide). Also, fewer Black students at Wynnebrook are chronically absent (absent 15 or more days of the school year). In 2018–2019, 13% of Wynnebrook's Black students were reported as chronically absent (compared to 25% of Black students in Florida and 22% of all students statewide).

Successes for Wynnebrook's Black students are visible in classroom projects, attendance data, discipline data, individual reading

Figure 3.3 Comparison of Science Performance

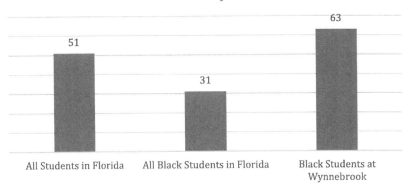

Percentages of Students Achieving Proficient or Advanced Performance in Science (2018– 2019)

accomplishment data, school performances, and state assessment data. The school's focus on both academic skills and relational skills prepares students to succeed far beyond elementary school. Black students at Wynnebrook exude optimism about their academic futures. As one Black male student asserted, "My parents believe I can succeed. My teachers believe I can succeed. So I believe I can succeed, as well . . . all the way through high school and college."

History, Background, and Demographics

Located in West Palm Beach, Florida, Wynnebrook Elementary is a highly rated public elementary school serving preschool, kindergarten, and students in first through fifth grades. The school is part of the Palm Beach County School District, the tenth largest district in the nation. The school opened in 1966 and served predominantly White families; however, in the following 15 years, many White families moved farther west to less-populated areas. Throughout the 1980s and 1990s, the numbers of Black and Latinx students at Wynnebrook grew, and the percentage of students meeting low-income criteria also grew. Today, 94% of Wynnebrook's students meet federal free- or reduced-price lunch criteria, 50% of the students identify as Latinx or Hispanic, and 42% identify as Black or African American. Only 7% of Wynnebrook's students are White or Caucasian.

Even though Wynnebrook opened over 50 years ago, only five individuals have served as the school's principal. When Jeff Pegg became Wynnebrook's fourth principal in 1999–2000, over 80% of the students were Latinx or Black. In the next few years, the percentage of students of color grew to 90%.

When he arrived at Wynnebrook, Principal Pegg was astonished to hear teachers express their fear of Black students. He learned that teachers were especially afraid of a group of 70 Black students who were bused from a community along Florida's eastern coast. The students had become known as "the green bus students" because their school bus was named "the green bus." While teachers feared Wynnebrook's Black students in general, there seemed to be a higher level of fear of the green bus students.

Often, problems with green bus students started on their long bus rides to and from Wynnebrook. Rather than waiting for problems to occur and be reported to him after the fact, Principal Pegg decided he would ride the green bus along with the students. "So I got on the bus, and I sat right next to two of the students who had the biggest reputation for being troublemakers," explained Principal Pegg.

During these bus rides, the principal acquired a deeper understanding of the world of the green bus students. "I got to see and understand a whole lot," Principal Pegg shared. "For example, we'd ride along, and it wouldn't be long before we'd see drug deals going down in front of us. It was right in front of the students. The bus driver would say, 'They see this stuff all the time.'"

The principal would also use these bus rides as opportunities to meet the parents of green bus students. "We made connections with parents that we never would have made otherwise, because they would pick their kids up at bus stops." Eventually, green bus students started asking Principal Pegg to ride their bus. So he made a deal with the students. "All right, if you have four great days with no bus referrals, I'll ride the bus with you on Friday," he negotiated. The students perceived the principal's presence as a reward, and the principal ended most weeks riding the green bus.

Even though Principal Pegg was shocked and dismayed by the fear teachers expressed, he recognized the importance of listening and putting systems in place to minimize or eliminate problems. He explained:

> Adults were fearful because they let the kids run the school and there were no systems for anyone to follow. Adults were too afraid to hold the kids accountable. We put systems in place to hold everyone accountable, adults and students. Everybody had to be part of the solution.

The Wynnebrook Code of Conduct became a foundation upon which many of the systems were built. The Code of Conduct stood as a teaching tool to help everyone understand how their actions, or inactions, influenced their success and the success of others at Wynnebrook. When teachers reported a difficult situation, they knew the principal and/or another member of the school's leadership team would immediately join them in their classrooms. Typically, when leaders arrived, ensuing conversations focused on the Code of Conduct. "I am respectful. I am responsible. I am a peacemaker. I am prepared." These conversations gave students an opportunity to learn from their behavior, make corrections, and remain in the classroom environment successfully.

Instead of promoting a negative, accusatory tone, suggesting, "You did this or that," leaders used the Code of Conduct to open channels of communication, encouraging students to reflect and identify alternative ways of addressing their feelings and concerns. In other words, students were not simply admonished for inappropriate or unproductive behaviors; instead, they were encouraged to talk about how they might have chosen a more respectful or responsible approach. In addition, students were challenged to consider how they could better prepare themselves to serve as peacemakers when conflicts arise. Teachers saw school leaders model respectful and effective responses to difficult situations and learned to emulate these strategies. In this way, teachers also learned how to be peacemakers.

"It's just about giving kids love and respect," Principal Pegg explained. "Nobody respected the kids, because the kids didn't act as if they respected the adults. Sometimes, we've got to give respect first. Well, not just sometimes. All the time," he emphasized.

Shortly after coming to Wynnebrook, Principal Pegg hired Suzanne Berry to be a first-grade teacher. In 2008, she was promoted to serve as the school's assistant principal. Eight years later, in 2016, when Mr. Pegg received a district-level leadership position, Ms. Berry was promoted to serve as principal at Wynnebrook. Clearly, Mr. Pegg did not leave succession up to chance, and in response, Principal Berry continued to emphasize and build upon the foundation he had established. As a result, achievement has continued to grow.

Distinguishing Values, Goals, and Strategies

When Principal Pegg started as principal at Wynnebrook, there were teachers who were "afraid to walk in the school's hallways." Additionally, Principal Pegg quickly learned that many of Wynnebrook's Black students could not read and were not developing literacy skills. Principal Pegg recalled visiting classes during literacy instruction. He shared:

> I will never forget when I visited third-grade classrooms. The students (most of them students of color) had basal readers in front of them. So I asked this one young man to read to me, and he struggled so much that I ended up reading to him. I noticed the same with most of the other students. They struggled so much to read the words there was no way

they were likely to get the meaning. So later I talked to the teachers, and I asked, "Do you understand a good majority of these students can't read the basal reader you put in front of them? Do you realize they are not able to read most of the words and they certainly don't comprehend what they're reading?" The teachers responded, "Of course, we know. They [the students] came to us that way."

The principal explained that Wynnebrook teachers were assigning reading tasks but not teaching students how to pursue those tasks successfully. Teachers used the basal readers the district provided because they did not have other tools to teach reading. Teachers were providing the best "instruction" they knew how to provide, especially considering the "academic deficiencies" they perceived in Wynnebrook's students of color.

Principal Pegg confessed that he was tempted to challenge his teachers and ask, "What are you going to do to change this situation?" However, he recognized that, first, he had to ask himself, "What are you going to do to change the situation?" Just as Principal Pegg recognized that everyone had to share accountability for changing the social climate and culture at Wynnebrook, he also recognized that everyone had to share accountability for changing the academic culture of the school. Although he was a new principal who inherited old problems, Principal Pegg understood he would need to be the first person to accept accountability for bringing about change. Neither Principal Pegg nor Principal Berry referred to the term *reciprocal accountability*; however, in this instance and in many others, both leaders modeled the concept of reciprocal accountability as a core value at Wynnebrook. Fink (2014) explained:

[Reciprocal accountability] means that if school or district leaders are going to hold teachers or principals accountable for something, then those leaders have an equal responsibility to ensure that teachers and principals know how to do what they are expected to do.

(p. 1)

Before Principal Pegg or Principal Berry expected Wynnebrook teachers to enact change, these leaders considered what they themselves would do to ensure teachers had the support they needed (time, materials, training, etc.) to implement the change successfully. Before Wynnebrook leaders could expect teachers to be accountable for teaching their students to behave as scholars, the leaders knew they needed to establish school-wide expectations for scholarly behavior (the Code of Conduct). The leaders knew they needed to open lines of communication with the parents of the green bus students. As well, the leaders knew they needed to provide immediate assistance and constructive modeling when teachers needed help restoring order.

Principal Pegg recognized that changes in literacy instruction were not likely unless teachers were given better tools for teaching reading. He utilized the school's Title I funds to purchase sets of reading materials that allowed teachers to help each individual student advance their reading level. "Oh yeah, the teachers thought I had lost my mind. I boxed up all those basal readers and got rid of them," Principal Pegg chuckled. Today, Wynnebrook teachers access a well-organized stockroom filled with reading materials that address the full range of student reading levels. Many of the books reflect the backgrounds and cultures of Wynnebrook's students.

Also, Principals Pegg and Berry knew that teachers needed high-quality, intensive, and sustained professional development so they were prepared to provide effective literacy instruction that accelerated the progress of students who were reading far below grade-level standards. They ensured that professional development, focused on the state's literacy standards, became central to teachers' professional learning at Wynnebrook.

Principals Pegg and Berry knew that Wynnebrook teachers needed time to plan and prepare for the high-quality literacy instruction they expected in every classroom. To provide teachers more time, Principal Pegg stopped asking teachers to supervise students in the school cafeteria before classroom instruction began. "I supervised the kids from 7:00 to 7:30 so the teachers could go straight to their classrooms to get ready for the day," he explained. "Later, I was able to hire additional support personnel to help supervise the kids early in the morning," he added.

Perhaps most importantly, Principal Pegg and Principal Berry understood that Wynnebrook teachers needed to work together to plan high-quality instruction that would lead Wynnebrook's students (most of whom were students of color) to deep levels of understanding of important concepts in mathematics, science, literacy, and other subjects. The school did not have systems or structures to support such collaboration, so the leaders began intensive efforts to establish strong professional learning communities (PLCs) at Wynnebrook.

52

Through reciprocal accountability, Wynnebrook has created an environment where teachers have a high likelihood of leading Black students (and all other students) to impressive levels of academic success. A Wynnebrook teacher explained:

> Administrators here work to remove barriers for teachers, so all we have to do is focus on teaching. The administration works day and night to make sure that's all teachers have to worry about. Then, we teachers remove the barriers for our students. We provide them with what they need to be successful, regardless of homelife. There is a sense of community here. We all support each other so that everyone succeeds.

Challenges

The route to establishing reciprocal accountability at Wynnebrook Elementary was neither smooth nor easy. While Principal Pegg believed in the concept, in 1999 and the early 2000s, there were leaders in the school district's central office who seemed unfamiliar with the idea. Even when Wynnebrook was improving instruction rapidly, there were school district administrators who criticized the school for failing to implement district policies and procedures.

Principal Pegg recalled:

> I remember this district administrator coming in here and dragging us over the coals for stuff. She said, "You've got to do this and this and this and this." I threw my book down, and I said, "Why won't somebody ask me about my Black males?" Performance was improving! Really improving! But they were only concerned about whether we were doing all the things they wanted us to do.

Many principals might have quickly abandoned the things they knew were working for students to appease their supervisors; however, Principal Pegg and Principal Berry were determined to stay focused on what they were doing to build the capacity of teachers to teach Wynnebrook's students challenging academic standards.

For example, district curriculum experts developed a scope and sequence that specified when teachers were expected to teach specific concepts and skills. When district leaders insisted that Wynnebrook follow the prescribed scope and sequence, then–Assistant Principal Berry recommended that Principal Pegg take a different course of action. Based on Ms. Berry's suggestion, Principal Pegg convened the school's teachers and said, "This is what the district provided, but I want you to look at it and map it out. I want to see what makes sense to you. You need to determine what will work for our students." Principal Pegg recognized that the district wanted teachers to teach every standard specified by the state, even if the standard had limited value in preparing students to develop strong literacy, numeracy, or science skills.

Marzano (2003) emphasized that leaders needed to help educators focus on a viable curriculum. The curriculum is not viable or teachable if there is more to teach than can be taught in the minutes, hours, and days available for instruction. While many state, district, and school administrators seem to be comfortable ignoring this logic, Principal Pegg refused to ignore the obvious. The teachers appreciated the trust and respect demonstrated by their school leaders, and they worked earnestly to refine the scope and sequence in ways they believed would result in Wynnebrook students mastering the most important academic standards. Mr. Pegg argued, "If it didn't make sense to the teachers, it wasn't going to work anyway."

Similarly, district leaders developed math assessments they expected all schools to use. Principal Berry explained how the district's assessments did not necessarily test the math content teachers had taught, and the district assessment might give little or no attention to state standards that had been the focus of considerable teaching. As a result, the district assessment did little to help teachers know how to refine their teaching. Principal Berry shared, "Instead of using the district assessment, our teachers constructed our own common assessments. We looked at the standards, and prior to teaching each unit, the teachers would determine what students should be able to answer to show us they had mastered the standard." Wynnebrook teachers determined what they needed to teach and how they needed to teach it so their students would have a high likelihood of demonstrating mastery on the common assessments they created. Principal Berry admitted, "We almost never used the district assessment."

The district continued to insist that schools follow their procedures; however, the Wynnebrook principals resisted (sometimes quietly and sometimes more assertively) when they perceived that the mandates detracted from their teachers' capacity to serve students well. Then, in 2016, the dynamic between Wynnebrook and the district office reversed course. Principal Pegg recalled receiving a visit from one of the district's regional superintendents. The regional superintendent explained that the district superintendent, Dr. Avossa, upon reviewing school-level data, wanted to know more about Wynnebrook's successes. District leaders determined they needed Mr. Pegg on their team as an instructional superintendent. Mr. Pegg agreed to join them but indicated that Wynnebrook would be best served with Ms. Berry as principal.

While the district bureaucracy posed significant challenges, building teachers' capacity to provide effective, engaging instruction presented an even greater challenge to Wynnebrook's leaders. Wynnebrook (like many schools) succeeds only to the degree teachers believe that, together, they can educate every student they have the privilege to serve. According to Donohoo (2017), "When a school staff shares the belief that through their collective actions, they can positively influence student outcomes, student achievement increases" (p. xv). In fact, research by Goddard et al. (2000) revealed that a school team's collective efficacy is even more powerful than socioeconomic factors in predicting student achievement.

When Mr. Pegg began serving as Wynnebrook's principal, teachers were not efficacious about their ability to teach the school's students, especially the school's Black students. In truth, some of the teachers may not have believed that any teacher could successfully educate Wynnebrook's Black students. Principal Pegg and his leadership team understood their role in helping Wynnebrook teachers believe they could teach Black students (including the green bus students) to learn challenging academic standards. Each teacher would need to believe this, even though many students were performing two or three years below grade level, even though many students did not behave as teachers would have liked, and even though most of the school's learning materials did not respond to the students' strengths or needs.

Wynnebrook took a vital step toward realizing a sense of collective efficacy when Principal Pegg sent three of his team members (including Ms. Berry) to a weeklong seminar on professional learning communities. "Most people didn't know what professional learning communities were back then, and people had not heard of Rick DuFour or Becky DuFour," explained Principal Pegg. After the initial professional development, Principal Pegg accompanied other Wynnebrook educators to subsequent sessions, even as the real work was commencing back at school.

"We realized we had to totally revamp our master schedule and organize time to maximize the focus on literacy," explained Principal Pegg. As well, leaders developed the necessary structures for regularly scheduled teacher collaboration. This teacher collaboration became the engine for building teachers' belief in their capacity to teach Wynnebrook students well.

Principal Berry explained that teachers knew what was written in state standards but "were all over the map regarding what the standards actually meant." She added, "It was so eye-opening to see one standard, one sentence, and how many different views teachers had about what the standard meant." She explained that PLC meetings provided opportunities for teachers to reach deeper understandings of what students needed to learn. She claimed, "Teachers would say, 'This is what the kids need to understand! We've got to make sure the kids know how to do this!'" As they came to know exactly what their students needed to learn, teachers were no longer willing to follow a prepackaged guide, script, or workbook.

PLC meetings became venues where teachers worked together to create common formative assessments. Principal Berry explained, "Once teachers understood the standards, they were ready to determine what kind of tasks students should be able to complete to show they had really mastered the standard." Each common assessment became the destination toward which each teacher on the team would focus. By establishing a clear sense of the destination *before* teachers planned and provided instruction, teachers began to develop a greater sense of efficacy.

Common formative assessments at Wynnebrook generated another important advantage. Principal Pegg explained:

> When four or five teachers worked together to create a common assessment they were all going to administer on the same day, teachers had a new reason to support each other and work together. Nobody wanted to fall behind, and nobody wanted to let their colleagues fall behind.

In many public schools, teachers feel and act like independent contractors. Each teacher does their best to teach their students, isolated from their peers within their individual, self-contained classrooms. At Wynnebrook, a different culture emerged in which teachers felt a responsibility to one another. Principal Berry explained, "The teams would eat lunch together and spend additional time together. Instead of complaining about what Johnny did, they talked about how a lesson went, what worked well, and what didn't help get students to learn the content."

Principal Pegg added, "The teachers learned that they could help each other succeed. If they talked to each other and listened to each other, they could really help each other succeed at teaching our kids." Principals Pegg and Berry were willing to support Wynnebrook teachers in whatever ways were necessary; however, they also knew that teachers could be a powerful support to one another. One Wynnebrook teacher explained:

> We all want to help one another. The relationships we have together as colleagues are so important because we can share and there is no embarrassment. There's no, "Oh, my kids did that, and I am sad," or "Yours did well and I am embarrassed," or "I don't want all this information put out there." Everybody is together saying, "How can we support all our students as a grade and then as a school?" I think the sharing and the level of comfort and the relationships among our colleagues when we are planning are everything.

Throughout Wynnebrook Elementary, one sees evidence of powerful collective efficacy. The specific teaching strategies that work impressively well to help students understand concepts in one classroom can also be observed in the classroom next door or down the hall, because teachers have worked together, planned together, shared their best ideas with one another, and helped one another through fears and frustrations. Wynnebrook teachers described the trust they built in one another. One teacher explained, "I know my colleagues want me to succeed. That means a lot. That makes me want even more to help them succeed. Our trust in each other is amazing."

Recognitions

Wynnebrook Elementary has received numerous awards recognizing the academic accomplishments of the school's students. Every year, over the past 18 years, the Florida Department of Education has designated Wynnebrook as an "A" school because of the students' high levels of achievement on state assessments, as well as their high levels of growth each year. In 2011, and again in 2016, Wynnebrook won the Exceeding Expectations Award from the East County Technical Assistance Center. In the school's front office, a framed page from the US Congressional Record, dated January 3, 2017, acknowledges Wynnebrook's many accomplishments. Congress noted that even though 94% of Wynnebrook's students met low-income criteria and almost 90% of the students were students of color, Wynnebrook's performance on state assessments ranked 19th among the 124 elementary schools in the relatively affluent Palm Beach School District.

In 2017, Wynnebrook received an America's Best Urban Schools Award, recognizing multiple indicators of academic success for every demographic group of students. Wynnebrook is one of only nine schools in Florida to win the America's Best Urban Schools Award.

It is important to note that Wynnebrook has been recognized for many other accomplishments. For example, the school received the Palm Beach County School District's Golden School Award, recognizing the school's exemplary volunteer programs. In 2016, Florida's Tax Watch, an independent, nonpartisan, and nonprofit public policy research institute, awarded its Principal Leadership Award to Principal Jeff Pegg. In November 2018, Principal Berry accepted a School of Excellence Award from the Florida PTA. Also, in 2019, Florida Atlantic University's Green School Recognition Program awarded Wynnebrook a Green School of Quality Award.

On a wall in Principal Berry's office, she has posted a piece of work from a first-grade student. The document simply states, "Dear Ms. Berry, thank you for calming me down today. I love you, Ms. Berry." When asked about the document, Principal Berry shared, "It's all about the kids, isn't it? It's about their lives and their futures." She added, "At the end of the day, you have to believe in your school. You have to be willing to step outside the box, and you have to be willing every now and again to get a little crazy and speak up on behalf of your school."

What It Is and What It Isn't: Factors That Have Influenced Success at Wynnebrook Elementary School

What It Is: Creating Safe Environments for Everyone

Wynnebrook leaders understood that teachers are not likely to teach well if they feared their students. Leaders did their part to establish systems and structures that made school safe for teachers. Also, leaders consistently modeled appropriate, respectful ways to engage with students and teach students how to resolve conflicts and interact with others constructively. At Wynnebrook, teachers learned how to use the school's Code of Conduct to *teach* students how to behave as scholars. Teachers reinforced countless examples of students modeling the Code of Conduct so that students came to see themselves as respectful, responsible, and prepared peacemakers.

What It Isn't: Perpetuating Ineffective Rule-Based, Punishment-Focused Systems

In many schools, teachers are afraid to interact with Black students (especially Black male students). Rules are not designed to teach students how to interact with one another successfully; instead, they are designed to make adults feel like they are in control. Often, misbehavior is ignored until it is perceived as a crisis. Then, teachers and administrators feel justified in suspending or expelling Black students.

What It Is: Providing Students Access to Literature That Resonates with Their Lives

At Wynnebrook, teachers led students to get excited about literacy. Teachers taught important literacy standards, often by allowing students to read material that resonated with students' concerns, experiences, and backgrounds. Students discovered that printed words, sentences, and paragraphs held meaning in their lives. Wynnebrook leaders made sure that teachers had access to abundant reading materials (at appropriate reading levels). These materials reflected the backgrounds, cultures, and interests of Wynnebrook's students.

What It Isn't: Limiting Focus to Literature with Little Relevance to Black Students

In many typical schools, Black students find little reward in reading. They struggle to decode words that have little or no meaning to them. Even when they understand the words, the concepts or experiences seem alien to their lives. Often, Black students never experience the power and the magic of written language, because they are only asked to read content they find boring and meaningless.

What It Is: Leaders Assuming Responsibility for Providing Support

As Wynnebrook's leaders identified changes that teachers needed to make to improve teaching and learning, the leaders first considered what they needed to do to support teachers. School leaders assumed reciprocal accountability by considering how they could support teachers in understanding and implementing changes. For example, leaders considered how they could "take things off teachers' plates," freeing up teachers' time to plan and implement the desired changes. Leaders provided teachers professional learning experiences, modeled desired practices, and reinforced teachers' positive efforts.

What It Isn't: Mandating without Supporting

Often, teachers receive many directives and little support to help them implement the directives. Some leaders assume that teachers 1) understand specifically what leaders want them to do, 2) understand why the directive is beneficial to students, 3) know all they need to know to implement the directive well, and 4) have all the support they need to implement the directive well. Of course, if these assumptions were accurate, a great majority of teachers would have implemented the directives before they were asked to do so. Often, the lack of reciprocal accountability results in "leaders" not "leading" anybody.

What It Is: Ensuring Sufficient Time to Teach Content Well

Wynnebrook's leaders tried to ensure that teachers did not endeavor to teach more state standards than could be taught well in the time available. Despite district pressure, school leaders allowed teachers to determine which standards were most important to long-term student success. Leaders encouraged teams of teachers to sequence the standards in ways that made sense to the teachers. Leaders wanted teachers to understand that it was more important to build student understanding than it was to "cover" everything listed in state standards.

What It Isn't: "Covering" Content without "Teaching" Anything Well

Unfortunately, many leaders insist that teachers abide by district-created scope and sequence charts, even though schools have years of experience doing so with lousy learning results for students of color. As a result, teachers feel compelled to touch upon each concept or skill listed in the curriculum documents without any expectation that their students will achieve a deep understanding of anything.

What It Is: Maximizing Time for High-Quality Teacher Collaboration

Educators at Wynnebrook developed a collective sense of efficacy concerning their ability to help students of color learn challenging academic content well. Professional learning communities provided a powerful engine for building this collective efficacy. Teachers learned to support one another in ways that helped them become increasingly effective educators. Leaders made sure that teachers had abundant time for collaboration. Additionally, leaders supported teachers in starting with the end in mind by helping teachers develop common formative assessments before they began teaching concepts (Wiggins & McTighe, 1998). Teachers and leaders worked to build a culture of trust and support, nurturing teachers' commitment to help one another and their willingness to learn from one another.

What It Isn't: Token Collaboration / Token Collaboration Time

In many schools, teachers experience token collaboration, during which teachers plan their lessons without any clear sense of what students should learn or any clarity about how they will determine if learning has occurred. As a result, collaboration does not lead teachers to reflect upon their practices and refine their lessons in ways that lead students to deeper levels of understanding. In some schools, leaders initiate something they call a professional learning community, amid toxic environments where there is more suspicion than trust. Unless and until substantial trust exists, collaborations are generally not "professional," do not result in much "learning," and never generate any real sense of "community."

References

Donohoo, J. (2017). *Collective efficacy: How educators' beliefs impact student learning*. Corwin.

Fink, S. (2014, January 24). *Reciprocal accountability: How effective instructional leaders improve teaching and learning*. https://k-12leadership.org/reciprocal-accountability-how-effective-instructional-leaders-improve-teaching-and-learning/

Goddard, R. D., Hoy, W. K., & Hoy, A. W. (2000). Collective teacher efficacy: Its meaning, measure, and effect on student achievement. *American Education Research Journal, 37*(2), 479–507.

Marzano, R. J. (2003). *What works in schools: Translating research into action*. Association for Supervision and Curriculum Development.

Wiggins, G., & McTighe, J. (1998). *Understanding by design*. Alexandria Association for Supervision and Curriculum Development.

O'Farrell Charter High School

San Diego, California

We studied a poem by an African American writer. I don't remember the author's name, but the moral of the poem was that people may originally put you down or box you in, but when they box you in, that's your time to grow and get better at what you want to do. You need to perfect what you're going to do to succeed in your life.

— Andrew, O'Farrell High junior

O'Farrell pushes me to go beyond easy goals and go beyond the expectations and the standards. There's just a lot of support.

— Tina, O'Farrell High School junior

At O'Farrell, they prioritize us going to college and having a good future for ourselves. I think they give us resources that other schools don't give to their students.

— Nate, O'Farrell High School junior

My home base teacher supports me with things at home so I can focus on school. If something going on at home is affecting your schoolwork, he'll help you overcome it. Teachers at O'Farrell do that for us, and that support gets us to where we are today.

— Jaliya, O'Farrell High senior

My favorite teacher is Mr. M because he's my home base teacher. He's supportive of all his students, regardless. We

DOI: 10.4324/9781003277910-5

didn't talk to each other for a whole year, and he still wanted the best for me and still tried to get through to me. I'm stubborn, but he doesn't give up on his students. He always brings enthusiasm to teaching. He gets to know his students, and that makes you want to learn from him.

– Jaliya, O'Farrell High senior

One of my dearest colleagues told me that if you don't get their hearts, you'll never get their heads, and I think that's the best piece of advice. Relationships are the foundation of everything. You need to know your students even better than you know your content. It doesn't matter if I could write the best essay or if I know the AP exam inside, outside, and backward. I need to know why that content matters for my students. I need to know those students sitting in front of me right now. Why does this content matter to them?

– English teacher, O'Farrell High

Often, high school students feel valued if they're academically successful. We want all our students to be academically successful, but not everyone is at first. We still get all students to feel valued because we believe every student needs an adult at school who knows and cares about them. I think that's easier to accomplish at an elementary level, and it gets harder as kids get older. When students get to high school, they can have a terrible year because of multiple reasons, and suddenly their academics dive, and the only person who notices is maybe their counselor at the end of the year. So at O'Farrell, every student has a home base teacher who takes care of them for four years. The home base teacher is responsible for their students. The home base teacher looks out for them academically, socially, emotionally. When students come to school upset, the home base teacher is the one who notices. The home base teacher will listen, care, and take supportive action. Home base is a big part of why students feel valued at O'Farrell.

– Brian Rainey, principal, O'Farrell High

Unlike some charter schools, magnet schools, and private schools, O'Farrell Charter High School does not use selective admissions criteria to limit enrollment to students who have histories of academic success. The school is open to all who meet the minimum age requirements and live within the boundaries of the San Diego Unified School District. When admission requests exceed the number of available slots, a random computer lottery is held, with preference given to siblings of currently enrolled students and staff members' children.

O'Farrell boasts a 100% graduation rate, high rates of academic success on state assessments, and high percentages of students who take Advanced Placement classes and pass Advanced Placement tests. As the preceding quotes suggest, Black students at O'Farrell Charter High School are succeeding because of a blend of caring relationships, deliberate efforts to help students develop and pursue important goals, rigorous academic offerings, and powerful supports that help students achieve challenging academic standards and reach their goals.

Some may assume O'Farrell's successes are attributable primarily to the special characteristics of charter schools. In truth, O'Farrell's small enrollment makes it easier for educators to create and sustain the powerful relationships that form the foundation of the school's success; however, it should be noted that many small high schools do not generate the levels of success achieved by O'Farrell's Black students. As well, it should be noted that determined and committed teams of educators in large traditional public schools can emulate the most successful practices found at O'Farrell High if they embed the appropriate supports for students and the appropriate support for school staff.

Accomplishments and Achievements

All demographic groups of students at O'Farrell High perform at outstanding levels on multiple indicators. Black students at O'Farrell High perform at higher levels than high school students throughout California. Students in California take the California Assessment of Student Performance and Progress. As shown in Figure 4.1, in the 2018–2019 academic year, 57.27% of students in California high schools performed at the proficient or advanced level in English. In contrast, only 38.43% of California's Black high school

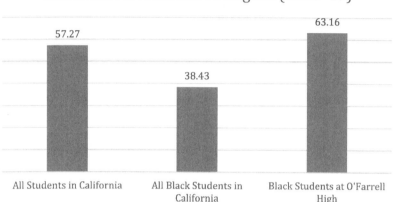

Figure 4.1 Comparison of English Performance

Percentage of Students Achieving Proficient or Advanced Performance in English (2018–19)

students performed at the proficient or advanced level. However, 63.16% of O'Farrell High School's Black students performed at the proficient or advanced level in English. Black students at O'Farrell High outperformed students in general throughout California and substantially outperformed Black students in California.

The academic performance of O'Farrell High School's Black students in mathematics is similarly impressive. As illustrated in Figure 4.2, 32.34% of California's high school students performed at the proficient or advanced level in mathematics. In contrast, only 14.27% of California's Black high school students performed at the proficient or advanced level. Impressively, 47.37% of O'Farrell High's Black students performed at the proficient or advanced level in mathematics. O'Farrell High's Black students are three times as likely to perform at the proficient or advanced level in mathematics than other Black students in California.

Admission to a University of California (UC) or a California State University (CSU) campus requires students to successfully complete the following courses: a) two units of history or social science, b) four years of English, c) three years of mathematics, d) two years of laboratory science, e) two years of language other than English, f) one year of visual and performing arts, and g) one year of a college preparatory elective that can include an additional course from any of categories a through f. These

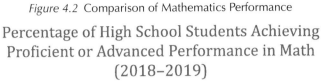

Figure 4.2 Comparison of Mathematics Performance

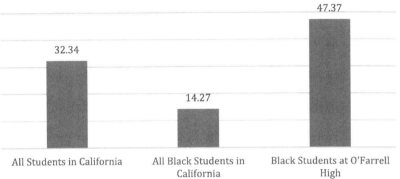

requirements (commonly referred to as "A through G" requirements) must be completed with a grade of C or higher for students to be eligible to be considered for admission at UC or CSU campuses (see www.cde.ca.gov/ci/gs/hs/hsgrtable.asp). In many California school districts, A through G requirements exceed high school graduation requirements. Throughout California, only 43.6% of high school graduates met the A through G requirements in 2021, whereas at O'Farrell, all their graduates meet the A through G requirements.

In addition to meeting California's A through G requirements, many Black students at O'Farrell are completing Advanced Placement courses. Twenty-four percent of O'Farrell's Black students are enrolled in Advanced Placement courses (compared to 15% of Black students in California).

History, Background, and Demographics

O'Farrell Charter High School is part of the O'Farrell Charter School (an elementary school, middle school, and high school) located in the Skyline/Encanto area of San Diego, California. In 1959, O'Farrell opened as a traditional junior high school in the San Diego Unified School District. During the late 1960s and 1970s, many White families left Southeast San Diego, and O'Farrell Junior High served predominantly Black students. However, in the late 1970s and 1980s, many Black families chose to avoid O'Farrell because of the school's negative reputation associated with violence and low academic achievement. As Black families sent their children to schools outside of Southeast San Diego through San Diego Unified's Voluntary Ethnic Enrollment Program (VEEP), O'Farrell Junior High served increasing numbers of Latinx and Asian families who moved into the area to find affordable housing. The demographic changes did not change O'Farrell's reputation, as gang violence and low achievement persisted. In 1994, the San Diego Unified School District converted O'Farrell into a charter elementary and middle school.

The new charter school was designed based upon middle school concepts promoted by Fenwick (1987) and the Carnegie Corporation of New York (1989). Improvement, however, was not instantaneous. Brian Rainey, the founding and current O'Farrell High School principal, recalled when he was one of the O'Farrell Middle School history teachers. He described a trip he and his fellow O'Farrell Middle School teachers took to meet the history teachers at the high school to which most O'Farrell students transferred. The high school history teachers told the middle school educators, "We always know your kids because they're dressed the best, but they are the worst students."

The comments from the high school teachers distressed Mr. Rainey and some of his colleagues and led them to focus intently on improving the quality of their academic offerings. Conversely, some of the O'Farrell Middle School teachers did not think their students could achieve better academic outcomes. Even though there was not universal agreement, eventually, the focus on academic excellence resulted in considerable improvements. For example, in 2006–2007, the school achieved an Academic Performance Index (API) score of 720, based on student performance on state assessments in a system where the California Department of Education considered an API score of 800 as the goal for all schools.

The parents of O'Farrell Charter Middle School students wanted O'Farrell to continue serving their children after eighth grade. Mr. Rainey volunteered to lead the effort to create a ninth-grade program. As a result, O'Farrell offered ninth grade for students in the 2010–2011, 2011–2012, and 2012–2013 school years. The ninth-grade program was housed in portable classrooms on a field adjacent to the middle school.

As services to ninth-grade students continued, Mr. Rainey and his colleagues planned the expansion of services through grade 12. Also, a permanent new high school facility was designed. In 2013–2014, the school provided services for tenth-grade students. In 2014–2015, the school served eleventh-grade students, and in 2015–2016, O'Farrell High School graduated its first class of seniors. In May 2016, a new facility for the O'Farrell Charter High School opened its doors.

The new high school is an attractive set of small buildings connected by grassy areas and wide sidewalks. The buildings are named after different universities to emphasize O'Farrell's college-going culture. The high school's proximity to the middle school and elementary campuses facilitates opportunities for high school students to serve as role models and mentor younger children.

Approximately 580 students attend O'Farrell Charter High School (among the 1,850 who attend the K-12 O'Farrell Charter School). Over half (53%) of the high school's students identify as Latinx or Hispanic. Approximately 20% of the students identify as Filipino or Asian, and approximately 16% identify as Black or African American. Nearly 63% of the school's students meet free- or reduced-price meal eligibility criteria. It should be noted that although O'Farrell Elementary and O'Farrell Middle School claim many academic successes, only O'Farrell High School met the eligibility criteria for the National Center for Urban School Transformation's America's Best Urban School Award. O'Farrell High School is the focus of this chapter.

Distinguishing Values, Goals, and Strategies

Two values resonated throughout discussions with administrators, teachers, parents, and Black students at O'Farrell High: 1) a commitment to building relationships and 2) a commitment to ensuring that all students make progress toward ambitious academic goals. These values are commonly mentioned in many school mission statements, but they rarely influence the daily practices and routines found in high schools. At O'Farrell, however, these values have influenced practices, policies, routines, procedures, job responsibilities, and everyday interactions in ways that promote the engagement and empowerment of all students, and especially Black students.

O'Farrell Charter High School is structured upon the belief that all students will learn challenging academic concepts and skills if they are educated in a community that knows, values, and respects them. Unlike schools that merely express a philosophical interest in strengthening adult/student relationships, educators at O'Farrell High have structured schedules and job responsibilities to ensure that each student will feel known, valued, and respected by at least one teacher.

When students enter ninth grade at O'Farrell High, they are assigned a home base teacher. Each home base teacher is assigned a maximum of 30 students, and every O'Farrell teacher serves as a home base teacher. All students meet with their home base teacher each school day at 8:00 a.m. for 25 minutes. Students retain the same home base teacher throughout their four high school years. Teachers and students reported that the activities occurring during home base are designed to help students and teachers learn about each other, build a sense of community, strengthen positive character traits, and address social and emotional issues.

Home base, however, is not a traditional advisory class during which teachers take attendance, deliver announcements, and fulfill other administrative responsibilities. Home base is designed to build, strengthen, and sustain relationships among students and between students and teachers. Home base teachers assume important roles that teachers in typical high schools are not asked to assume. For example, home base teachers assume responsibility for meeting and getting to know the parents of their home base students. Principal Rainey explained that each home base teacher is the primary point of contact for students' parents. He emphasized, "When a parent has an issue, they don't call or email me, they call the home base teacher." O'Farrell students reported that their home base teachers knew their parents and were comfortable communicating with them. Similarly, O'Farrell teachers clearly assumed responsibility for reaching out to parents and building positive relationships. One teacher explained:

> Nobody likes a call home from a teacher when they've never even met you. So I think it's important, at the beginning, to tell them how much I enjoy their students or what I really admire about their students.

Additionally, home base teachers assume responsibility for continuously monitoring the grades of their home base students in all classes at O'Farrell. This requires teachers to maintain frequent communication with each other. In many high schools, parents do not learn that students are falling behind until the semester is ending, and it is too late to intervene in ways that could ensure academic success. At O'Farrell, teachers utilize their home base responsibilities to intervene early and work with parents, students, and teachers to ensure that students succeed in classes.

Home base teachers even serve as problem solvers and disciplinarians when their home base students have difficulties in other classrooms. Principal Rainey compared O'Farrell to typical schools by saying:

> At most schools, if a teacher gets upset with a student and kicks them out of class, the student goes to the office. Well, that rarely happens here, but if a teacher does send a student out of class, the student doesn't go to the office. The student goes to their home base teacher, because the home base teacher is like their mom or dad on campus. They're not just the disciplinarian; they are the coach, the advocate, the cheerleader. The home base teacher will communicate with the other teacher and determine the best way to resolve the situation.

Principal Rainey explained that O'Farrell teachers hold one another accountable for treating all students fairly and with respect. Teachers help one another learn strategies for dealing with difficult situations. As well, home base teachers hold their students accountable for modeling the character traits that are the focus of home base lessons. O'Farrell parents were delighted by the impact of home base on their children's success. "So it's like a big family," one parent shared and then added, "Home base is fabulous for us. For me, it's home base!"

Home base, however, is just a foundation upon which O'Farrell educators build supports for helping students achieve ambitious goals. Emphatically, Principal Rainey explained:

> Our focus is on empowering students. We have a preamble to our Falcon Way. It says, "I have the power to create a great life for myself." It's on the front of the theater in gigantic letters. It's on the front of my office. It's something we want students to believe: they have the power to create a great life for themselves.

Principal Rainey believes that if we truly intend to empower students, we cannot create policies, procedures, and rules that lead students to feel incapable of success. He explained:

> I think the biggest problem in education is that people either don't understand human nature or they just act as if it isn't real. Teenagers are teenagers and not widgets, and you can do things that will break them. In education, we take kids who are really struggling in mathematics and double-block them in math. You want to kill their spirit and make them spend twice as much time doing the thing that makes them feel stupid? Why would you do that? We don't understand teenagers. You would think we would remember what it was like to be a teenager.

At O'Farrell, educators have decided that empowering students to create a great life for themselves means working with teenagers in ways that motivate them to invest sustained effort. Motivating teenagers is very different from forcing students to endure repeated failures. Instead, at O'Farrell High School empowering students to create a great life for themselves means 1) leading all students to see that they can make meaningful, step-by-step academic progress; 2) teaching all students clearly and precisely what is required for them to achieve a great life for themselves (including graduation and postsecondary education); and 3) providing all students a quantity and quality of individualized support that makes step-by-step academic progress a regular experience and the attainment of postsecondary admission inevitable. O'Farrell educators acknowledge that some students might not choose to pursue education at a four-year university or even a two-year college; however, they are committed to ensuring that all students will graduate well positioned to have a choice.

Leading students to believe they can make meaningful, step-by-step academic progress when they have suffered repeated academic failure is difficult. An O'Farrell teacher shared that some of her students of color entered ninth grade reading substantially below grade level. She explained that when students cannot make sense of the texts in front of them, the impact can be devastating. In response, O'Farrell teachers decided to use reading inventories to determine student Lexile (reading) levels.

In the high school, we give the inventory three times a year to know how to support and challenge students. If I know their Lexile level, I can determine how to best help students learn and develop literacy. So I don't use it, per se, to give one student a less-challenging text but to know, for this student, this text is going to be particularly challenging. So what type of front-loading or prework can I do to help them learn from that high-level text? It also allows me to measure how much students' reading skills are growing throughout my course. This also helps students self-monitor. Students see their Lexile level increase. Also, this enables us to celebrate growth.

O'Farrell students see themselves making authentic academic progress. Students see that excellent and caring support from their teachers, combined with their own hard work, results in real academic success. They start to believe, "Maybe I do have the power to create a great life for myself!"

As mentioned previously, only 43.6% of California's high school graduates meet the A through G requirements for admission into a University of California or California State University campus. In contrast, all O'Farrell graduates meet the A through G requirements. This success is not accidental. One of the O'Farrell teachers explained that the success is a result of a series of pivotal decisions that have influenced many aspects of life at O'Farrell. She explained that the decisions were made early in the development of the high school:

> We were four trailers on a dirt field when I started: one teacher per content area. And so I feel like I had the privilege to make powerful decisions to build the culture of the high school and these high expectations that we have for all students. This might seem small, but getting rid of the D in our grading system was a pivotal decision, because the UC and CSU don't accept the D [students must complete the A–G requirements with a grade C or higher]. So when students earn a D, they might pass your course in high school but not be eligible to apply to colleges in their senior year. We didn't see a point to the D, so we got rid of it. We have set high expectations for all our students, and we make sure everyone

graduates A through G compliant and can apply to the UC and Cal State School systems.

The teacher continued to explain that she and her O'Farrell High colleagues knew that when students did not earn an A, B, or C, teachers still needed to ensure that students learned critical academic content. This consensus among O'Farrell teachers resulted in another pivotal decision. She explained:

> We got rid of the D. So if a student doesn't earn an A, B, or C, they must attend summer school to fix the grade. But more importantly, they must go back to the content and re-engage with what they did not learn during the school year.

These decisions dramatically reduced the likelihood that O'Farrell students would pass classes without learning the concepts and skills that were essential to success in the subsequent course. The decisions dramatically increased the likelihood that all O'Farrell students would learn content that would allow them to advance successfully to upper-level and Advanced Placement courses. Students who might have struggled as ninth graders learned that they could, with effort, master rigorous academic content.

A third pivotal decision at O'Farrell focused on the use of new resources. Principal Rainey explained that he has consistently utilized additional funding to reduce adult-to-student ratios in foundational classes, particularly ninth-grade courses. He has even chosen to use short-term federal funding to hire temporary teachers in mathematics, English, and Spanish. Why ninth-grade classes? "Because it's about skill building and laying a foundation," Principal Rainey explained. He added, "When you don't get a foundational piece right, you can struggle for years." At O'Farrell High, educators have used their resources to make sure that ninth-grade students develop strong understandings of the key concepts that are the building blocks for success in more advanced classes.

Often, in more typical high schools, ninth-grade classes are crammed full of students, while advanced classes serve relatively small numbers. Many ninth graders do not earn passing grades, they do not earn high school credits, and too often, they do not graduate. If they are allowed to take tenth-grade classes (perhaps because they "earned" a D), their chances of success in the tenth-grade course are minimal, because they have not learned crucial foundational concepts and skills. At O'Farrell, Principal Rainey has endeavored to use resources in ways that lower class sizes, provide opportunities for coteaching, or position adults to provide other supports to help ensure students have successful experiences in ninth-grade classes.

It is also important to note that O'Farrell provides additional supports to help students succeed in their classes. For example, O'Farrell High is an AVID (Advancement Via Individual Determination) National Demonstration School. Through AVID, students learn organizational skills, study skills, note-taking skills, and other skills that help them succeed in rigorous courses, while also preparing them to succeed in postsecondary education. Through AVID, O'Farrell provides students tutorials that maximize the likelihood that students will develop deep understandings of key concepts. As a father of an O'Farrell senior shared, "The AVID program has provided many children a pathway to success." He continued by explaining, "A lot of children fall away because they can't get back on track. AVID gives students a path to stay on track, even when things get tough."

Many schools that claim to have a "college-going culture" do not have a college-going curriculum. Many schools that offer a college-going curriculum do not offer the quantity and quality of support that will lead all students to succeed in this rigorous course of study and be guaranteed excellent choices beyond high school. At O'Farrell High, educators have deliberately built constructive relationships with students and parents. At the same time, educators ensure that all students will learn the key concepts and skills associated with a rigorous academic curriculum and benefit from the supports they need to succeed in every course.

Challenges

When Principal Rainey opened O'Farrell High School, he explained, "I had a small group of six teachers. I got to pick my math teacher, which was great. I did not get to pick my English teacher, which was not great." Like thousands of principals everywhere, Principal Rainey did not start with a team he perceived as ideal. Nonetheless, he opened the school and 1) worked to create early successes that would set the tone for more successes, 2) developed systems for building the capacity of staff to learn, grow, and support one another, and 3) provided a balance of support and pressure for teachers who were not serving students well.

Principal Rainey sought to create some early successes by building a positive, exciting culture at O'Farrell. He pointed out:

> I had this small group of six teachers, and I had a chance to craft a culture and say, "Look, we're absolutely going to hold these kids to the highest standard academically and behaviorally, but we're also going to support them so they succeed."

In many schools, such a statement might be included in a principal's speech at the beginning of the school year but never results in tangible changes in programs, practices, or routines. Even with his small team of teachers, Principal Rainey faced challenges in helping colleagues decide how they would hold students accountable to high academic and behavioral standards. In fact, as a new principal, Principal Rainey likely struggled to develop consensus on the meaning of such expectations and the nature of supports students would need to succeed. Nonetheless, Principal Rainey helped teachers plan how they could develop and use home base, best utilize the supports of AVID, eliminate D grades in ways that ensured all students would learn critical academic content, use Lexile levels to build students' literacy skills, and implement other practical changes that would hold students accountable to the highest academic and behavior standards and provide all students the support they needed to succeed.

Principal Rainey could have spent all his time focused upon the teachers who posed the greatest challenge, but instead, he recognized the importance of supporting a group of teachers who were eager to help students of color excel. By doing so, O'Farrell High School achieved some important early successes. Principal Rainey claimed:

> By our second year, we had very good scores in math and history. But in our third year, we did something no one thought possible. In our third year, our algebra scores were the highest in the city: higher than one of the most prestigious suburban schools. And our history scores tied for the highest.

The early successes demonstrated how O'Farrell students could excel and how O'Farrell teachers could work together in ways that ensured student success. The successes sent the message to students and their parents that college entrance and success were attainable and likely if students persisted toward their ambitious goals.

While the early successes were important, Principal Rainey knew he and his team would need to continue building their capacity to empower O'Farrell's students to excel. Principal Rainey focused on professional development initiatives that built the capacity of O'Farrell teachers to relate to, understand, and promote the success of students of color. Teachers described how they learned (both through professional development opportunities and through their roles as home base teachers) how their own experiences growing up were often different from the experiences of Black and Brown students at O'Farrell. One teacher explained, "I've learned to listen better to my students." Another shared, "I've learned to talk about the issues that my students want to talk about, like institutional racism and Black Lives Matter." Another teacher summarized, "We don't back down from teaching our students the concepts they need to succeed in college and in life, but we've learned to teach many of those concepts in ways that our students will see as meaningful and relevant."

Teachers and the principal discussed the importance of implicit bias training. Principal Rainey explained that the training was not designed to shame or blame anyone; instead, it was designed to help staff members better understand their students, better understand themselves, and better understand how their students might perceive them. Through focused, meaningful professional development, O'Farrell educators had the opportunity to learn how to reach and teach O'Farrell students more effectively.

Principal Rainey explained how much of O'Farrell's professional development is provided by O'Farrell teachers. Through their roles as home base teachers, O'Farrell High School teachers know much more about one another's teaching practices than do teachers in most high schools. Teachers have learned to share their most effective teaching practices in ways that elevate teaching effectiveness throughout the school.

Through professional development, guidance, and support, Principal Rainey helped many teachers grow and improve. He nurtured a climate in which teachers feel responsible for helping one another grow and improve. Nonetheless, Principal Rainey admits there have been a couple of times when things have not worked well and teachers have been dismissed.

He shared, "I cannot accept when people do things to other people's kids that they would never tolerate for their own kids." He explained that he was willing to support and help every teacher. He said, "I have a duty to invest in teachers and help them succeed"; however, he acknowledged that he also had a duty to protect students from teachers who did not have high expectations for their success.

Recognitions

O'Farrell's first ninth-grade class matriculated in 2011–2012, making O'Farrell a relatively new high school. However, the school has achieved many important recognitions. The National Center for Urban School Transformation awarded O'Farrell High School the America's Best Urban School Award in 2015. In 2017, San Diego's Association of African American Educators (AAAE) recognized O'Farrell's achievements in fostering equity in educational opportunities and outcomes for African American students. Both the America's Best Urban Schools Award and the award from AAAE celebrated the academic successes of O'Farrell's students of color.

Advancement Via Individual Determination (AVID) named O'Farrell High School a National Demonstration School in 2018. At that time, there were over 6,400 AVID schools; however, there were only 120 AVID National Demonstration Schools (and only a few charter schools that had earned National Demonstration School status). National Demonstration Schools are identified through a rigorous process as exemplary models of the best AVID strategies and methodologies.

Consistently since 2017, US News and World Report has designated O'Farrell High School as one of America's Best High Schools. The rankings are based on four-year graduation rates and student performance on state assessments and college-level exams.

Additionally, in 2019, O'Farrell High School was one of five high schools in the nation featured in the book *Five practices for improving the success of Latino students* (Theokas et al., 2019). O'Farrell was featured in the book because of the many indicators of academic success for the Latinx students served at the school.

O'Farrell High School has been recognized by a wide array of entities based on abundant evidence of academic excellence achieved by students of color. These recognitions are impressive; however, they are not as impressive as the confidence, character, eloquence, and sense of efficacy exhibited by O'Farrell's students of color who have come to believe that they have the power to create a great life for themselves.

What It Is and What It Isn't: Factors That Have Influenced Success at O'Farrell Charter High School

What It Is: Structuring School to Support the Development of Relationships

Success begins with relationships. Black children (like all children) will invest impressive effort when they believe teachers are committed to helping them excel. Building relationships, however, is not always easy, especially when children have experienced scant evidence that adults are committed to helping them succeed. At O'Farrell, educators built relationships through persistent, sustained, and sincere effort to listen and learn from students and their families. Educators structured time into the school schedule, and they took on specific responsibilities to ensure they built powerful, positive relationships with students and families. As educators learned about their students, they used what they learned to reshape how they taught challenging concepts and skills. They found ways to make content more accessible and meaningful to Black students.

What It Isn't: Accepting Proxies vs. Grappling with the Centrality of Building Relationships

Some teachers and administrators believe reducing class sizes will build better teacher-student relationships and lead Black children to believe that teachers are committed to helping them excel. However, in some schools, Black children may be taught in classrooms with only a dozen children but teachers sustain the same climate and culture they generated when their classroom held 40 students.

Our systems of education (especially our systems of high school education) have been structured in ways to suggest that caring relationships are optional. Some teachers might be considered outstanding educators because they "teach the standards" without any regard for the needs of students. In some schools, teachers may believe that their job does not require them to build relationships with students and certainly does not require them to build relationships with families. Until systems change, practices change, and hearts change, children are not likely to change their perceptions of us and positive relationships will not emerge.

What It Is: Insisting Students Learn the Skills Essential to Their Continued Academic Progress

Black children, like all children, are motivated by real, meaningful success. At O'Farrell, educators encourage Black students to boldly envision the life they desire. At the same time, however, O'Farrell educators help Black students understand what is required (short-term and long-term) to achieve their goals. O'Farrell educators recognized that it is disingenuous to allow students to pass a course without the requisite knowledge and skills to proceed to the next course in the sequence. At the same time, O'Farrell educators recognized the importance of ensuring that students always had viable routes to acquiring the knowledge and skills they needed to succeed.

What It Isn't: Giving Students Misleading Information about Their Preparedness

At some high schools, Black students have impressive grade point averages; however, they complete few rigorous courses because 1) graduation requirements are minimal and 2) good grades in lower-level courses do not prepare students for success in higher-level courses. Often, these students perform poorly on state academic assessments and college entrance exams. If they are admitted to colleges and universities, they are not as successful as they could be because they were not appropriately prepared. In such cases, systems have lied to students and their parents. Grades suggest that students will have opportunities to create good lives for themselves when they have not been adequately prepared for success.

What It Is: Focusing on and Celebrating Progress Toward Meaningful Goals

Education is fundamentally about progress. At O'Farrell, educators help students conceptualize goals that are meaningful to them, and they help students see the progress they are making (course by course, Lexile level by Lexile level, skill by skill, concept by concept) en route to their goals. Success is not accidental; it is planned meticulously. Students observe themselves making progress, and their progress motivates them to invest greater effort.

What It Isn't: Failing to Acknowledge and Build Upon Progress

At some schools, individual progress is invisible to students and invisible to the system. Students may learn two, three, or four important concepts, but the test covered eight concepts and the student earned an F. Students may have developed important new skills in mathematics, but the state assessment simply identifies the student as "Below Basic." Systems persistently deliver the false message "You are not capable of learning" when, in fact, students are inherently capable.

What It Is: Creating Early Successes in High School

At O'Farrell, educators recognized that ninth grade is pivotal. If students do not experience strong academic growth in ninth grade, their chances of graduation and postsecondary education diminish dramatically. Therefore, O'Farrell leaders invested time, energy, and resources to maximize the likelihood that ninth-grade students would learn the academic content and skills necessary for their success in the years ahead.

What It Isn't: Accepting High Rates of Ninth-Grade Failure

At some high schools, it is easy to predict that large percentages of ninth-grade students of color will not earn sufficient credits to become tenth-grade students. Nonetheless, leaders continue to pack large numbers of students into ninth-grade classes and fail to provide teachers supports that might be useful to increase student success. Often, more experienced, accomplished teachers are "rewarded" with assignments to teach juniors and seniors, and newer teachers are required to prove their merit with students who might have the greatest needs.

What It Is: Building a Team

Rarely, if ever, do leaders start with the perfect team of educators. O'Farrell High School was no exception. However, O'Farrell leaders recognized the importance of working with educators to build a team committed to making a powerful difference in the lives of students. Principal Rainey dedicated energy to constructive, meaningful dialogue that built upon the strengths of individual teachers and groups of teachers. He helped the team take important steps toward early successes that set the tone to many subsequent successes for O'Farrell. He continued to support teachers and hold them to high expectations while acknowledging their efforts and celebrating their accomplishments.

What It Isn't: Waiting and Hoping

Some leaders claim, "We could accomplish ___ if only I had a better ___ teacher." While the assertion might be true, waiting for the right teacher to arrive is wasting precious time. By actively and constructively engaging with the school team, leaders nurture a climate and culture that helps less-effective teachers grow and improve. Leaders should assume responsibility for creating an environment in which continuous, professional growth is likely. Of course, leaders should also be prepared to respond when individuals demonstrate an unwillingness to invest the time and effort necessary to improve. Often, the primary issue is not the quality of an individual teacher but, rather, the extent to which the school's culture develops, nurtures, and sustains great teachers.

References

Carnegie Corporation of New York. (1989). *Turning points: Preparing American youth for the 21st century*. The report of the task force on education of young adolescents. (ERIC Number ED312322). Retrieved from ERIC website: https://eric.ed.gov/?id=ED312322

Fenwick, J. J. (1987). *Caught in the middle: Educational reform for young adolescents in California public school*. Report of the superintendent's middle grade task force.

Theokas, C., Gonzalez, M. L., Manriquez, C., & Johnson, J. F. (2019). *Five practices for improving the success of Latino students*. Routledge.

Concourse Village Elementary School (PS 359)

New York City Department of Education, District 7 Bronx, New York City, New York

People at this school are much more respectful than they are at other schools. Everybody here is really nice, and nobody is rude. Here, they accept every single child. So whoever comes to the school, they're welcome.

— Idara, fourth-grade student at Concourse Village Elementary

I like going to school here because we can socialize, and the teachers are nice. They are kind to us. I like going to school here, because they make learning fun.

— Marissa, fourth-grade student at Concourse Village Elementary

One of the books we're reading in fourth grade is The Tiger Rising. It's about this boy, Rob, who had a rash, and he was getting bullied. And there was a girl named Sistine who was also getting bullied, but she stood up to the bullies. I like the book because I think it's about learning to stand up for one another and help one another. It's a really good book.

— Leonard, fourth-grade student at Concourse Village Elementary

The great thing about being departmentalized is that I got to meet with the second-grade team and the third-grade team.

DOI: 10.4324/9781003277910-6

This allowed me to discuss the second-grade standards and determine what I could do for my scholars to help them master the standards and prepare them for third grade. The collaboration was important in helping me see the connection between the standards so I could ensure my scholars would get ahead.

– second-grade teacher at Concourse Village

My mom has a saying, "The fish rots from the head first." If your leadership is not the best, how can your staff be the best? A lot of people in leadership roles go into work and it becomes just a job and it's not something they're passionate about. Here, Mrs. Sorden looks at the children who attend this school as her children. She looks at each child as if she birthed that child. Okay, I'll be honest, because at first I thought, "Oh, this is going to be a pit stop. It's a public school, and I'm not too keen on the public school system." But when my husband and I saw the way the principal treats the kids here, that was very heavy. We said, "Oh, our son is staying here."

– parent of a third-grade student at Concourse Village Elementary

I model a lot. I'm the happiest when I'm in the classrooms. I love teaching. So I model for teachers how I plan the lesson. I model how to teach concepts. I model a positive attitude about what we believe our children can achieve. I model by how I treat children, how I interact with them, and how I hold myself to the same expectations to which I hold our teachers. I model respect for the children in front of me, because that is what they merit. I walk the talk.

– Alexa Sorden, principal, Concourse Village Elementary

The first line of the scholar's creed at Concourse Village Elementary reads, "I am a Concourse Village scholar, destined for success." From prekindergarten through fifth grade, Concourse Village students recite the creed daily. Each day, they experience a school culture, curricula, and instructional strategies designed to ensure their success. The welcoming smiles, the sincere acknowledgments of scholarly habits and cooperative behavior, the rich discussions about the characters and themes in recently read literature, the excited buzz of students engaged with one another in hands-on projects, the frank and open discourse about issues with social and cultural relevance to both the neighborhood and the nation, and the calm, gentle assuredness of teachers and administrators all reinforce the message, "Yes, you, child, are destined for success." Evidence of student success permeates the school's learning data.

Accomplishments and Achievements

Black students at Concourse Village Elementary perform academically as if they are destined to succeed. As shown in Figure 5.1, across the state of New York, fewer than half (45.4%) of elementary students achieve at the proficient or advanced level in English language arts on New York State's Student Achievement Assessment. Slightly more than one-third (35.3%) of New York's Black elementary school students achieved proficient or advanced levels of performance in English language arts in 2018–2019. In contrast, 85% of Black students at Concourse Village achieved at the proficient or advanced level in English language arts. Black students at Concourse Village were more likely to achieve proficient or advanced levels of performance than Hispanic, White, or Asian students in New York State and more than twice

Figure 5.1 Comparison of English Language Arts Performance

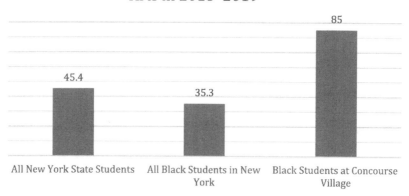

Percentages of Students Achieving Proficient or Advanced Performance in English Language Arts in 2018–2019

as likely to achieve grade-level proficiency than Black students elsewhere in New York State. Furthermore, it is important to note that, at Concourse Village, 35% of Black students performed at the advanced level in English language arts (50% performed at the proficient level, and 35% performed at the advanced level). At Concourse Village Elementary, Black students are developing critical literacy skills with impressive levels of mastery.

The academic performance of Concourse Village's Black students in mathematics is even more striking. As illustrated in Figure 5.2, 49% of New York's elementary students perform at the proficient or advanced level in mathematics. In contrast, only 34% of the state of New York's Black elementary school students perform at the proficient or advanced level. Impressively, 96% of Concourse Village's Black students perform at the proficient or advanced level in mathematics. Black students at Concourse Village outperform every racial group in the state of New York in mathematics. Black students at Concourse Village are more than twice as likely to perform at the proficient or advanced level in mathematics as Black students elsewhere in New York State. In New York State, 41% of Black students performed at the "Below Basic" level in mathematics. In contrast, not one Black student at Concourse Village scored "Below Basic." Conversely, 15% of New York State's Black elementary students performed at the advanced level in mathematics. At Concourse Village, however, 58% of the school's Black students performed at the advanced level in mathematics.

Figure 5.2 Comparison of Mathematics Performance

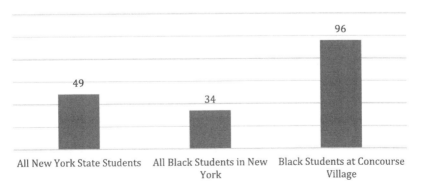

Percentages of Students Achieving Proficient or Advanced Performance in Math in 2018–2019

A visitor to Concourse Village classrooms would not be surprised to learn about the students' outstanding performances on state assessments. One need only see Concourse Village first graders reading and understanding chapter books or watch kindergarten and first graders learning coding skills and engineering concepts to observe how Concourse Village students develop academic confidence beginning in the primary grades. Visitors might also observe intermediate-grade students discussing how the recession of 1893 led White property owners in Harlem to rent their empty apartments to Black families, igniting White flight. These conversations reflect students' ability to read informational texts, identify pivotal details, and discuss their implications with deep understanding. Similarly, visitors might listen to Black students utilizing pictures to explain to one another what "4 × 1/3" means and looks like and hear them clarify why different algorithms for addressing the problem make sense, demonstrating that Concourse Village students can do much more than solve random math problems. They can reason mathematically and use mathematics to solve real problems in their world.

Parent surveys administered by the New York City Department of Education rate Concourse Village highly for the presence of effective school leadership, collaborative teaching, trust, rigorous instruction, strong family-community ties, and a supportive learning environment. Average daily attendance is consistently high, and suspensions or other disciplinary actions are very rare. At Concourse Village, student achievement on state assessments is the logical result of a positive school culture, rigorous academic curricula, and engaging instruction. Principal Sorden emphasized:

> We don't test prep at all. The word doesn't even come up in our building. We ensure that the curriculum is rigorous throughout the entire year, starting in prekindergarten. We emphasize good teaching. We don't emphasize testing. I don't put that pressure on my students or on my teachers.

Parents are particularly impressed by the rigor of the curricula and the quality of the instruction their children receive. One parent explained:

> I said to my kid, "You're seven! How do you know this?" If this is what they're giving our kids in second grade, imagine

what they're going to give them in fifth grade. Imagine what their reading level will be! There's no limit at Concourse Village saying, "This is a public school, so we're going to dumb it down." No, it's like, "This is a public school, and we're still going to hold you accountable for achieving great things." That was big for me. Yeah. I'll be honest. It changed my perspective on public schools.

History, Background, and Demographics

Located in the poorest congressional district in the nation (NY-16), South Bronx's Concourse Village Elementary School (PS 359) is in the New York City Department of Education's District 7. Concourse Village Elementary resides in a campus that was constructed in 1969 and opened in the 1969–1970 school year as PS 156. The Department of Education closed PS 156 in 2008, determining it to be persistently dangerous and consistently low-performing academically. The school reopened as PS 385, but in 2013 the school was phased out once again due to continuing poor performance. Alexa Sorden was hired to serve as a middle school principal in another district in 2012 and, as a result of her success, was given the opportunity to lead Concourse Village Elementary School, PS 359, in 2013.

Principal Sorden shared that when she began serving as principal, the school's physical learning environment was "unkept, messy, and not student-centered." She explained how the interior walls in parts of the building were painted in dark, drab colors, accentuated with black borders. She further reported, "Immediately, I brightened the building with primary colors, new furniture, and positive messages throughout the school." Today, classrooms at Concourse Village are clean, cheerful, and attractively decorated. Electronic smart boards, laptop computers, and other technological aids are used regularly to illustrate concepts and engage students in thoughtful conversations. Principal Sorden proudly described the "differentiated" furniture she acquired for her students. "The classroom furniture is set up to give our students choice based on how they learn best," she explained. Classrooms offer students a variety of choices in desks and seating, including gaming chairs, because "many of the students (boys mainly) like to rock while they're working." The atmosphere is orderly, yet as one student explained, "It's comfortable here. You can be yourself."

Concourse Village Elementary serves approximately 340 students (from prekindergarten for three-year-old children through grade 5). Almost two-thirds (63%) of the students identify as Latinx or Hispanic. One-third (33%) identify as Black or African American. Approximately 87% of the students qualify for free- or reduced-price meals, and 15% of the students are experiencing homelessness.

Many of the students at today's Concourse Village Elementary learn in the same classrooms that served their older siblings or cousins ten years ago. However, today's students benefit from a dramatically different school experience. All the students, and particularly the Black students, emanate a sense of efficacy about their academic potential and a sense of optimism about their future.

Distinguishing Values, Goals, and Strategies

When leaders regularly and persistently articulate clear and consistent expectations, these expectations can influence the shared values of a school. When asked what she expected to see in classrooms at Concourse Village, Principal Sorden responded:

> When I enter a classroom at Concourse Village, I expect to see students leading small groups and students leading whole groups. I expect to hear students' voices. I expect to see teachers engaging with students in a thoughtful manner. I expect to feel a sense of love and respect. I expect to see students annotating texts. I expect to see students engaging in respectful debates about important questions or topics and using evidence to support their assertions. I expect to see smiles. I expect to see students who look as if they know that the classroom is their learning space and it was designed for them. I expect to see students taking risks by asking questions or giving answers to questions they had not anticipated. I expect to see students feeling joy. I expect to see students feeling a sense of order and intentionality. And if I don't see all I expect, I will be most concerned if I don't see the sense of joy, love, and safety. The other ideas about things like leading student discussions or probing student thinking could be

part of the normal learning curve for teachers. With time and professional development, they could get there. I have more flexibility in those areas. But the sense of joy, love, and safety, those are nonnegotiables for me.

Principal Sorden's comprehensive response centers first on students feeling joy, feeling loved, and feeling like the adults around them care enough to keep them physically and emotionally safe, while simultaneously caring enough to lead them to academic success. Gay (2010) explained that, "Caring interpersonal relationships are characterized by patience, persistence, facilitation, validation, and empowerment for the participants" (p. 49). Principal Sorden wanted all students, in every classroom, to experience relationships of this nature. Throughout Concourse Village Elementary, teachers have embraced Principal Sorden's expectation. One can observe students lying on the classroom carpet as they read a novel or write a report. Students can be seen sitting in their gaming chairs, using their iPads, and discussing how they might use mathematics to solve a real problem in their neighborhood. Similarly, one could listen to primary-grade students share how they relate to the challenges characters face in Judy Blume's *Freckle Juice* or hear how intermediate-grade students draw parallels between the personal identity struggles articulated in Nikki Grimes's *Garvey's Choice* and the struggles they face as they endeavor to pursue their dreams. All students, and specifically Black students, act as if they believe that Concourse Village is a place created to nurture their success and well-being.

Teachers at Concourse Village have used the school's core values to build a positive, warm, accepting culture throughout the school. While we were observing one Concourse Village classroom, we quietly asked a Black boy, "What are your classroom rules? Where are the classroom rules posted?" At first, he looked bewildered, and then he eagerly explained, "Oh! You mean our core values: integrity, perseverance, optimism, willingness, empathy, and respect. It spells I-POWER. Those are our core values in every classroom. We don't need rules because we have core values here."

The young man was correct. At Concourse Village, neither teachers nor students appeared to need stated lists of rules. We observed dozens of examples when teachers used the school's core values to reinforce positive student behavior. We heard teachers make statements such as, "I love the way you are willing to try this hard task," "Thank you for showing respect for your classmate by listening carefully to her answer," "You are so good at demonstrating perseverance by trying other ways to solve the problem until I'm able to help you." Conversely, we did not hear teachers tell students to "be quiet, stay in your seat, raise your hand," or follow other traditional classroom rules found in most American schools. In traditional classrooms, many times each day, Black and Brown students hear reminders about how they don't follow the rules, can't be quiet, or refuse to stay in their seats. Ultimately, the message they receive suggests they aren't good students and, certainly, aren't the favored students. At Concourse Village, Black and Brown children are inundated with frequent and sincere affirmations of their positive characteristics. Students worked hard to earn more positive comments, and teachers were happy to acknowledge the core values manifest in their students day to day.

The PBIS program (Positive Behavior Interventions and Support) is another important tool Concourse Village teachers use to create classroom environments and a school-wide environment in which all students feel accepted and valued. Of course, there are thousands of schools that claim to use PBIS; however, in many schools, the quality of implementation among classrooms varies greatly and minimizes the impact of the positive efforts on the part of some teachers. For example, a student is not likely to feel accepted and valued in science class if, in the previous hour, the reading teacher demeaned him because he blurted an answer before the teacher acknowledged him. In many schools, the thin veneer of positive statements and rewards hides strict, too often arbitrary, rules that are most important to teachers. At Concourse Village, however, teachers use both verbal praise and tangible rewards to frequently reinforce core values and other positive behavior. Often, teachers praise individual students for their scholarly behavior or award "power dollars" that students can use when they visit the classroom treasure chest. As well, teachers praise groups of students for their collaborative efforts and provide collaboration points that can also be used for treasure chest prizes. Finally, when students leave their homeroom classes, other Concourse Village teachers (e.g., art teachers, physical education teachers, science teachers) can award entire classes "Ellie" tokens (Ellie is an elephant, the schools' mascot) that accumulate and earn opportunities for special parties and events. The quantity and quality of positive recognition and reward make Concourse Village students trust that the adults value and believe in them. We heard multiple Black students say, "Our teachers like us," as if it were a phenomenon unique to Concourse Village. Teachers expressed pride in the way they consistently used PBIS and the school's core values to create a positive culture throughout Concourse Village.

Even with the core values and the PBIS systems, Concourse Village would not likely have such a pervasive, positive culture without the powerful involvement of Principal Sorden. Her frequent classroom visits, her monitoring, and her modeling helped to make joy, love, and safety ubiquitous nonnegotiables throughout the school. Relentlessly, she supported and guided teachers to create environments in which all students were likely to experience joy, love, and safety. Boykin and Noguera explained, "Students learn through relationships" (2011, p. 28). Principal Sorden has integrated this wisdom into her work with teachers.

In addition to her affective expectations, Principal Sorden expects all her students to experience curricular rigor in ways that will empower them to succeed in life. At Concourse Village, New York's state standards do not exist as end targets; rather, they are the building blocks teachers utilize as they develop rigorous and engaging curricula, motivating students to reach even higher levels of learning and achievement. At Concourse Village, strong positive relationships between teachers and students are one side of the coin; the other side is effective teaching focused on challenging academic concepts.

Departmentalization has been an important tool for increasing curricular rigor throughout the school. One Concourse Village educator explained how teachers are challenged to develop the levels of expertise required to teach rigorous academic standards across multiple subject areas. She shared that departmentalization provided her the chance to focus on developing expertise in one or two areas. Another teacher explained that departmentalization allowed her to work with her colleagues across grade levels (vertically) to develop deeper understandings about how the standards required at one grade level connect to the standards students should learn at subsequent grade levels. As teachers worked together to help one another understand grade-level expectations, they helped one another build content knowledge and better understand important nuances about curricular expectations. Vertical collaboration became an important source of ongoing, job-embedded professional development. Teachers were able to learn from their colleagues within a low-risk atmosphere in ways that immediately influenced the daily lessons they provided students. One educator explained how departmentalization and vertical collaboration helped: "[It] allowed me to see the importance of being able to master your practice. I became a better educator for my students, and in turn, that allowed them to be successful."

Vertical collaboration also influenced curricular consistency throughout Concourse Village. For example, fourth-grade math teachers knew that fifth-grade math teachers depended upon them to ensure that students mastered specific concepts and skills before they left fourth grade. Third-grade English language arts teachers knew they had a responsibility to build upon (not just reteach) the literacy concepts and skills that second-grade English language arts teachers helped students master. One Concourse Village educator explained:

> When I started teaching, math was not my strength, or at least I did not think it was my strength. Through departmentalized collaboration, I was able to master the content. I can break down the standards from kindergarten through fifth grade because I was given the opportunity to understand the concepts that need to be mastered. I really started understanding what my students need to master before they come into my grade and what they need to master while they are with me to be successful in the year to come.

Departmentalization has helped elevate the rigor of curricula at Concourse Village, and it has also helped tailor the curricula to Concourse Village's students. Yes, teachers make sure they teach New York's state standards, but teachers deliberately design curricula that will resonate with their Black and Brown South Bronx students. One Concourse Village educator explained:

> Here, we create the curriculum. And while we're creating it, we're thinking, "Who are our kids?" Our kids are Muslim, they're Black, they're Latino. They live in an urban setting. So we've created a Bronx curriculum. This is a curriculum made for our students. Every summer, every year, we look at our kids, we look at who's coming, who's going, and we think, "We can even do more. We can center our students more. It could be more about them."

Concourse Village teachers, with the support of the school's administrators, are constantly revising and improving curricula so that students are more likely to relate to the challenging standards teachers want them to understand. Concourse Village teachers recognize that their Black and Brown children can learn challenging concepts and skills, but first, teachers must help their students see how these concepts and skills are relevant to their lives. When children see themselves and their lives in the literature they read, in the science they explore, in the mathematical problems they seek to investigate, and in the art, music, and drama they experience, they are much more likely to develop deep understandings.

Consistent with Principal Sorden's expectations, throughout Concourse Village classrooms, one can see students engaging in literature that features Black and Brown characters who represent impressive traits. Of course, students also read literature featuring other characters; however, teachers are very purposeful in selecting literature with themes they believe are important to their students. As well, throughout the school, one can see students engaging in science projects, in social studies conversations, and in solving mathematical problems that Black and Brown children in the South Bronx are likely to find interesting and relevant.

Additionally, throughout the school, one sees students annotating texts, even in the primary grades, in English language arts, science, social studies, and even mathematics. Principal Sorden explained, "We don't have to wait for the state standards to tell us to teach what our students are ready to learn." Similarly, one can see students analyzing, debating, discussing, comparing, inferring, sequencing, drawing conclusions from, and making sense of both fictional and nonfiction texts written at or above students' grade level. Regularly scheduled collaboration continues to provide powerful opportunities for teachers to learn from one another, always building upon the strengths of their students.

Challenges

When Alexa Sorden became principal, she knew that Concourse Village would not change unless the school's culture changed. Changing personnel was insufficient because negative school cultures, like bacteria in the air, can infect new teachers and new support staff. Toxic patterns of interaction tend to replicate themselves without regard to who might be the current teachers occupying various classrooms. To Principal Sorden, changing the school's culture meant changing the ways teachers and other school personnel interacted with students, changing the ways students interacted with one another, and changing the ways adults at school (teachers, support staff, administrators, and parents) interacted with one another. If the culture failed to change, any other substantive change would be difficult or impossible.

Just as Principal Sorden wanted teachers to change the culture of their classrooms by celebrating the positive attributes and accomplishments of their students, she sought to change the culture of the school by acknowledging and celebrating the positive actions of teachers. Principal Sorden spent considerable time in classrooms, supporting teachers by acknowledging their efforts to create a positive and supportive culture for students. She praised teachers for using the core values to call attention to students' strengths and maximize the likelihood that students would strive to exhibit those characteristics more frequently.

Principal Sorden recalled one of her observations of a lesson in a second-grade classroom. She heard the teacher encourage a student, "Come on, you got this! Persevere!" The student replied, "You think I can do it?" The teachers responded, "Of course! You can do anything!" The student's eyes began to water. Principal Sorden discreetly asked the student to step outside with her into the hallway so she could discover why he looked upset. She asked, "Are you okay?" and he replied with an emphatic "Yes!" But Principal Sorden said, "You look like you're going to cry." He then responded, "It's just that no one ever believed in me."

The child's unexpected response brought tears to the principal's eyes, and she assured him he was indeed destined for success. In that moment, she knew the importance of doing all she could to help teachers change the culture of the school so that every student might know that the adults at school believed in them.

Unfortunately, there were times when acknowledging and celebrating the positive was insufficient. Principal Sorden explained that one of her early challenges focused upon individuals who acted in ways that were oppositional to the culture she knew needed to exist at Concourse Village. She explained that she needed to establish a culture in which everyone believed that Concourse Village students could achieve amazing learning outcomes. Unfortunately, she learned that some staff members believed that students of color could not excel. She explained:

> I don't like the word "can't." When I hear a teacher say, "My students can't . . .," I'll say, "OK, they haven't mastered that skill yet, so tell me what lessons you need to teach so that my

children can master the skill they haven't acquired yet." If the teacher says they don't know what lessons need to be taught or if they say they don't know how to teach those lessons, that's a different conversation. But for a teacher to say that someone can't, I've never really understood that.

Specifically, Principal Sorden explained that in 2013, she had a primary-grade teacher who did not believe her students of color could meet the expectations that had been outlined. Principal Sorden had rallied her team of teachers to focus on aligning their instruction to Common Core Standards. She insisted that teachers resist the temptation to water down expectations, "regardless of a student's classification or economic status." She issued the charge, "We will make sure our students persevere and are able to go as far as they can, because we cannot possibly know the limits of their abilities." The principal explained that she expected students at every grade level to be able to re-read and annotate texts to highlight key concepts. She expected students to quote texts to justify their responses. She told her teachers, "A kindergarten student could read something at his grade level, but if I ask him, 'How do you know that?' he should be able to point to the text that substantiates his response."

There was, however, a first-grade teacher who did not embrace these new expectations. Principal Sorden described the situation:

> So I had set forth the expectations about what I wanted to see students doing. I remember walking into the class of this first-grade teacher whose class was predominantly Black. She wasn't following the expectations I had set forth. So I said, "I'm not sure why you're doing something completely different." (She was having students fill in the blanks in sentences.) And I said, "I'm not sure where this came from and why you would deviate from the curriculum plan." She never specifically said, "These Black students cannot do this," but she said, "I know you have expectations, but the students are not there yet. They're not ready for that." I asked, "Do you have data to indicate they're not there yet? I need to see how this decision was made." She said, "Well, I've been teaching for a while in this community, and I know all the deficits they're coming with." (This was the third week in September.)

Principal Sorden let the teacher know that neither the students nor the community had deficits that prevented her from "giving students what they deserved." In the following days and weeks, the principal provided abundant in-class support to the teacher. "I modeled many lessons to show that my students could meet the expectations we had for them," the principal explained. "Ultimately, she didn't like all the support I was providing, so she resigned. I refused to accept that my students were going to get less than what they deserved," Principal Sorden asserted.

La Salle and Johnson explained that "[b]elief systems are the foundation of every decision made in a school system" (2019, p. 83). If Principal Sorden had spent most school days in her office, responding to district emails, she might have never known she had a first-grade teacher who believed that Black and Brown students "were not ready" to engage in thoughtful literacy tasks. If she had chosen to ignore the first-grade teacher's disregard for the curriculum plan, she might have inadvertently encouraged other disbelieving teachers to revert to less-challenging expectations. If she had not stepped into the first-grade classroom, provided support, and modeled teaching approaches that generated positive results for students of color, the first-grade teacher, and perhaps other teachers, would have concluded that Principal Sorden delivered great speeches but did not really believe they could change learning outcomes for Black and Brown students. The culture at Concourse Village would not have changed as the principal hoped, because the toxic belief system that had poisoned the school for years would have gone unchallenged. The principal's vision of equity and excellence would never have been realized.

Recognitions

Teachers, support staff, administrators, parents, and students have worked diligently to improve learning outcomes for Concourse Village students. The hard work has generated multiple awards and recognitions.

In each year, from 2014 through 2018, the New York City Department of Education has recognized Concourse Village Elementary as a Showcase School for Exemplary Practices. As a showcase school, Concourse Village has welcomed visitors from throughout New York City who want to learn more about the school's successes.

In 2017, the Accelerate Institute awarded Concourse Village and Principal Sorden the National Award for Transformational Leadership. The award honors transformational urban school principals who, for four consecutive years, demonstrate accelerated results in schools that serve a sizable percentage of urban, low-income, and minority students. The award recognizes the important and challenging work of school leaders who give students a chance by believing in them.

The following year, 2018, the US Department of Education awarded Concourse Village Elementary the coveted Blue Ribbon Award for Exemplary High-Performing School Award. It is worth noting that the US Department of Education confers three types of Blue Ribbon Awards: Exemplary Improving Schools, Exemplary Achievement Gap Closing Schools, and Exemplary High-Performing Schools. Most winners of the Exemplary High-Performing School Award are schools in affluent communities where multiple indicators suggest that student performance is among the top schools in the state. Concourse Village is one of the few nonselective urban public schools to win the Blue Ribbon Award for Exemplary High-Performing Schools.

Concourse Village Elementary has also been recognized by the George Lucas Foundation's Edutopia as a School that Works. In 2019, 2020, and 2021, Edutopia has featured various Concourse Village practices in short video presentations. The presentations address a wide array of topics, such as the Google Form Concourse Village administrators sent to parents each week to assess family wellness during the pandemic, the strategies a Concourse Village teacher used to teach her students digital art concepts, and the three-read protocol used by Concourse Village math teachers to help students demystify challenging word problems (see www.edutopia.org/school/concourse-village-elementary-school).

Additionally, in 2020, the National Center for Urban School Transformation (NCUST) awarded their Gold America's Best Urban Schools Award to Concourse Village Elementary. The award acknowledged that all demographic groups at Concourse Village demonstrated outstanding academic success on multiple indicators.

Parents, students, teachers, support staff, and administrators are justifiably proud of the recognition the school has received. Nonetheless, the awards have not diminished the urgency to keep improving. The school's assistant principal explained:

> From our first year (2013) until now, a lot has changed. When you have those kids in front of you, things change. You realize,

this looked good on paper but it's not good enough anymore. You learn and you evolve, which is what is expected. There's no way you can remain successful by doing the same exact thing every year. It's not happening. The world and the students are constantly evolving. So we do a lot of reflection. We do a lot of research. We work together, and we expect ourselves to get better. Improvement is nonnegotiable.

Principal Sorden reminded us of the first line of the school's scholar's creed: "I am a Concourse Village scholar, destined for success." She added, the last line is, "Ultimately, my achievements will leave a lasting impression on the world." At Concourse Village, the school community will keep improving because they are determined to leave a lasting impression on the world.

What It Is and What It Isn't:
Factors That Have Influenced Success at Concourse Village Elementary School

What It Is: Leading Students to Feel Joy, to Feel Loved, and to Feel Safe

At Concourse Village, educators are committed to leading students to feel joy, to feel loved, and to feel safe. The goal is to influence how each student feels about themselves and their capacity to learn and succeed academically. Teachers want every student to feel as if their joy, well-being, and success are the primary reasons Concourse Village exists. How do teachers know if they are successfully leading students to experience joy, well-being, and success at school? They ask their students! Based on student responses, educators continuously improve upon their efforts to make learning exciting, intriguing, joyful, and meaningful for each student. Students find they do not need to become somebody else to be valued, appreciated, respected, and loved at Concourse Village; instead, teachers are committed to helping students be the beautiful, brilliant people they already are and help them grow to achieve the successes they are destined to achieve. This culture is the foundation of the school's success.

What It Isn't: Treating Students Politely and Respectfully

Often, educators think they have done all that should be necessary when they have created a polite, respectful classroom environment. Teachers might reflect upon their behavior as educators and think, "I'm doing quite a bit to demonstrate my respect and appreciation for each student." However, some students (and especially some students of color who have experienced negative classroom cultures) might perceive that the polite, respectful environment hides the teacher's true belief that the student is merely tolerated, not valued. As well, some students might conclude they are tolerated as long as they closely follow the teacher's rules. Often, Black students feel the rules were established to promote the success of other students with different backgrounds. Often, in this type of culture, Black students drift to the margins to avoid conflict with the teacher. Even when teachers have good intentions, Black students rarely feel joy, feel loved, or feel safe in such classrooms.

What It Is: Teaching Rigorous Academic Content Every Day

As a starting point, teachers at Concourse Village focus on ensuring that their students learn Common Core Standards. Often, teachers add more rigorous content to deepen students' understanding of important concepts and skills. Teachers try to ensure that their students have more than surface-level familiarity with the standards. Teachers want their students to discuss, analyze, evaluate, synthesize, and exhibit other cognitive skills while demonstrating their depth of understanding of important concepts. Teachers believe that when their students achieve this level of fluency with academic standards, they will naturally perform well when they are given state assessments. As well, Concourse Village educators believe their students need and deserve opportunities to enjoy, art, music, physical education, coding, and a variety of other endeavors.

What It Isn't: Focusing on Test Preparation

In some schools, educators (often influenced by administrators) think that the best way to ensure that students of color perform well on state assessments is to give them plentiful opportunities to take practice tests so that students develop test-taking skills. While some of these approaches might generate modest increases in scores, they do not increase the likelihood that students will be prepared to apply the content in ways that will help them succeed in more advanced courses or in real-world application of the information.

What It Is: Focusing on, Acknowledging, and Rewarding the Positive

At Concourse Village, teachers are constantly looking for opportunities to acknowledge and reinforce students' efforts to exhibit the school's core values. Attention to the positive minimizes the need to focus upon the negative. The persistent attention to the positive makes each classroom an exciting place because students are constantly being acknowledged for being impressive scholars with outstanding character. More importantly, students of color are convinced that the positive messages they hear from their teachers are genuine and accurate: they are indeed scholars who are destined to succeed.

What It Isn't: Focusing on Negatives

In some schools, educators have developed rules that maximize the extent to which teachers feel comfortable or the extent to which teachers feel in control. Sometimes these rules seem to fit poorly with the physiological, social, and emotional needs of children and adolescents. Some students of color (especially boys) feel like classroom rules set them up for failure. When students are acknowledged only when they misbehave or break the rules, they receive the subtle message that they are not good students, their chances for success in school are slim, and their presence in the classroom is not desired. In response, some students of color are quite willing to show their disdain for the teacher's rules by defiantly challenging the teacher.

What It Is: Building the Capacity of Elementary Teachers to Teach Rigorous Content

At Concourse Village, leaders recognized that teachers are not likely to teach rigorous content well if they don't have a deep understanding of the content. Also, leaders recognized that it is very difficult for teachers to develop deep understanding of the content across several academic disciplines. So school leaders implemented departmentalization in grades 2 through 5 so each Concourse Village teacher could focus on developing expertise in only one or two content areas. Frequent vertical collaboration meetings provide teachers a supportive venue for building their content expertise along with their colleagues. Teachers learn how each grade level should help students develop the knowledge and skills that will lead students to high levels of academic success.

What It Isn't: Expecting Elementary Teachers to Teach Challenging Concepts across All Subjects

In many elementary schools, teachers are expected to teach all state standards to all their students. There is often an implicit assumption that teachers have the requisite content knowledge to teach rigorous content standards across multiple disciplines. Often, schools do not offer teachers any regular opportunities to build their content knowledge, so teachers perceive that they must assess their own curricular needs and devise their own strategies for addressing their curricular needs.

References

Boykin, A. W., & Noguera, P. (2011). *Creating the opportunity to learn: Moving from research to practice to close the achievement gap.* ASCD.

Gay, G. (2010). *Culturally responsive teaching: Theory, research, and practice* (2nd ed.). Teachers College Press.

La Salle, R. A., & Johnson, R. S. (2019). *Shattering inequities: Real-world wisdom for school and district leaders.* Rowman & Littlefield.

6

Paul Laurence Dunbar Young Men's Leadership Academy

Fort Worth Independent School District, Fort Worth, Texas

The dream team is what we call our teachers here, because they make our dreams come true. They work hard so we can accomplish our dreams. I think Mr. White [the principal] came up with that name. The teachers go above and beyond to make sure we can achieve our dreams.

– Ezra, eleventh-grade student at Young Men's Leadership Academy

I get motivation and enthusiasm from teachers and from my brothers every day. The atmosphere here is just different. You want to come to school because you know you're welcome here, you have a place here, and you have a purpose here. It's nice to come to school every day knowing that your day is going to be full of things that will help get you where you're going in life and not just plain stuff that doesn't help at all.

– Kevin, tenth-grade student at Young Men's Leadership Academy

I wish all schools showed the students the attention they need. Parents are sending their kids to school, assuming that the teachers, the principals, and the counselors are watching over them and helping them become better people. I think schools should basically copy what YMLA does. YMLA is doing what parents really want schools to do.

DOI: 10.4324/9781003277910-7

YMLA gives kids the attention they need to grow and be a better person.

> *— Carl, tenth-grade student at Young Men's Leadership Academy*

I know that not every school can scrape together the best of the best teachers to make their own dream team, but if they just mirrored some of the things teachers did here, other schools would be so much better. Teachers should meet and greet their students and ask, "How's your day going?" And then connect with students on an individual basis because those connections motivate students to listen to what you're trying to say and open their minds to learning.

> *— Darryl, eleventh-grade student at Young Men's Leadership Academy*

One very important thing that should never go away is our culture. Our culture here is so important. I can't stress it enough. The culture of brotherhood is like none other. I have a brother at home. We talk a lot, but I'm not as close to him as I am with some of the people here. They push me to become a better person, they help me better myself, and I do the same thing for them. It's an experience I don't think we could get anywhere else.

> *— Ezra, eleventh-grade student at Young Men's Leadership Academy*

I tell the team, my name is on the report card, so if the kids are failing, I'm failing too. If I'm owning the data, what are you owning? You control your classroom. There's a direct correlation between teaching and learning. If the young men aren't learning, we've got to look to see how you're teaching and how you're adjusting to the needs of the students. This approach just keeps people honest. We're always celebrating growth. We're always praising our students and our teachers. For anyone who may not believe that our young men can achieve, I make it hard for them, because I tell my teachers, "That's me

in your classrooms. I see myself in your students, so you can't
tell me our Black kids can't perform. You just can't tell me that."
— Rodney White, principal, Young Men's
Leadership Academy

The Paul Laurence Dunbar Young Men's Leadership Academy (YMLA) in Fort Worth, Texas, prepares leaders. The school's motto, "Expected to learn and entitled to achieve," is a rebuttal to all who might assume that a secondary school, serving predominantly male students of color, would serve students "expected to fail" and "entitled to the next stop on the school-to-prison pipeline." To the contrary, the principal, teachers, and support staff have thoughtfully considered how they can support students through their middle school and high school years (grades 6 through 12) and position them for both admission into and success through postsecondary education.

Students at YMLA are expected to learn rigorous academic concepts and skills. Simultaneously, YMLA students are expected to develop important character traits, such as perseverance, resilience, integrity, honesty, and personal accountability, as they prepare to assume leadership roles in their communities. Students learn they are "entitled to achieve" as they exhibit these fundamental characteristics.

Accomplishments and Achievements

Black students at YMLA achieve at levels that prepare them to earn admission into four-year colleges and universities, win scholarships, and succeed in rigorous postsecondary programs. Over 1,200 high schools in the United States are considered dropout factories because they fail to graduate one-third or more of their students. While only 16% of the nation's students identify as Black, 40% of the students enrolled in dropout factories are Black (Alliance for Excellent Education, 2015). In stark contrast, 100% of the Black students served at YMLA graduate.

YMLA students must work hard to graduate. Students matriculate through a college preparatory curriculum that includes English language arts, mathematics, science, history, fine arts, physical education, and world languages. YMLA students are more likely to complete Advanced Placement courses in mathematics, science, and other subjects than high school students throughout Texas. Over 70% of YMLA's grades 11 and 12 students take at least one Advanced Placement (AP) or International Baccalaureate (IB) exam. As well, YMLA students are more likely to complete dual-enrollment courses, through which they earn both high school credit and college credit. Many of YMLA's Black graduates attend respected four-year universities, such as Baylor University, Texas Christian University, and the University of Texas at Austin.

The academic success of YMLA's Black students is apparent in student performances on state assessments. High school students in Texas take end-of-course state assessments in English I, English II, algebra I, biology, and US history. On each assessment, the percentage of YMLA's Black students who perform at grade level or above is higher than the overall percentage of students in Texas who perform at grade level or above.

For example, as illustrated in Figure 6.1, in 2018–2019, 44% of high school students in Texas scored at grade level or above on the English I end-of-course assessment. Only 31% of Black students in Texas scored at grade level or above on the English I test. In contrast, 47% of the Black students at YMLA scored at grade level or above on the English I assessment.

Results for the English II end-of-course assessment were similar (see Figure 6.2). In 2018–2019, 48% of high school students in Texas scored at grade level or above on the English II end-of-course assessment, while only 35% of Black students in Texas scored at grade level or above on the same test. In contrast, 50% of the Black students at YMLA performed at grade level or above.

Figure 6.1 2018–2019 English I End-of-Course Assessment

Percentages of Students Achieving At Grade Level or Above on English I End-of-Course Assessment

44%	31%	47%
All Texas Students	All Black Texas Students	Black Students at YMLA

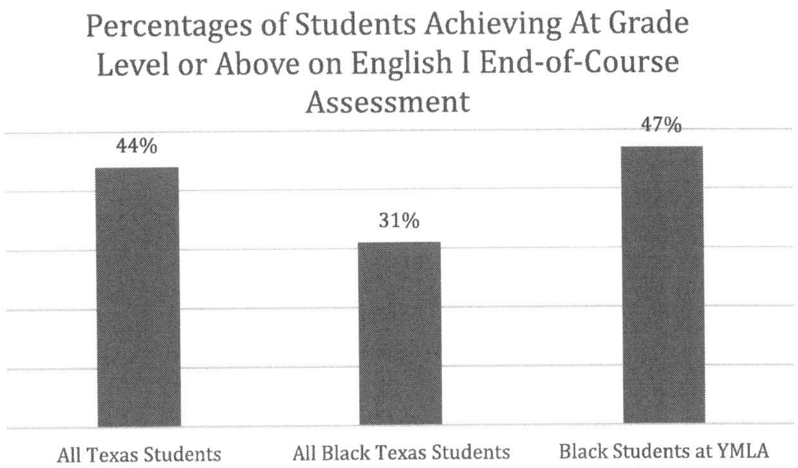

Figure 6.2 2018–2019 English II End-of-Course Assessment

Percentages of Students Achieving At Grade Level or Above on English II End-of-Course Assessment

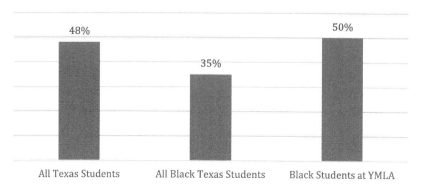

Figure 6.3 2018–2019 Algebra I End-of-Course Assessment

Percentages of Students Achieving At Grade Level or Above on Algebra I End-of-Course Assessment

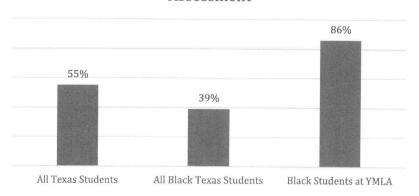

The results were more dramatic in algebra I, biology, and US history. As shown in Figure 6.3, Black students at YMLA were much more likely to perform at grade level or above than students in Texas, in general. While 86% of Black students at YMLA performed at grade level or above on the algebra I assessment, only 55% of Texas high school students, and only 39%

of Black Texas students, scored at grade level or above. Approximately two-thirds (66%) of White students in Texas scored at grade level or above, so YMLA's Black students outperformed Texas's White students by 20 percentage points. By performing at grade level or above in algebra I, YMLA students are better prepared to excel in more advanced mathematics courses and are more likely to be accepted into and succeed in four-year universities.

YMLA's Black students had similar successes in biology. Figure 6.4 shows that 59% of Texas high school students performed at grade level or above on the biology end-of-course assessment. In contrast, only 45% of Black high school students in Texas performed at grade level or above on the same test. Once again, however, the performance of YMLA's Black students was substantially better. Almost seven out of eight (87%) Black students at YMLA performed at grade level or above in biology. In comparison, only three of four White students in Texas (75%) performed at grade level or higher on the biology end-of-course assessment.

Finally, YMLA's Black students outperform Texas averages on the state's US history end-of-course assessment. Figure 6.5 shows that 70% of Texas high schools performed at grade level or above on the US history end-of-course assessment. Only 59% of Black high school students in Texas performed at grade level or above of this test. In comparison, 85% of YMLA Black students performed at grade level or above on the state's US history end-of-course assessment.

Figure 6.4 2018–2019 Biology End-of-Course Assessment

Percentages of Students Achieving At Grade Level or Above on Biology End-of-Course Assessment

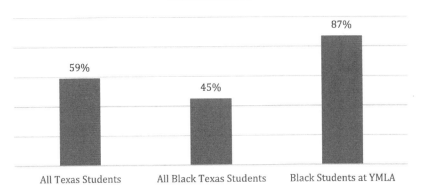

All Texas Students   All Black Texas Students   Black Students at YMLA

Figure 6.5 2018–2019 US History End-of-Course Assessment

Percentages of Students Achieving At Grade Level or Above on US History End-of-Course Assessment

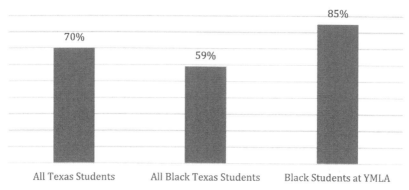

It is interesting to note that, while YMLA's Black middle school students perform well academically, YMLA's middle school student success data is not as impressive as the high school student success. At YMLA, student successes build as students spend time immersed in the YMLA culture. When students are treated as though they are "expected to learn and entitled to achieve," the impact over time is powerful.

History, Background, and Demographics

The Paul Laurence Dunbar Young Men's Leadership Academy is located in a historically Black neighborhood in the Fort Worth Independent School District in Fort Worth, Texas. The school opened in 2012 as the district's first school dedicated exclusively to nurturing the success of male students in both the classroom and life. The district's board of trustees repurposed Dunbar 6th Grade Center (a well-respected school) to house the new secondary, single-gender school.

YMLA serves approximately 365 students in grades 6 through 12. Over half (53.2%) of the students identify as Black or African American, and 41.1% identify as Hispanic or Latino. Fewer than 3% of the students identify as White. Approximately 79% of the students meet eligibility criteria for free- or reduced-price meals.

When Rodney White was selected to serve as principal of the new YMLA, he immediately addressed various misconceptions about the purpose of the school. "Some people thought this was going to be a reform school," he shared. "In fact," he added, "one parent wanted to know when she would be able to pick up her son," because she assumed that her child would live in a dormitory at the school. Some people in the African American community were not pleased to lose what they perceived as a successful sixth-grade center to acquire a "reform school for boys on the way to prison."

Principal White shared that some friends and colleagues questioned his judgment for accepting the principalship at YMLA. "People told me YMLA was a career breaker. They asked, 'Why would you sign up for that? How are you going to motivate those guys? How are you going to keep them from fighting each other every day?'" Principal White explained that the criticisms helped inspire the school's motto: "Expected to learn; entitled to achieve." He emphasized, "That's our motto, and all the young men here know it. You're expected to learn, and you're entitled to achieve. We're going to college here!"

Regularly, YMLA students recite the academy's creed:

I am a scholar of Paul Laurence Dunbar Young Men's Leadership Academy.
I will seek knowledge.
I will speak the truth.
I am destined for success in everything I do.
The decisions I make today will affect my tomorrow.
I am accountable to myself, my brothers, my family, and my community.
I am a scholar of Paul Laurence Dunbar Young Men's Leadership Academy.
We are our brothers' keepers.

The creed is apparent in the interactions among students, the interactions among teachers and students, the content of courses, and the focus of extracurricular activities. The creed is both an affirmation of the strengths of Black students and a reminder of the school's commitment to build upon those strengths in ways that position YMLA scholars for leadership.

Distinguishing Values, Goals, and Strategies

When YMLA was established, the Fort Worth Independent School District was led by the district's first Black superintendent. "It was my luck,"

Principal White mused, "this school was in his neighborhood, the neighborhood in which he grew up. So he was very tough on me." Principal White explained that the superintendent was honest and clear about his high expectations for student achievement. The superintendent made clear that student performance at YMLA could and should improve.

Principal White continued to explain that the Fort Worth District utilized a series of interim assessments to monitor the progress of schools and predict student performance on state assessments in the spring. At that time, YMLA served only middle grades. It was one of 30 middle schools in the district. When the first interim assessment was administered, Principal White received a phone call from the superintendent. The conversation emphasized that YMLA's interim assessment scores were ranked 27th out of the district's 30 middle schools. Principal White recalled, "The superintendent reminded me about his expectation that student performance at YMLA could and should improve."

The pressure would have caused some principals to immediately begin applying for positions in other school districts; however, Principal White took a series of actions that align tightly to four lines of the YMLA Scholar's Creed:

> I will speak the truth.
> I am destined for success in everything I do.
> The decisions I make today will affect my tomorrow.
> I am accountable to myself, my brothers, my family, and my community.

Instead of withholding information about the school's performance on the interim assessment, he chose to "speak the truth" in a manner that emphasized that YMLA students were "destined for success." By being transparent about the data that influenced how others perceived YMLA, YMLA's teachers, YMLA's students, and YMLA's leaders, he provided everyone an opportunity to make decisions today that would affect their tomorrow. He gave everyone an opportunity to be accountable to themselves and to the entire school community.

Principal White chose to share the data with his students in ways they could understand. He helped the students understand what the data meant and how the data led others to incorrect assumptions about YMLA and incorrect assumptions about them. He emphasized that YMLA was a leadership academy, and YMLA students were expected to model leadership. After establishing this context, Principal White shocked the group by specifying his expectation: "So our goal is top five. Say it with me guys, 'Top five!'"

The principal announced how he expected teachers to develop and share plans that would help YMLA students advance toward becoming one of the top five middle schools. As well, he asked students to meet and establish personal commitments and group commitments that defined how they would help YMLA move toward becoming one of the district's top five middle schools. In the following weeks, teachers defined commitments related to new peer tutoring programs and morning meeting competitions. Students made public commitments during their morning meetings. Seemingly, everyone wanted to share responsibility for elevating the community's perception of YMLA.

After the next interim assessment, Principal White shared that YMLA moved from 27th to ninth among the district's middle schools. By the end of the first year, the school scored among the top two or three middle schools in Fort Worth in each subject area. Principal White used the dramatic improvements to emphasize that YMLA students were indeed destined to succeed. Making data transparent and calling upon all stakeholders to share accountability for the school's success became important strategies for elevating the success of YMLA students. Principal White claimed, "Showing the data, showing that we believe, and showing that we're going to be relentless became a turning point, because that's when I started to see adults at the school believe our kids could do it. As well, I started seeing belief from the students and the parents that, okay, this school might be on to something."

In addition to focusing attention on important concerns reflected in the school-wide data, at YMLA, students are taught to carefully monitor data about their individual academic progress. Principal White explained that the Fort Worth Independent School District has a computerized system that allows students to see their grades "in real time, 24 hours a day, seven days a week." At YMLA, school personnel have helped students develop the habits of regularly reviewing their data, developing action plans to improve their grades, and monitoring their implementation of these action plans. In a concrete way, YMLA students learn how they can determine their academic destiny.

Another key YMLA strategy emphasizes acknowledging and celebrating positive behavior. Principal White recognized that there were too many discipline issues when YMLA started. He admitted that there were too many young men, and particularly African American young men, who were being removed from classes and sent home. The school turned to Positive Behavior Interventions and Support (PBIS) for strategies to reinforce the positive behavior traits exhibited by YMLA scholars.

Similar to the implementation of PBIS in successful schools, all school personnel engaged in the process of acknowledging and rewarding the positive student behavior they wanted to see. YMLA teachers described how they were responsible for reinforcing the school's high ideals among all YMLA students, not only the students they were assigned to teach.

At YMLA, however, the PBIS system was also implemented with some atypical components. Principal White explained:

> We wanted to create a culture of brotherhood and get students to buy into it. We wanted students to understand that this is not a normal school where you're fending for yourself. Here, everybody looks out for one another. We are our brothers' keepers.

All YMLA students are assigned to one of four prides. Each pride operates like a fraternity or a house. When school personnel reward positive behavior, in addition to rewarding individual students, they also reward the pride. Additionally, school personnel can issue demerits to individuals and to the pride.

Principal White speculated, "Behavior issues are low because the young men know that their behavior affects them, and it also affects their brothers." Some students who have long histories of disciplinary incidents may be numb to the impact of individual disciplinary actions; however, Principal White explained:

> When those points are tallied, students are accountable to their brothers, because their brothers will wonder, "What could you have done, brother, to help us earn more merits so we could have gone to the ice cream party or we could have earned the additional free time?" There are far fewer discipline issues when you have kids supporting good behavior and teachers building confidence by issuing merits that say, "You did this right!"

By focusing primarily on positive behavior, YMLA has achieved a substantial reduction in disciplinary incidents; however, the students are adolescents, and many are enduring a wide array of challenges. Principal White explained that when students have difficulties, he and his colleagues seek to help students understand how they could handle situations constructively. YMLA teachers and administrators help students reflect upon their choices and their actions so they recognize, "The decisions I make today will affect my tomorrow."

After serious conversations about a student's bad choices, the student might ask, "Am I going to get suspended?" Principal White explained that usually his answer is, "No, I need you to get back in that room and show who you are and how well you can do. I expect you to make this right." Teachers and administrators then follow up in ways that reinforce the positive decisions the student makes and acknowledge the student's positive leadership.

While the framework of PBIS is important, teachers emphasized how they assumed important roles in developing and sustaining a positive environment through their everyday interactions with students. For example, one teacher described the importance of avoiding judgment and talking to students in a respectful tone. Another teacher agreed and added, "Students won't learn from people they don't like, and they won't learn from people who don't like them in return." One YMLA teacher summarized the importance of positive relationships with students by insisting teachers should not waver from their high expectations; at the same time, they should not waver from their efforts to build and sustain positive relationships. The teacher emphasized, "If the relationships are genuine, a teacher can demand just about anything from their students."

A Black male math teacher explained that building caring relationships takes time and effort. He explained that, as an engineer, he sees all his students as individual projects. He has an image of what each student can be and wants to help him build his life from the foundation up. He takes the time to learn where his students were raised and who their parents are. Further, he endeavors to learn about the issues that might be weighing on his students or the possibilities that might lift them up. This investment in time pays rich dividends as he pushes students to soar academically.

Ferguson (2002) found that students were more likely to work hard when they believed their teachers cared about them. In addition, he found the relationship between students' perception of teachers' caring and students' effort to perform academically was strongest among students of color. Black male students at YMLA emphasized the power of the caring relationships they experienced at YMLA. For example, two Black students described a teacher who cared in ways that were particularly important. One student explained that when he experienced a death in his family, the teacher helped him talk through his feelings. The other student explained how the teacher's care and support helped him greatly improve his reading and writing skills. A tenth-grade student communicated the power of teacher caring at YMLA by saying, "There's no comparison between the teachers and support system at YMLA and my previous schools. Students at YMLA are treated with respect in and out of the classroom."

YMLA's learning culture is further distinguished by the teachers' collective commitment to persist until students develop understanding and mastery. In many schools, if a student receives a low grade on an assignment or a test, the grade is recorded in the teacher's grade book. The student's experience ends here, absent any opportunity to improve the grade or learn the concepts they did not master. In contrast, at YMLA, if a student earns a low grade, they are encouraged to go back and correct the work, not merely by changing answers, but with explanations for *why*. When they exert the effort required to understand the concept and understand how they erred, students receive a revised grade. A student emphasized, "The teachers at YMLA keep working with you until you 'get it.' That makes all the difference."

Challenges

Principal White reported his first major challenge involved finding the best teachers for YMLA. He knew he needed teachers who believed in the capacity of male students of color to excel. He said, "I'm looking for teachers who love kids. Even more, I'm looking for teachers who love my kids!" Also, he explained how he needed teachers who could teach male students of color well, that is, teachers who knew their content and how to deliver it in ways that created positive learning experiences for male students of color.

It is important to note that teachers at YMLA have played an important role in developing the "dream team." When a vacancy occurs, Principal White encourages the school's teachers to help him identify candidates who they believe have the capacity to be excellent additions to the team. He explained, "Nine chances out of ten, my team is not going to recommend someone who's going to cause an issue or be ineffective."

Encouraging teachers to tap other effective teachers works as a recruitment strategy at YMLA, because YMLA teachers feel supported by their principal. If teachers were not excited about the level of support they received from the school's administration, they would be less likely to encourage colleagues to join YMLA's faculty. One experienced YMLA teacher explained that she appreciated having a supportive administrator, something she did not enjoy in her previous teaching positions. She indicated Principal White's high expectations were coupled with his trust in teachers' capacity to make a powerful difference in their students' lives. She underscored how YMLA teachers, with the support of leadership, created the necessary conditions to maximize students' success. When teachers believe they enjoy an outstanding work environment, they are much more likely to be persuasive when they approach esteemed colleagues about applying to work with them.

Principal White also explained how he encourages current YMLA teachers to help him assess candidates' knowledge, skills, and abilities. He emphasized that the skills required to answer interview questions are not the same as the skills required to teach adolescent boys. In addition to interviewing candidates, the dream team observes each candidate teaching a lesson. Finally, before making a hiring decision, Principal White, YMLA teachers, and YMLA students provide the candidate with feedback about the lesson they taught. By observing how candidates respond to feedback, administrators and teachers get a sense of the candidate's willingness to grow and improve. As well, the process reveals information about how the candidate respects the voices of colleagues and students.

These extensive interview, observation, and feedback processes have increased the likelihood that YMLA hires strong teachers; however, Principal White realized that even outstanding teachers are likely to need ongoing, job-embedded support to ensure YMLA students achieve at high levels. At YMLA, frequent observations and detailed feedback form a backbone of support designed to help teachers address a few specific concerns of special import to YMLA students. Both administrators and teachers engage in regular classrooms visits, thus providing teachers regular opportunities to learn about factors that influence the success of students of color. Teachers observe these factors coming to life in their colleagues' classrooms. The first and primary factor is student engagement. Principal White emphasized:

> Here at YMLA, teachers know that the young men need to be actively engaged. We know that, for most boys, direct instruction isn't going to be effective if it goes beyond 15 minutes. So we believe in creating awesome models of a gradual release of responsibility so that our young men are engaged.

Classroom observations and feedback at YMLA underscore students' active engagement in learning. Principal White emphasized, "We want to see our young men doing, creating, and discussing. We don't want to see them just sitting and listening."

Secondly, Principal White explained that observation and feedback are designed to ensure that every lesson focuses on a challenging academic objective aligned to rigorous academic standards. Teachers at YMLA commit to ensuring that their students benefit from instruction that is at least as rigorous as instruction provided to students in affluent communities "because we want our young men to be prepared to compete." Walk-through observations and feedback processes (involving both teachers and administrators) are designed to look carefully at what students are expected to learn during a given lesson. Observers note the manner in which teachers present a clear and specific learning objective, align their instruction to this objective, and then utilize formative assessments to determine whether the lesson objective was achieved. Observers also examine the degree to which the teacher aligns the instructional activities and the formative assessment to the stated objective. Principal White explained, "Once the objective, the activities, and the formative assessment mesh, you usually have a good lesson with good engagement and alignment. We try to keep it simple." Principal White explained:

> I tell teachers we are not moving on until we have mastered the content. Learning is built upon foundations. If you move on without establishing a strong foundation, you can't expect success down the road. I know the district has a scope and sequence chart, and I know they tell us to stick to it, but if the young men aren't learning, we don't stick to it. Our teachers know they're not going to feel the heat from me. But when

students have mastered it, then it's time to move on. Or if kids already know the content, don't spend too much time on it. Let's move on and teach them things that they don't know.

Leaders at YMLA have helped teachers learn that student success is not accidental; success is likely when teachers specify a clear and rigorous learning object, pursued through aligned, engaging learning activities, and targeted toward a formative assessment that provides useful information about the extent to which students have mastered the specified objective. By persistently focusing on these few critical elements in walk-through observations, leaders have helped teachers see the connections between their teaching practices and student learning results. Principal White believes it is important to promote the "transparency of data" so that educators see how their teaching practices influence learning. He emphasizes, however, "We highlight the data in a way that is not punitive. We're always celebrating growth, and we're always praising."

Efforts to hire strong teachers at YMLA have been fruitful. As well, efforts to help YMLA teachers focus on improving a few essential concerns has been instrumental; however, Principal White admits that processes have not always worked the way he envisioned. He explained:

> This might sound strange, but one of our biggest victories was achieved when I removed a teacher the first semester after we opened. He wasn't invested, and he didn't believe in the kids. So before Christmas, I let the team know he wouldn't be with us anymore. And the team was shocked. They never saw it coming. I'm sure some of them saw some of the same issues I saw, but they didn't expect I would do anything about it. They didn't even know the gentleman was on a growth plan. I'm very cordial with everyone. I praise publicly and have rough conversations privately. But when they heard he wasn't returning, everyone realized I was serious about all the things we were saying about getting our young men to college. That helped us develop our culture of transparency of data and do what we needed to do in classrooms to get our young men to succeed. Some teachers decided they didn't want to be here, and they left. But some thought, "Okay, I'm in a place where I can really work and see results."

Recognitions

YMLA students are not alone in considering their teachers a dream team. For example, a YMLA STEM teacher received the Lockheed Martin Chair for Excellence Award. Similarly, a YMLA English teacher received the Chase Chair for Teaching Excellence Award.

YMLA has achieved several distinctions from the Texas Education Agency (the State Department of Education in Texas). The school has earned an "A" rating based largely upon student performance on the state's academic assessment. As well, YMLA earned the distinction of being in the top 25% of Texas schools in closing achievement gaps.

Both in 2015 and 2018, YMLA earned the National Center for Urban School Transformation's America's Best Urban Schools Award. This distinction was earned in recognition of the school's outstanding learning results for both Black and Latinx students.

In 2021, GreatSchools.com recognized YMLA as one of 1,838 public high schools to receive the College Success Award. The award recognizes and celebrates schools across the country that excel at helping students enroll and succeed in college. Award winners are determined based on data related to college preparation (including four-year graduation rate and college entrance examination scores), college enrollment, and college performance (including the percentage of students who require remediation in college and the percentage of students who persist to college graduation). Also, Common Sense, a national nonprofit organization dedicated to helping students and families thrive in media and technology, named YMLA a Common Sense–Certified Campus.

What It Is and What It Isn't: Factors That Have Influenced Success at Young Men's Leadership Academy

What It Is: Students Work Hard to Graduate When Graduation Is Meaningful

Almost all Black students at YMLA graduate; however, to earn a diploma, YMLA students must work harder and achieve more than students at many urban schools. At YMLA, students work hard to meet rigorous graduation requirements because they know that a YMLA diploma represents a meaningful accomplishment. Students know that when they graduate, they will be prepared to pursue a wide variety of academic and career choices.

What It Isn't: Making Graduation Easy

Many schools have watered down courses and graduation requirements to make it easier for Black students to succeed; however, in such schools, Black students recognize that a diploma is a ticket to nowhere. Students know when they are not acquiring transcripts that will enable them to earn admission into four-year colleges and universities. As well, students know when they are not learning the concepts and skills necessary to prepare them to succeed in postsecondary education. In such situations, if students do not have parents pushing them to graduate, they are more likely to decide that the pursuit of graduation is not worth their effort.

What It Is: Creating and Maintaining Pathways to Success

Black students at YMLA are more likely to be successful because teachers help ensure that students always have opportunities to grow, learn, and succeed. Often, before teachers give students an assignment or a test, they work with students to be certain that students understand the essential concepts and skills so their success is likely. However, even when students do not successfully complete the assignment or the test, teachers help students understand their misconceptions and offer students opportunities to demonstrate their mastery of the content. YMLA students know that their teachers will keep working with them as long as they keep trying to learn and succeed.

What It Isn't: Creating Dead Ends for Learning

In many secondary schools, Black students frequently find themselves at dead ends. The student submits an assignment or test; the teacher gives the assignment or test a "D" or "F" grade. The grade is entered into the grading system, and the class moves to the next topic. The student never knows why they earned a low grade. They do not have an opportunity to master skills that might be building blocks for developing future skills. Often, students recognize that they have little or no opportunity to offset the damage to their end-of-course grade caused by the low assignment grade. As a result, students often realize they have reached an academic dead end. They no longer have a reason to exert effort.

What It Is: Students Work Hard When They Have the Information Needed to Influence Their Destiny

At YMLA, educators provide students information about their individual and group academic performance. Educators help students and parents understand key data points and know how to use the information to influence their individual and group academic performance. At YMLA, when Black students are performing at levels lower than they desire, they learn that they have the power to influence their success through focused, deliberate action.

What It Isn't: Assuming Students Know How to Influence Their Academic Success

In many schools, Black students feel that educators have created a game they cannot win. Often, when Black students try to succeed, they do not have adequate information about what they need to learn, so their efforts are unsuccessful.

What It Is: Helping Teachers Understand How Their Efforts Influence Student Learning

At YMLA, leaders have consistently focused on a few critical factors that influence student learning. Specifically, classroom observations and feedback have focused upon 1) the extent to which all students are actively engaged in learning, 2) learning is focused on a specific, rigorous academic objective,

3) lesson activities are likely to lead students to master the objective, and 4) the teacher checks to ensure that students have learned the objective well through a formative assessment. As a result, YMLA teachers have learned that their actions can and will influence the success of their students.

What It Isn't: Promoting the Assumption of the Teacher's Neutrality in Student Learning

In too many schools, educators have come to believe that they "taught it" but Black students did not do what they needed to do to "learn it." The belief is perpetuated when White middle-class students seemed to have successfully "learned it," even if the success is due to factors that have little to do with the instruction the teacher provided (e.g., factors such as student prior knowledge, access to resource materials, support from parents who have the time, resources, and prior knowledge to ensure their child's success). The assumption of teacher neutrality is bolstered when school leaders promote random acts of professional development by following the educational fad du jour, instead of consistently reinforcing a small set of powerful teaching practices that influence the likelihood of student success.

References

Alliance for Excellent Education. (2015, November 10). *Number of annual high school dropouts falls by 250,000, new report finds*. https://all4ed. org/press_release/number-of-annual-high-school-dropouts-falls-by-250000-new-report-finds/

Ferguson, R. (2002). *What doesn't meet the eye: Understanding and addressing racial disparities in high-achieving suburban schools*. North Central Regional Educational Lab.

PART II

How Schools Can Engage and Empower Black Students

At Patrick Henry Elementary/Intermediate School in East Harlem; Maplewood Richmond Heights High School in St. Louis; Wynnebrook Elementary in West Palm Beach, Florida; O'Farrell Charter High School in San Diego; Concourse Village Elementary in the South Bronx; and Young Men's Leadership Academy in Fort Worth, Texas, educators have come together to create schools that generate outstanding academic outcomes for Black students. As Chenoweth (2007) suggested, if we want to know "Can it be done?" the answer is simply, "It's being done [now!]" (p. 1).

We did not hear educators from these six schools refer to themselves or their schools as antiracist; however, we see each of these schools as "a powerful collection of antiracist policies [practices and programs] that lead to racial equity and are substantiated by antiracist ideas" (Kendi, 2019, p. 20). Educators deliberately worked with students, families, and communities to create justice for the Black students they felt privileged to serve. They replaced cultures, curricula, and instructional practices that rarely served Black students well with cultures, curricula, and instructional practices that were fine-tuned to resonate specifically with the students at their schools.

While we recognize the difficulties inherent in changing decades and centuries of ineffective, even oppressive, practices, we contend the factors that contributed to the success of these six schools can become the norm in any school or school district where a critical mass of citizens, educators, and educational leaders commit to ensuring that Black students excel. The change may not be quick or simple, but "it's being done" now. So it can be done in schools and school districts throughout our nation.

DOI: 10.4324/9781003277910-8

125

All six schools featured in this book benefitted from outstanding principals who were committed to the success of Black students. There is no alternate route to success. Every community that wants their Black students to excel must ensure that Black students benefit from effective leaders who commit to their success in school and their success in life. Chapter 7 synthesizes our leadership findings, describing the nature and caliber of leadership required, and the implications for various stakeholder groups who play roles in selecting, preparing, and supporting school leaders.

Similarly, in all six schools, we found "dream teams" comprised of impressive teachers, teacher leaders, and support staff. In Chapter 8, we describe how these dream teams recreated "school" as a place where Black students felt they belonged, where Black students felt loved and valued, and where Black students experienced joy. In all six schools, the dream teams implemented structures that fostered the development of healthy, positive, and caring relationships between and among teachers, students, and families. The dream teams created powerful and positive transformational cultures that inspired the energy and effort of Black students, celebrated their beauty, and cultivated their brilliance. In addition, Chapter 8 describes the implications for teachers, parents, school leaders, district leaders, policy makers, and institutions of higher education committed to ensuring that all Black students benefit from similar practices.

In Chapter 9, we describe how dream teams at each of the six schools established clear pathways for the academic and social success of Black students. Black students realized their success was likely because dream teams developed curricular paths that students recognized as relevant to their lives, their communities, and their aspirations. Dream teams developed and refined instructional approaches that helped Black students know they could master advanced concepts and skills. Teachers and administrators created early on-ramps to those pathways so Black students would feel empowered, as if they were ahead of the pack instead of perpetually feeling as if they were behind the eight ball. As well, pathways were meticulously planned to help students through the most challenging transitions, and pathways were well marked to help students avoid dead ends and remain on course toward their personal and professional goals. Chapter 9 emphasizes the issues stakeholders must address to ensure the development of clear pathways for the success of all Black students.

References

Chenoweth, K. (2007). *"It's being done": Academic success in unexpected schools*. Harvard Education Press.

Kendi, I. X. (2019). *How to be an antiracist*. One World.

7

Ensuring Black Students Benefit from Effective Leaders Committed to Their Success

Many factors contribute to the development of outstanding schools where all demographic groups excel. However, researchers have concluded: "Indeed, there are virtually no documented instances of troubled schools being turned around in the absence of intervention by talented leaders. Many other factors may contribute to such turnarounds, but leadership is the catalyst" (Leithwood et al., 2004, p. 5).

If every Black student in America benefitted from the persistence of Principal Berry; the student-focused integrity of Principal Grawer; the whatever-it-takes attitude of Principal Pantelidis; the student-centered decision-making of Principal Rainey; the powerful, loving presence of Principal Sorden; and Principal White's unyielding belief in the capacity of every student to succeed, we would open millions of doors and change the trajectory of millions of lives. "Leadership is the catalyst" in every school that dismantles routines, procedures, programs, norms, teaching behaviors, rules, policies, and other practices that were not designed to lead Black students to academic success. Theoharis wrote, "Exemplary leadership helps both to create the necessity for change and to make change happen" (2009, p. 8). This chapter describes the leadership required to lead others to both understand the necessity for change in schools that serve Black students and the leadership required to make the needed changes happen.

DOI: 10.4324/9781003277910-9

Key Leadership Attributes

Principals Berry (and her predecessor, Principal Pegg), Grawer, Pantelidis, Rainey, Sorden, and White demonstrated a number of essential leadership attributes:

1. They exuded a passionate belief in the ability of Black children to achieve outstanding learning outcomes, and by doing so, they led others to believe the same.

2. Persistently, they recognized the beauty, value, and brilliance of Black students and Black families and led others to see the same.

3. Their steadfast focus on the specific needs of Black students challenged others to direct their attention and their efforts similarly. Also, these leaders inspired trust by providing a quantity and quality of support that made stakeholders feel efficacious about educating Black students to their fullest potential.

4. They nurtured a culture of collaboration in which educators shared responsibility for ensuring the success of Black students.

5. Their consistent, honest concentration on data and evidence of growth for Black students led others to abandon excuses and adopt more effective approaches.

The Leader's Belief

Many leaders will affirm their belief in the capacity of Black students to achieve; however, when they do so, they may be envisioning the three Black children in the fifth-grade advanced reading group or the two Black students in the Advanced Placement chemistry class. They may not necessarily include the Black students who entered eighth grade with fourth-grade reading skills, the Black children who can't seem to stop blurting out answers, or the Black students who spend more time parked outside the assistant principal's office than they spend in English class. Black students need leaders who believe in their capacity to excel, even though they have been in classrooms or programs that did not promote their success. Black students need leaders who believe in them when others have not. Black students need leaders who believe in them even when they have stopped believing in themselves.

Please note that while children need school leaders who believe in their capacity to excel, the leader's belief is insufficient. Muhammad (2009) explained that leaders must influence the development of a positive school culture in which educators throughout the school believe in the ability of every student to succeed. Lezotte and Snyder (2011) specified that leaders needed to influence the extent to which school personnel believed that 1) all students had the ability to succeed and that 2) the school personnel had the capacity to enable all students to succeed. Similarly, Johnson et al. (2017) emphasized how leaders face the central challenge of cultivating belief among all stakeholders.

The school leaders featured in this book boldly demonstrated their belief in a manner that was visible to teachers, parents, students, and even district leaders. If Principal Sorden had quietly ignored the first-grade teacher who did not believe her Black students could annotate text, her silence would have eventually communicated that Concourse Village teachers did not need to believe that Black students could excel. If Principal White had quietly ignored the low expectations of the teacher he eventually removed, he would have relinquished his responsibility to hold all teachers responsible for acknowledging the potential of every student at Young Men's Leadership Academy. The leaders featured here understood that every decision they made and every action they took would be scrutinized by stakeholders as they considered, "Does this principal believe in the capacity of Black students to excel *enough* that she/he will expect me to change what I believe and what I do?"

At these six schools, each principal's belief in the capacity of Black students to excel served as a moral imperative. Each principal's actions illustrated Principal Sorden's words: "I refused to accept that my students were going to get less than what they deserved."

Recognizing the Beauty, Value, and Brilliance of Black Students

Parents of Black students at Patrick Henry Preparatory School in East Harlem emphatically shared that Principal Pantelidis was committed to ensuring their children's success. Similarly, Black students at Maplewood Richmond

131

Heights High School in St. Louis reported that Principal Grawer valued their opinions and ideas. "He always asks what we think," one student noted. In all six of the schools featured in this book, leaders recognized and illuminated the beauty, value, and brilliance of Black students.

To know and understand the beauty, value, and brilliance of Black students, leaders of the six featured schools invested time in listening to Black students and Black families. Principal Sorden greeted students and parents as they entered Concourse Village and asked questions that reflected her sincere interest in their lives. Principal Pegg rode the green bus and listened to the stories of Wynnebrook's Black students, and when the bus arrived in the Black community, he met with parents and listened to their hopes and concerns. Principals at all six schools were known to regularly "check in" with their students to determine what they were learning, why students perceived the content was important, how they were feeling about school, what was important in their lives, and what neighborhood issues might be impinging upon their ability to focus on their classroom activities and assignments. Principals at all six schools were not strangers to the living rooms of their Black students. Principals saw the beauty, value, and brilliance of their Black students, in part, because they took the time to know their Black students and their families.

Scheurich (1998) described schools where students of color excelled as "loving" because of the way in which leaders valued, respected, and appreciated the children and families they served. Wood (2019) argued that loving and caring approaches are essential as we endeavor to create schools in which Black students succeed. He stated, "Bringing love into the educational system involves embracing a new educational paradigm that truly values the intelligence, worth, and morality of Black minds" (Wood, 2019, p. 7).

At the six schools featured here, love was not an abstract or passive notion. At Wynnebrook Elementary, Principal Pegg was clear when he stated, "It's just about giving kids love and respect." At YMLA, Principal White was unambiguous when he exclaimed, "I'm looking for teachers who love my kids!" At Maplewood Richmond Heights, Principal Grawer insisted, "We tell them [our students], 'We love you,' every day." At O'Farrell, Principal Rainey explained, "You keep that bar as high as you would for your own children, and you help them get there, you help fill in the gaps, you get somebody to teach them who knows and loves them." At Patrick Henry, on several occasions, we heard Principal Pantelidis say, "We love our kids. We would do anything for our kids." At Concourse

Village, Principal Sorden made abundantly clear, "The sense of joy, love, and safety, those are non-negotiables for me."

By seeing the beauty, value, and brilliance of Black students, by loving Black students for who they are, leaders *lead* teachers, counselors, school secretaries, coaches, social workers, cafeteria workers, custodians, nurses, instructional aides, assistant principals, parents, and the student population to act in loving ways. This loving leadership operates as a formidable force in generating the positive transformational culture necessary to ensure the success of students of color (Johnson et al., 2019).

Inspiring Trust

"Every leadership action builds or erodes trust" (Tschannen-Moran, 2014, p. 21). Leaders in the six featured schools continuously strove to build trust. Stakeholders never had to guess their principal's motives in the six schools featured in this book; instead, stakeholders were much more likely to conclude that every decision was focused upon the best interests of students. Teachers, parents, and students knew that Principal Rainey's decisions about graduation requirements were based firmly on a commitment to ensuring that every graduate would have an opportunity to attend and succeed in college. At Patrick Henry Preparatory School, personnel, from preschool through eighth grade, had confidence that Principal Pantelidis's decisions were grounded in his commitment to ensuring that every student would be well-prepared to enter and succeed in New York City's best high schools. When Principals Berry, Grawer, Sorden, or White visited classrooms, school personnel trusted their feedback was rooted firmly in the best interests of students, even in cases when they did not necessarily agree with or appreciate their comments.

Unfortunately, trust is in short supply in many schools across our nation. Too often, teachers, counselors, support staff, parents, and students do not know why or how decisions are made. Too often, stakeholders assume that decisions are made based upon the self-interests of administrators. As a result, stakeholders may be unenthusiastic about implementing an administrator's strategy, not because the idea is poor, but because stakeholders assume the idea is based on the principal's self-interested whim or the bureaucratic concerns of district office administrators. The absence of trust within school communities often diminishes the likelihood that meaningful, constructive changes occur, even when leaders have sound intentions for students of color. Muhammad and Cruz (2019) underscored the importance of connecting with stakeholders in a trustworthy manner.

> A transformational leader needs the very essential ability to connect with others' emotions. Facts and objective evidence alone do not inspire people; people need to connect with their leader on a personal level and know that their leader has not just an intellectual connection but also an ethical connection to their purpose.
>
> (Muhammad & Cruz, 2019, p. 6)

Tschannen-Moran (2014) explained how leaders build trustworthiness through their benevolence (caring, demonstrating positive intentions, extending goodwill), honesty (showing integrity, telling the truth, being authentic), openness (sharing important information, sharing decision-making), reliability (being consistent and dependable), and competence (problem-solving, resolving conflict, pressing for results). The everyday actions of leaders either increase or diminish the extent to which stakeholders perceive the leader's motives as benevolent, their words as open and honest, and perceive their actions as reliable and competent.

Leaders who fail to engender trust in ways that allow them to connect with others, teach others, and inspire others find themselves unable to create and sustain the changes they envision. While leaders may have outstanding reasons for asking educators to change their practice, dozens of factors may prompt resistance, even among individuals who would like to see their students of color excel. For example, La Salle and Johnson (2019) explained how change aversion exists as a safety mechanism of the human brain. Humans will avoid change they perceive as good and worthwhile if they fear they might not be able to implement the change successfully. They warned, "When leading equity initiatives, remember that many people will naturally react with fear about how the change could affect them personally" (La Salle & Johnson, 2019, p. 59).

To combat change aversion, equity-focused leaders must inspire stakeholders to trust that they will have everything they need to implement important changes successfully. Johnson, Uline, and Perez specified:

> Leaders who influence outstanding results for all demographic groups help stakeholders believe they have abundant support and,

consequently, abundant capacity to succeed. . . . Teachers are willing to pursue the lofty expectations of their administrators when they
perceive they have everything they need to meet and exceed those
expectations (e.g., training, materials, time, exemplar work samples,
no-risk opportunities to try, feedback, technological support, peer
support, and support for addressing students' non-academic needs).

(Johnson et al., 2019, p. 119)

At the same time leaders at all six schools expected educators to pursue
ambitious changes in school culture, curricula, and instruction, the leaders
minimized change aversion by providing abundant support, helping educators believe they could implement changes successfully. For examples,
teachers at Wynnebrook and Concourse Village benefitted from abundant
opportunities to observe their school leaders encouraging students of color
to adopt positive, scholarly behavior. Teachers at Patrick Henry Prep and
O'Farrell Charter High benefited from excellent professional development
that helped them rethink how they could teach challenging academic
standards in ways that resonated with the backgrounds and concerns of
students of color. Teachers at Maplewood Richmond Heights High and
Young Men's Leadership Academy received ongoing support from both
administrators and colleagues as they learned to deliver instruction in ways
that were more likely to lead Black students to master challenging academic skills. To generate essential change, the leaders of these six schools
inspired educators to trust they would not allow them to fail. Instead, leaders inspired educators to trust that their primary goal was to ensure every
educator would succeed in their efforts to help every student reach their
highest potential in school and life.

Because trust matters; race matters. Black leaders in the schools featured here committed to earning the trust of White district leaders and White
teachers. White leaders in these six schools committed to earning the trust
of Black teachers, students, families, and community members. It is important to note, however, that race does not preclude the development of trust.
Regardless of their race, the leaders of these six schools *earned* the trust of all
stakeholder groups each and every day. To earn trust, leaders could not hide
from racial issues. Instead, leaders had to be willing to support open, honest conversations about race. According to Singleton (2015), "Courageous
Conversation fortifies the passion, practice, and persistence educators need
to build racial consciousness and impact more profoundly their schools'

learning environments" (p. 67). At all six schools, leaders created environments in which students, teachers, parents, and community members were able and willing to discuss concerns about race in ways that strengthened trust and built the school's capacity to serve Black students well.

Nurturing a Culture of Collaboration

School leaders cannot accomplish substantial changes in teaching and learning for Black students without the active, regular, and sustained involvement of other school personnel. "In order to properly address the myriad of challenges facing schools today . . . educators need to work with like-minded individuals with a common goal to help them conquer their obstacles" (Muhammad & Hollie, 2012, pp. 67–68).

Leaders at the six schools featured in this book were masterful at creating a culture of collaboration. Of course, leaders expected their teachers to teach Black students well. Additionally, however, leaders expected their teachers to share responsibility for supporting one another in improving the teaching of Black students. Collaboration was an engine of change. Teachers learned from one another, they supported one another, and they assumed responsibility for helping one another elevate learning outcomes for all groups of students.

Principals Pegg and Berry dedicated time and invested professional development resources to ensure that Wynnebrook teachers developed professional learning committees that challenged ineffective practices and dramatically improved the teaching of literacy. At Concourse Village and Patrick Henry, Principals Sorden and Pantelidis expected teachers to come together regularly and contribute to decisions about approaches for making curricula responsive to the needs of students of color. At Maplewood Richmond Heights High and YMLA, Principals Grawer and White expected teachers to work together in ways that ensured that students would benefit from instruction that would reliably lead students toward Advanced Placement courses and dual enrollment programs. At O'Farrell Charter High, collaboration was embedded into the fabric of teachers' responsibilities as they assumed home base assignments that made them the primary point of contact and chief collaborator for a group of students over a four-year period.

Spillane (2006) explained that schools require multiple leaders. Principals can maximize the likelihood that changes will happen, and will have desired effects, when they distribute leadership roles and responsibilities. In the absence of such distributed leadership, school personnel at the six featured schools might have been more likely to sit back and watch the principal's initiatives falter or fail. By nurturing a culture of collaboration and distributed leadership, school personnel were much more likely to share ownership of various initiatives and work together to ensure these changes benefitted students.

Focusing on Data and Growth

Leaders in the six featured schools were truth tellers. They told the truth about what Black students were learning and not learning. They told the truth about what was happening and not happening in classrooms that influenced what Black students learned. Perhaps, most importantly, leaders in the featured schools led other school personnel to become truth tellers who honestly reflected on their professional practice and constantly worked to improve learning outcomes for Black students.

Efforts to examine student data should be designed to generate meaningful improvements in teaching and learning for every child, thus advancing equity goals (Radd et al., 2021). Too often, leaders push teachers to review student data in ways that resemble looking through a window. As teachers peer through the data windows, they note what students did or didn't learn or understand. In contrast, in the six featured schools, leaders encouraged teachers to review student data as though they were looking into a mirror. As school personnel peered into the data mirror, they considered what they did or didn't do to influence the learning of students of color. They considered what they could have done to better influence the learning of Black students.

Leaders should engage school personnel in reviewing data as a means to improve student learning (Ash & Hodge, 2016). The most important benefits of data reviews will not be realized if conversations never evolve beyond "what they got right or wrong" to focus upon "what could be done to help students develop deeper understandings."

At all six schools, leaders sought to create what Principal White (at YMLA) referred to as transparency of data. Leaders helped school personnel understand that while learning results were, of course, influenced by student effort, learning results were also heavily influenced by the specific teaching practices that occurred in classrooms.

Leaders created environments in which school personnel felt comfortable sharing student learning data and sharing information about the teaching practices they employed that influenced the learning outcomes. La Salle and Johnson (2019) emphasized that leaders should "lead with a flashlight, not a club" (p. 51). At the six featured schools, leaders created a low-risk environment by avoiding using data as club and by emphasizing and celebrating growth. Leaders in these schools valued and celebrated improvements in teaching and corresponding improvements in learning results. Teachers knew they were not expected to achieve perfection in learning outcomes for their students of color. They knew; however, they were expected to learn from the performances of their students and continuously improve their teaching practices.

Empathy Interviews

Nelsestuen and Smith (2020) explained that empathy interviews are generally one-on-one interviews with a few open-ended questions. The questions are designed to elicit stories and help uncover unacknowledged needs. In this section, we provide some sample interview questions that might be used to acquire additional perspective about the extent to which Black students are benefitting from effective leaders who are committed to their success. In this chapter, we propose questions that can be asked of parents of Black students and of Black students in intermediate, middle, or high school grades. More information about conducting empathy interviews can be found at https://learningforward.org/journal/supporting-each-other/empathy-interviews/.

Questions for Parents of Black Students or Black Students in Intermediate, Middle, or High School Grades

1. Some school leaders act as if they passionately believe that Black students can achieve outstanding learning outcomes. Do leaders at this school passionately believe that Black students can achieve outstanding learning outcomes? What has happened to make you think they do or do not believe in the capacity of Black students to excel academically?

2. At this school, what have school leaders done to bring attention to the academic successes of Black students? How have school leaders helped everyone see that Black students can excel?

3. Describe something leaders at this school have done that you think builds trust among Black families regarding the school's commitment to their children. Describe something leaders at this school have done that you think might have eroded trust among Black families regarding the school's commitment to their children.

4. What would you like to see school leaders do to bring attention to the academic successes of Black students at this school? How would you like school leaders to help everyone get a deeper sense of the ability of Black students at this school to grow academically and achieve at high levels?

Implications

All stakeholders have a role in ensuring that Black students benefit from effective school leaders who are committed to their success. If any group of stakeholders fails to assume their role, the likelihood that Black students will benefit from effective school leaders is diminished.

Implications for Parents

- Reinforce and celebrate the words and actions of district leaders, school leaders, and teacher leaders who exhibit the characteristics described in this chapter. Good leaders have many professional choices, so make sure leaders who support the education of Black students know they are appreciated.

- Help other parents understand the leadership characteristics described in this chapter. Too often, parents buy into popular media notions that suggest that schools that serve Black students need leaders who act like prison wardens.

- Volunteer to serve on committees that are interviewing candidates for leadership roles. Look for the leadership characteristics discussed in this chapter when reviewing candidates. Especially consider the extent to which candidates demonstrate that they recognize the beauty, value, and brilliance of Black students, inspire trust, and nurture a culture of collaboration.

- Meet the district leaders who supervise the principal of your child's school. Share your understanding of the leadership characteristics that Black students need. Ask what the district is doing to acquire leaders who model these characteristics. Ask what the district is doing to build the capacity of current leaders to model these characteristics.

Implications for School Leaders

- Dedicate time each week to listen to Black students and their families. Learn about their concerns, their interests, their needs, and their hopes. Always communicate your appreciation of their openness. Let students and parents know you value them.

- Make sure your communication (both oral communication and written communication) regularly expresses your belief in the capacity of Black students to excel and your belief in the capacity of educators at your school to ensure the success of Black students.

- To bolster your belief in the capacity of Black students to excel, seek out and visit schools where Black students achieve impressive learning results. Strive to learn from other outstanding school leaders.

- Even though trust is an essential leadership commodity, there is no professional title that automatically generates trust. This is especially true in communities that have suffered because of the untrustworthy behavior of people in positions of authority. You must endeavor to earn trust through your daily actions. Strive to model benevolence, honesty, openness, reliability, and competence so that you earn the trust of school personnel, parents, students, and the broader community.

- Check how well you have communicated the reasons for your actions by asking stakeholders (e.g., teachers, support staff, parents, students) to share their thoughts about the reasons behind your most recent decisions.

- Whenever you ask anyone to commit to changing their work processes or work behavior, ask what support they need to successfully meet your expectations. Be prepared to find ways to provide whatever support is necessary to help the people you depend upon, and who depend upon you, succeed.

- Strive to demonstrate your commitment to supporting adults at your school as they seek to help Black students succeed. Help others know you are dedicated to helping them become outstanding teachers, counselors, paraprofessionals, etc. When others conclude that your goal is to prove their incompetence or inadequacy, your capacity to influence their constructive engagement is greatly limited and their behavior is much more likely to become toxic.

- Maximize the time available for regular constructive collaboration focused upon improving teaching and learning at your school. Ensure that collaboration is focused in a manner that will lead to better learning results for Black students.

- To the extent possible, participate in collaboration meetings actively and regularly, especially when teams have minimal experience working together toward the goal of helping one another improve learning outcomes for students of color. Ensure that collaboration occurs in an atmosphere that engenders trust among all participants.

- Encourage members of the school team to assume leadership roles in collaborative efforts. Often, people are more likely to learn from colleagues they trust than from outside "experts."

- Encourage collaboration opportunities that allow teachers to learn from one another's teaching in classrooms. Nurture a supportive environment in which teachers see one another as colleagues who are committed to helping one another help students of color succeed.

- Monitor your use of time and steadily increase the amount of time you spend in classrooms. Remember that you probably are not leading anything or anybody when you are in your office or at the district office.

- When in classrooms, pay attention to Black students. Note the extent to which they are feeling valued, respected, capable, and loved. Note the extent to which they are actively engaged in learning. Note the extent to which they are showing evidence that they are understanding challenging academic concepts. Share feedback focused on these issues. Share feedback in a manner that acknowledges teacher effort and celebrates student growth. Limit suggestions to one or two issues that are likely to make a powerful difference for students of color.

● Carefully monitor a wide array of data points that address the extent to which Black students are succeeding at school (e.g., attendance, discipline referrals, suspensions, performance on formative assessments, grades, mastery of important standards). Use data to acknowledge and celebrate growth and improvement. Also, use data to highlight issues of concern and engage stakeholders in planning improvement strategies.

Implications for Teachers

● Know that most of the implications for school leaders described prior apply to teachers in various teacher leadership roles. As a teacher leader, you are a model. Others will learn from you, so make sure you are modeling a strong belief in the capacity of Black students to excel. Make sure you model listening to Black students (and their family members) and seeing their beauty, value, and brilliance. Make sure colleagues see you as someone who is persistently focused on ensuring the success of Black students. As a collaborator, make sure colleagues know that you are committed to helping your colleagues lead Black students to outstanding levels of success.

● Reinforce and celebrate the words and actions of district leaders, school leaders, and colleague teacher leaders who exhibit the characteristics described in this chapter. You have an important role in creating a professional community focused upon improving the lives of Black students.

● Help other teachers understand the leadership characteristics described in this chapter. Strive to contribute to a culture in which everyone is focused upon providing what Black students need to excel.

● Volunteer to serve on committees that are interviewing candidates for leadership roles. Support candidates who demonstrate the leadership characteristics discussed in this chapter.

● Remember that if you believe in the capacity of Black students to excel, you are in a special position to lead. Prepare yourself to assume greater leadership (in your existing role or in new roles). Strive to learn from teacher leaders and administrators who are endeavoring to make a positive difference for Black students.

Implications for District Leaders

- Develop a deep understanding of the school leadership needed to improve outcomes for Black students. Study this chapter. Visit and learn from school leaders who exemplify these characteristics.

- To bolster your belief in the capacity of Black students to excel, seek out and visit schools where Black students achieve impressive learning results. Strive to learn from outstanding school leaders within and beyond your district. Create opportunities for the school leaders you support to visit schools (within your district or beyond your district) where Black students achieve impressive learning results. Too many district leaders assume that the performance of Black students in their district schools is good, acceptable, or even outstanding because it is a smidgen better than the performance of Black students in another school or is a fraction better than it was the prior year. Create a level of institutional cognitive dissonance that inspires constructive change by immersing yourself in schools that demonstrate the capacity to lead Black students to excel.

- In whatever district role you play, first, avoid taking actions that make it more difficult for school leaders to implement the recommendations specified in this chapter. For example, keep in mind that every minute you require school leaders to spend completing district reports or attending district meetings may represent minutes that could be spent in classrooms helping teachers improve outcomes for Black students.

- In whatever district role you play, consider your opportunities to use your position in a way that builds the capacity of school leaders to pursue the leadership practices described in this chapter. For example, consider your opportunities for helping school leaders examine data in ways that highlight the needs of Black students. Consider your opportunities for helping school leaders work with their teams to engage in constructive planning to address those needs and increase the likelihood of student success.

- Reconsider and redesign the role of assistant principals, especially in schools that serve large concentrations of students of color. Often, the assistant principal role perpetuates school dysfunctions that do not serve Black students well. Specifically, many assistant principals serve as disciplinarians. When there is an assistant principal in the school office, teachers feel comfortable removing students from class and asking the assistant principal to deal with issues that often stem from the teacher's difficulty establishing a positive relationship with students or from the teacher's difficulty providing instruction that students perceive as relevant and engaging. Because the school disciplinarian rarely works with teachers to improve instruction, the role rarely prepares individuals to become principals. Instead, districts should structure the assistant principal role in a way that focuses squarely on helping teachers improve learning. Instead of sitting in an office, waiting for the stream of discipline referrals, assistant principals should be in classrooms, noting which students are not engaged and supporting teachers in increasing student engagement. Assistant principals should develop skill at helping teachers build stronger, more positive relationships with students (especially Black students) in ways that prevent discipline problems and maximize the likelihood of student success.

Implications for Institutions of Higher Education

- Individuals who prepare school leaders must have a deep understanding of the school leadership needed to improve outcomes for Black students. This is true for all institutions that prepare school leaders and is especially true for institutions that profess a commit to advancing social justice. Institutions that prepare school leaders should examine the knowledge, skills, and dispositions of the individuals who share responsibility for preparing leaders and determine how they can build the capacity of those individuals to prepare leaders well.

- Individuals who prepare school leaders should spend time visiting and studying schools where Black students excel. Individuals who prepare school leaders should know this chapter and strive to deepen our understanding of school leadership that is a catalyst for the success of Black students.

● Candidates for school leadership credentials, certifications, or licensure should be required to spend time visiting and studying schools where Black students excel. It is exceptionally difficult for new leaders to establish a vision of excellence for Black students if all they have seen or experienced is educational mediocrity (or worse) for Black students.

Implications for Policy Makers

● Develop publicly accessible data tools that make it easy for the public to monitor the performance of schools on various indicators related to the success of Black students. The data tools should make it easy for parents, school personnel, and community members to understand how well various schools and school districts are influencing learning outcomes for various demographic groups. Data tools should feature attendance data, discipline data, literacy levels, mastery of algebraic concepts/skills and other foundational mathematical skills, development of a world language, participation in special education, completion of units required for graduation, completion of units required for postsecondary admission, and other important learning milestones. The public should be able to use such data tools to identify schools and districts that are leading Black students to excel. As well, the data tools should help communities identify schools and districts where improvement is needed. In schools that serve small numbers of Black students, safeguards should protect the privacy of individuals; however, data tools should help all schools feel accountable for leading Black students to excel.

● Policy makers should establish strategies for recognizing and celebrating schools and districts where Black students excel. As well, policy makers should establish strategies for recognizing and celebrating schools that demonstrate significant improvement in learning outcomes for Black students. When policy tools highlight school failures without highlighting successes, we reinforce the notion that Black students cannot succeed academically. Policy makers have a responsibility to celebrate educators and communities that ensure the success of Black students.

● Policy leaders must create incentives that encourage outstanding school leaders to work and stay in schools that serve concentrations of Black students. The goal of equity will not be achieved if we act as if policies that are supposedly "race-neutral" perpetuate a status quo that is all but equal. If school leadership is the catalyst for change, then we must maximize the likelihood that Black students benefit from outstanding school leaders if we want Black students to excel.

- Policy leaders must establish greater reciprocity in accountability systems. Too often, systems hold schools (and more specifically school leaders) accountable while ignoring the roles districts play in creating systems that make it difficult for school leaders to lead students of color to excel. When principals lead their schools to outstanding learning results for Black students, often their success comes despite (not because of) district policies, procedures, and practices. Many more school leaders could be catalysts of constructive change if they worked in districts that created and aligned supports to build their capacity to be outstanding leaders.

References

Ash, R. C., & Hodge, P. H. (2016). *Five critical leadership practices: The secret to high-performing schools*. Routledge.

Johnson, J. F., Uline, C. L., & Perez, L. G. (2017). *Leadership in America's best urban schools*. Routledge.

Johnson, J. F., Uline, C. L., & Perez, L. G. (2019). *Teaching practices from America's best urban schools: A guide for school and classroom leaders*. Routledge.

La Salle, R. A., & Johnson, R. S. (2019). *Shattering inequities: Real-world wisdom for school and district leaders*. Rowman & Littlefield.

Leithwood, K., Louis, K. S., Anderson, S., & Wahlstrom, K. (2004). *Review of research: How leadership influences student learning*. The Wallace Foundation.

Lezotte, L. W., & Snyder, K. M. (2011). *What effective schools do: Re-envisioning the correlates*. Solution Tree Press.

Muhammad, A. (2009). *Transforming school culture: How to overcome staff division*. Solution Tree Press.

Muhammad, A., & Cruz, L. F. (2019). *Time for change: Four essential skills for transformational school and district leaders*. Solution Tree Press.

Muhammad, A., & Hollie, S. (2012). *The will to lead, the skill to teach: Transforming schools at every level*. Solution Tree Press.

Nelsestuen, K., & Smith, J. (2020). Empathy interviews. *The Learning Professional, 41*(5), 59–62.

Radd, S. I., Generett, G. G., Gooden, M. A., & Theoharis, G. (2021). *Five practices for equity-focused school leadership*. ASCD.

Scheurich, J. J. (1998). Highly successful and loving, public elementary schools populated mainly by low-SES children of color: Core beliefs and cultural characteristics. *Urban Education, 33*(4), 451–491.

Singleton, G. E. (2015). *Courageous conversations about race: A field guide for achieving equity in schools* (2nd ed.). Corwin.

Spillane, J. R. (2006). *Distributed leadership*. Jossey-Bass.

Theoharis, G. (2009). *The school leaders our children deserve: Seven keys to equity, social justice, and school reform*. Teacher's College Press.

Tschannen-Moran, M. (2014). *Trust matters: Leadership for successful schools* (2nd ed.). Jossey-Bass.

Wood, J. L. (2019). *Black minds matter: Realizing the brilliance, dignity, and morality of Black males in education*. Montezuma Publishing.

Ensuring Black Students Belong, Feel Loved, and Experience Joy

When our NCUST teams visit schools where students of color achieve remarkable outcomes, often our subsequent conversations focus more on the amazing culture of the schools than on evidence of curricular rigor or instructional effectiveness. In our visits to each of the six schools featured in this book, while we often found astounding teaching and impressive academic rigor, our postvisit conversations often centered on the relationships, culture, and warm and loving environments we observed in classrooms. We marveled at how Black students at Maplewood Richmond Heights High School seemed to find joy in learning about challenging science concepts. We were awed by the eagerness of Black students at Wynnebrook Elementary to complete literacy assignments and receive feedback from their teachers. We were fascinated by the way teachers at Patrick Henry Preparatory School created an environment that made their Black middle school students eager to apply complex mathematical thinking to real-world problems. Often, we would hear ourselves exclaiming, "The students would do anything for those teachers!"

Ladson-Billings (2009) aptly described outstanding educators as *Dreamkeepers*: individuals who see beauty and brilliance in the children they serve, who nurture and support the beauty, and who enable the brilliance to flourish. In quoting Elizabeth Harris (one of teachers she featured), Ladson-Billings wrote, "God's little flowers, that's what I call then. Everyone a little different but everyone so sweet. And just like a garden, the classroom has got be a place that nurtures them" (Ladson-Billings, 2009, p. 97).

James Ford, the 2015 North Carolina Teacher of the Year and the program director for the Public School Forum of North Carolina, told *Education Week*:

DOI: 10.4324/9781003277910-10

> The relational part of teaching may very well be its most underrated aspect. . . . Our first job as teachers is to make sure that we learn our students, that we connect with them on a real level, showing respect for their culture and affirming their worthiness to receive the best education possible.
>
> (Sparks, 2019, p. 8)

The powerful impact of teacher-student relationships has been demonstrated in over 119 studies, with an effect size of 0.72 (more powerful than student's prior achievement, teacher professional development, student's home environment, phonics instruction, student's socioeconomic status, class management, and many other factors) (Hattie, 2009). Findings from one study revealed, when teachers increased the number of their positive comments and interactions to a level that was five times greater than the number of negative comments and interactions, their students demonstrated significantly less-disruptive behavior and were more likely to attend to academic tasks (Sparks, 2019). Noddings (2012) suggested that the power of teacher-student relationships rests in the centrality of caring to our efforts to help children and youth grow and learn.

Not only does a more welcoming atmosphere enhance learning, but it also helps children build self-esteem. "Schools must be a second home for children, orderly, attractive, warm, comfortable. Schools should be welcoming. But the major facet that creates climate is the attitude of the people who inhabit the building" (Villani, 1999, p. 103).

Scholars have emphasized how social, emotional, and cognitive learning factors are intertwined and interdependent (CASEL, 2005; Jones & Kahn, 2017). Teacher-student relationships have a substantial influence on the development of students' social and emotional skills and competencies. In turn, students' social and emotional skills have a powerful influence on their development of academic skills. Frey et al. (2019, p. 13) asserted, "We believe that the most important questions to ask about SEL [social, emotional learning] are not about which program to use, but about how teachers will integrate the tenets of SEL into the fabric of their lessons." In the six featured schools, social and emotional learning is far more than a supplemental program; social-emotional learning is interwoven throughout the fabric of teaching and learning as a hallmark of each school's culture.

In many schools, social, economic, and cultural differences between Black students and teachers make the establishment of strong and meaningful relationships more difficult (MacNeil et al., 2009). When schools fail to address this difficulty, the results can be devasting for Black students and "lead to a cascade of negative academic and behavioral transactions that can lead children to withdraw and become less motivated, leading to greater gaps in school performance and achievement" (Osher et al., 2020, n.p.). However, when the relationships between Black students and their teachers are positive, the impact on students' ability to regulate their emotions, behavior, and cognition can be powerful, resulting in stronger executive functions, along with skills and dispositions associated with engagement in learning and cognitive and academic skills (Osher et al., 2020).

While the power of teacher-student relationships is important for all students, Ferguson (2008) found that teacher-student relationships (and particularly teacher encouragement) have a significant impact on the effort of Black students. He wrote:

> Perhaps the most interesting finding here is the distinctive importance of teacher encouragement as a reported source of motivation for nonwhite students, especially African American students, and the fact that this difference is truly a racial difference, mostly unrelated to measures of SES [socio-economic status]. The special importance of encouragement highlights the likely importance of strong teacher-student relationships in affecting achievement, especially for African American and Hispanic students.
>
> (Ferguson, 2008, p. 226)

The research suggests we should not be surprised that Black students at all six featured schools spoke first and foremost about the caring environments created by their teachers. Black students (at all grade levels) believed their teachers cared sincerely about them. Black students were eager to pursue challenging academic tasks, rewrite papers, and complete complex projects because they felt encouraged, supported, cared for, and loved by their teachers.

This chapter describes how teams of teachers (with the support of their administrators and other support personnel) created learning environments that led Black students to feel belonging, to feel valued and loved, and to experience joy in learning. Furthermore, this chapter describes how various stakeholders can help ensure that all Black students have schools where they experience belonging, love, and the joy of learning.

Key Attributes of Schools Where Black Students Experience Belonging, Love, and Joy

In all six schools featured in this book, we found the following attributes:

1. School leaders and teacher leaders established teacher recruitment and selection processes that identified individuals who recognized the beauty and brilliance of Black students and their families. Leaders built "dream teams" by hiring teachers who demonstrated excellent capacity to create and sustain positive transformational cultures for Black students (Johnson et al., 2019).

2. Dream team members (with the support of their administrators and other colleagues) established and sustained systems and structures that built healthy, positive, and caring relationships among a) teachers and students, b) teachers and families, and c) students and other students.

3. School leaders insisted that everyone contribute to the development of school and classroom cultures in which Black students felt belonging, love, and joy. The development of a positive transformational culture for Black students became a nonnegotiable institutional priority.

Recruiting and Selecting Teachers

At the featured schools, principals and teachers described efforts to fill vacancies with individuals who had substantial capacity to help students of color feel a sense of belonging, love, and joy. Three factors stood out in school efforts to recruit and hire teachers.

First, leaders prioritized candidates' capacity to establish and develop relationships with students of color. For example, candidates who could not convince Principal White that "they loved kids and, even more so, loved YMLA kids" were not likely to receive employment offers. Similarly, candidates do not receive employment offers to teach at Concourse Village unless Concourse Village students, who sit in demonstration lessons, report that the candidate cared about them and wanted them to succeed.

Often, principals, district human resources personnel, and hiring committees are eager to hire candidates with impressive content knowledge.

Such expertise is valuable when the candidate can connect with students in ways that maximize the likelihood that students will become eager to learn the content. If the candidate is not likely to build a connection with Black students, it is not likely that Black students will benefit from the candidate's depth of knowledge.

Secondly, at the featured schools, selection processes often involved teachers and students, and sometimes parents from the school. The involvement of students and parents was important because it emphasized to students, parents, and the candidates under consideration that student and parent opinions were valued. The involvement of other teachers and school personnel was important because it communicated that the school was hiring someone to become part of their dream team. They were not simply seeking another math teacher or an individual to teach fifth grade.

Often, school and district hiring processes suggest the school is seeking an independent contractor who will be expected to enter their classroom, close the door, and teach their students. At the featured schools, hiring processes foretold a different expectation. If candidates were hired, they would be expected to be part of a collaborative team that was working together to make a difference in the lives of students of color. The team believed in their students, and the team believed in their collective capacity to improve teaching and learning for their students.

Finally, at the featured schools, selection processes required candidates to teach students. Candidates could not merely talk in an interview about their ability to relate to students of color; they had to demonstrate their ability to do so within the context of an actual lesson. At O'Farrell Charter High School, demonstration lessons revealed candidates' skills at relating to Black and Brown students and enabling them to understand rigorous academic concepts. At Patrick Henry Preparatory School, many of the individuals hired had been student teachers at the school, so Principal Pantelidis and other Patrick Henry educators had extended opportunities to determine if the candidate had the capacity to relate well with students and become a strong member of the PS/IS 171 dream team. At Concourse Village, the principal listened intently to the feedback provided by students. She wanted to hear from students how they perceived the candidate and the lesson the candidate taught. Yes, leaders wanted to ensure that candidates possessed content knowledge, but even more so, they wanted to ensure that candidates knew how to engage and empower students of color. Leaders wanted to make sure that candidates knew how to connect with Black students and create learning experiences that brought them excitement and joy.

Finally, it should be noted that leaders at all the featured schools described efforts to seek out, recruit, and hire teachers of color. They also reported varying levels of success, in large part because of the substantial competition for small numbers of qualified Black teaching candidates. Race matters because relationships matter and relationships are influenced by race. Conversely, it is important to note that race neither precludes nor ensures the capacity of teachers to help Black students feel valued and respected and experience belonging and joy. A teacher leader from one of the featured schools shared, "Ultimately, our students need and deserve teachers who recognize them as amazing people with unlimited potential. We look for colleagues who see that potential and will do whatever it takes to help our kids achieve their dreams."

Establishing and Sustaining Routines and Structures That Build Caring Relationships

To establish positive cultures and build caring relationships with Black students, educators in the featured schools constructed and maintained routines and structures that encouraged ongoing attention to relationships. While the schools endeavored to hire individuals who valued and respected Black students and Black families, leaders recognized the importance of building and strengthening regular opportunities to promote positive, caring relationships among teachers, students, and families.

To build relationships in ways that led Black students to experience belonging, love, and joy, teachers at all six schools frequently sought their students' input. Teachers asked students of color for their opinions. Teachers resisted the urge to make stereotypic assumptions about what made sense to students, what interested them, or what motivated them. Instead, teachers asked students for their opinions. When we observed classrooms, we heard O'Farrell Charter High teachers ask students, "What do you think about how this lesson is going?" We heard Patrick Henry Preparatory School teachers ask, "What do you think about what we're reading?" We heard Wynnebrook Elementary teachers ask, "Does this problem-solving approach make sense to you?" Not only did teachers ask, but they also listened. Students who had seemed disinterested perked up when they realized their teacher was seeking their expert advice on adjusting the lesson's direction. Students who had looked confused seemed to feel relieved when they had the opportunity to tell their teacher that the lesson no longer made sense to them. In our interviews with students, we frequently heard students proudly say, "My teacher listens to my opinion. My teachers care about what I think. Our teacher gives us choices." Aronson (2008) explained the power of the simple act of asking students their opinions:

> The everyday antiracist "move" I rely upon is to cultivate a mindset of insatiable curiosity about my students as individuals: who they are, the experiences they have had, what they think about things, and how they think. Curiosity is the diametrical opposite of stereotyping and prejudice, the assumption that you know who a person is, what they think, or how they will act simply because you know what category they belong to.
>
> (pp. 67–68)

In many ways, educators in the six schools built positive, caring relationships by establishing practices and routines designed to reinforce relational strengths and restore relationships that had been fractured. Teachers used holistic instructional strategies that prioritized the development of integrity and wisdom in children and youth (Howard, 2001). In addition to building students' academic/cognitive skills, teachers deliberately endeavored to develop students' social adaptability and moral judgment. Teachers at Wynnebrook learned to reinforce and celebrate students as they modeled the characteristics described in the school's Code of Conduct. For example, by celebrating students for being respectful with each other, educators helped shape a more positive culture among students. Similarly, teachers at Concourse Village acknowledged student efforts to model the school's core values. By focusing on positives and building upon strengths, Concourse Village educators were able to transform a persistently dangerous school into a place students called "respectful," where "nobody is rude."

At all six schools, when misbehavior occurred, educators did not rush to punish students. Instead, educators often used such incidents as opportunities to teach students how to engage constructively with others. For example, at Young Men's Leadership Academy, educators helped students reflect upon their choices and actions so they learned to handle difficult life situations well. Unfortunately, in more typical schools, "educators typically punish children of color without reflecting on the factors that may be motivating the misbehavior" (Noguera, 2008, p. 133). Too often, as we focus on establishing comfortable teaching environments for adults, we miss the opportunity to understand and respond constructively to what Black students need to succeed in the classroom and in life.

Black and Latino boys and young men are significantly more likely to experience suspension, expulsion, or other exclusionary discipline than other students (Wood & Harris, 2016). Losen and Martinez (2020) reported that for every 100 Black boys enrolled in secondary schools in 2015–2016, Black boys lost 132 days of instruction due to out-of-school suspensions. For every 100 Black girls enrolled in secondary schools in 2015–2016, they lost 77 days of instruction due to out-of-school suspension. The report also indicates that for every 100 White secondary students, they lost 21 days of instruction due to out-of-school suspension. In contrast, at all six of the featured schools, leaders were much less likely to use exclusionary discipline strategies and more likely to try to empower students of color by helping them manage difficult situations well.

For example, teachers at Maplewood Richmond Heights High discussed how building relationships and building trust require time and consistency, especially when serving students who have experienced many negative interactions with educators. The teachers recognized that distrust might not evaporate in a few weeks or even a few months. By providing opportunities for students to build a relationship with a teacher over a multiyear period, many of the featured schools increased the likelihood that strong, positive relationships would develop.

At O'Farrell Charter High School, the home base structure increased the likelihood that students would have the same teacher/advocate for all four high school years. Additionally, the home base structure ensured that time would be dedicated to building relationships with and among students each day. At O'Farrell, building relationships is not "other duties as assigned" or "an unpaid mandate." In contrast, at O'Farrell, building relationships between and among teachers, students, and families is an explicit part of every educator's job. Teachers embrace their home base duties just as they embrace their responsibility to teach mathematics, science, or literacy.

In *Maggie's American Dream*, noted child psychiatrist, James Comer (1988) described his childhood in segregated neighborhoods and schools. At that time, there was less of a need for schools to deliberately build connections to Black families because teachers and other school personnel were likely to live in the same neighborhood of the families they served. Maggie Comer was likely to see her son's teachers in the grocery store, at church, or at community events. There was less of a need to build trust between school and families because Black parents trusted that Black teachers had their children's best interests at heart. Black teachers were not afraid to talk with Maggie Comer because there was a shared understanding that the school and the family were working toward the same goal: the well-being and success of all Black children.

In the schools featured in this book, educators recognized that they could not assume that Black families trusted the school had their children's best interests at heart. One teacher acknowledged, "Some of our parents were in school themselves, a few years ago. And for some of them, school was horrible." Some families had little reason to believe that educators cared sincerely about their children. Some teachers had little or no experience talking with Black families and learning about their strengths, concerns, hopes, and dreams.

By structuring opportunities for educators to visit student's homes, engage in open conversations about community issues, laugh about family stories, and get to know each other, educators developed trust. As Principal Sorden and her teachers walked the neighborhood in the South Bronx, as Principal Grawer and the Maplewood Richmond Heights High teachers sat in living rooms with the families of their students, and as O'Farrell home base teachers built and sustained relationships with families over the course of four years, the schools endeavored to recreate the level of trust that Maggie Comer experienced with her children's teachers. Brown (2019) explained that building quality relationships with Black families requires more than regular, positive phone calls to parents (although such calls may be helpful). She emphasized that building relationships required a commitment to listening to Black parents and valuing their experiences and perspectives.

Of course, as educators in the featured schools listened to students and families, they often identified needs that extended beyond academic concerns. School administrators and teachers worked closely with school counselors and social workers to connect students and families with agencies that would address their physical, financial, emotional, and social needs. In several cases, when the services provided by existing social service agencies were inadequate, administrators, teachers, and counselors identified and pursued strategies for providing needed support. For example, the Maplewood Richmond Heights School District collaborated with local churches and community volunteers to establish Joe's Place, a home for teenage students experiencing homelessness in their community (see www.mrhschools.net/domain/34).

Before educators can build meaningful relationships with families, educators must first recognize and believe that families want the best for their children (Wood & Harris, 2016). Educators are not likely to establish trust with family members if they cling to myths suggesting that families of color do not care about their children. While many educators claim to support and encourage parental engagement, often our actions suggest that we don't believe parents have the capacity to help their child succeed. In these cases, we fail to acknowledge that human beings are unlikely to engage with people who don't value them.

It is important to acknowledge that many schools across the nation are strengthening their efforts to avoid punitive, exclusionary discipline practices. While this progress is important, it is grossly insufficient. There are far too many schools where Black students think their teachers believe they could do their jobs better and live happier work lives if Black students were not present. In stark contrast, at the six featured schools, Black students reported that their teachers miss them when they're not at school. "They call and ask if I'm OK," one Black Maplewood Richmond Heights High student shared with some amazement. Black students (from preschool through high school) believed their teachers were happy to see them at school and excited to see them learn.

It is especially important to note that leaders at the six featured schools invested time, effort, and resources in acknowledging and celebrating the strengths of students of color. By celebrating the character of Black students, by acknowledging their efforts to support their peers, by highlighting their capacity to model leadership, educators at the six schools influenced how Black students saw themselves and how they saw one another. As well, educators influenced how parents saw their children. Like Maggie Comer, parents of the students in the featured schools became convinced that their children could be leaders in the community and in the world. Parents felt their struggles to support their children were being recognized and were bearing fruit.

Insisting That Everyone Contribute to a Positive Culture for Black Students

Leaders at the six schools never stopped working to ensure that every student benefitted from a positive transformational culture. School leaders and teachers made impressive efforts to ensure each new teacher they hired embraced and enhanced a school-wide culture conducive to the success of Black students. In addition, principals and other school personnel developed an array of structures and systems to support the development of positive relationships between and among teachers, students, and families. Leaders ensured that all personnel contributed to a culture in which Black students experienced a sense of belonging, the feeling of being valued and loved, and a sense of joy as central to all these efforts.

Muhammad (2009) described how school cultures can grow toxic as "fundamentalists," who are committed to maintaining the status quo, resist the efforts of "believers," who are committed to promoting the success of all students (p. 29). While Muhammad outlined various steps leaders can take to neutralize fundamentalists or even convert them to believers, he also acknowledged that some fundamentalists are unlikely to change their point of view. According to Muhammad, "[They] are so deeply rooted in their opposition to change that it consumes and defines them." (Muhammad, 2009, p. 96). In other words, these protectors of the status quo are not likely to change their beliefs because, in their minds, such a shift would mean surrendering their purpose as flag bearers for those who resist believing all students can succeed.

Principals at the six featured schools were masterful at persistently building a critical mass of believers: individuals who were committed to ensuring students of color would experience belonging, love, and joy. By creating positive, supportive work environments where educators successfully educated students of color, these principals led educators who were "on the fence" and even some fundamentalists to become powerful believers. In cases where determined fundamentalists undermined collective efforts to create a positive transformational culture for students of color, leaders acted assertively, prudently, and promptly to neutralize or remove these negative influences.

Principal Rainey described a situation at O'Farrell Charter High School in which a teacher "wasn't willing to put in the effort or care enough about the kids to raise the bar and create a supportive environment for them." The principal explained, "I thought maybe I was being unreasonable, so I tried to show the teacher how to improve this way and that way, but the teacher didn't try." If Principal Rainey had allowed the teacher to continue unabated, the teacher might have become increasingly toxic to the school's learning culture and impeded student achievement. Ultimately, Principal Rainey refused to tolerate the teacher's behavior, questioning how a teacher would "do this to kids when they would never do this to their own kids." Principal Rainey followed procedures, and the teacher was removed. Each of the other five principals described similar stories that ended with a teacher being dismissed or deciding to leave.

To sustain a dream team, principals must be keepers of the dream (Olivero, 1980). When principals allow nonbelievers the space to foment toxicity, principals cause the believers to wonder what the principal truly believes. They wonder, "Will the principal support me when I step out in support of Black students? Why am I doing all this work to build the literacy skills of my second-grade students of color when, next year, they will be in third grade with a teacher who doesn't care about them? Why am I working so hard to get our Black parents to believe we truly care about their perspectives when I know that the teacher next door never listens to Black parents? Doesn't the principal notice that our students of color have a 75% chance of having a joyful experience in eighth-grade science because three of the four members of the science team have created these amazing community-based science lessons? Doesn't the principal see what a tragedy it is for the 25% who are being taught that science is all about reading a boring textbook and answering the questions at the end of each chapter?"

All six featured schools were successful because school leaders were committed to creating a culture in which all Black students experienced belonging, love, and joy. As Principal Sorden explained, "It's nonnegotiable." To maximize the likelihood that this culture developed, spread school-wide, and matured, leaders engaged in strong, inclusive processes to hire new dream team members. They provided routines, structures, and supports that encouraged ongoing attention to the development of positive relationships with Black students and Black families. Additionally, leaders took assertive action when school personnel acted in toxic ways that threatened the culture needed to ensure the success of Black students.

Empathy Interviews

Educators who are eager to create cultures in which Black students experience belonging, love, and joy should recognize that they are most likely to succeed if they ask the experts: their students and their students' families. These empathy interview questions are intended to help school teams learn how they can maximize the likelihood that Black students experience belonging, love, and joy at school. Even though several questions are listed, remember that successful empathy interviews usually focus on just one question at a time.

Questions for Black Students or Their Family Members

1. Question for Students and/or Their Family Members: Have you ever participated in the process of helping your school select a new teacher? If so, what did you like about the process? How might the process have been improved? If you haven't participated in the process of helping select a new teacher, would you like to participate in the future? What could be done to help you feel good about participating in the selection process?

2. Question for Students: Do you recall a time when a teacher asked you a question to get your opinion about how a lesson was going? For example, has a teacher asked you, "Is this lesson making sense to you?" If so, what happened? How did you feel about being asked to offer your opinion? Would you like if your teacher asked your opinion about lessons more often? Why or why not?

3. Question for Students: Does your teacher notice when you behave well? If so, what does your teacher say or do to let you know that the teacher noticed you were behaving? How does it make you feel when the teacher notices you behaving well? What would you like to see your teacher do when you are behaving well?

4. Question for Students: Does your teacher notice when you misbehave or make bad decisions? If so, what does your teacher say or do to let you know that the teacher noticed your misbehavior? How does it make you feel when the teacher has noticed your misbehavior? What would you like to see your teacher do when you misbehave?

5. Question for Students: Are there any adults at school who have a good relationship with you (who really know about you, your interests, strengths, concerns, and needs)? If so, who are those adults? What did they do to get to know you? What would you like to see happen so that more adults at school would get to know you well?

6. Question for Students and/or Their Family Members: When Black students misbehave at school, are teachers and administrators concerned mainly about punishing students, helping students learn how to succeed in school and in life, or both? Can you describe a situation that led you to think that the school's main focus was on punishing students or helping them succeed in school and in life?

7. Question for Family Members: What do teachers and administrators at this school do to reach out and get to know the families of Black students? What has worked well to build positive relationships with the families of Black students? What would you recommend teachers and administrators do to get to know the families of Black students better?

8. Question for Family Members: Do teachers and administrators at this school believe that Black families care about the success of their children? Can you think of something that has happened that made you think teachers and administrators truly believed Black families cared about the success of their children? If so, please describe what happened. Can you think of something that has happened that made you think teachers and administrators don't believe Black families care about the success of their children? If so, please describe what happened.

9. Question for Black Students and/or Their Family Members: Are there teachers at this school who don't like Black students? If so, what has happened to make you think they don't like Black students? Do you feel that school administrators are taking actions to change this situation? If so, what actions do you think are being taken?

Implications

All stakeholders have a role in ensuring that Black students experience belonging, love, and joy at school. Collectively, we must acknowledge that

Black students deserve nothing less. Collectively, we must acknowledge our shared responsibility in ensuring that all Black students benefit from such school cultures.

Implications for Parents

- Ask school leaders and district leaders how you can participate in processes for selecting new teachers at your child's school. Encourage school and district leaders to include demonstration lessons into selection processes. As you participate in selection processes, focus upon the ability of candidates to appreciate the beauty, value, and brilliance of Black students. Focus on each candidate's capacity to build relationships with you and with Black students.

- Volunteer to participate in empathy interviews focused upon improving services to Black students at your child's school. If school leaders do not know about empathy interviews, refer them to this book.

- Encourage your child to think about what teachers might do to help them learn. Often, children don't realize they have worthwhile opinions about what might help them learn well. So ask your child, "What could the teacher have done to help you understand that concept better?" Encourage your child to share their opinions with their teacher. If your child is reluctant to do so, consider talking with the teacher and encouraging the teacher to invite your child to share his or her opinions.

- Ask teachers and school leaders what they are doing to reinforce the positive behavior characteristics of children. Ask how they acknowledge and celebrate the personal and social strengths children exhibit. Encourage efforts to increase the acknowledgment and celebration of positive character traits.

- Ask school leaders to share data about the number of students who experience exclusionary discipline (including office referrals, in-school suspension, out-of-school suspension, exclusion from curricular or extracurricular activities, or expulsion). Ask to see these data disaggregated based on race and gender and ask to hear about the strategies the school is employing to reduce exclusionary discipline, in general, and the steps being taken to reduce disproportionate exclusionary discipline for Black students.

- Invite your child's teacher and/or school administrator to visit your home. The meeting does not need to be long, and there isn't a need for any specific agenda. The purpose of the meeting should be for the school personnel to get to know you and your family better and for you to get to know the school personnel better.

- If you are aware of a teacher at your school who creates a toxic environment for Black students, share your concerns with the school administrator. Ask the school administrator how they intend to monitor the situation and minimize harm to Black students.

Implications for School Leaders

- Establish teacher selection processes that engage existing teachers, students, and parents. Make sure that selection processes include opportunities to observe candidates teaching lessons to students at your school. Before processes begin, make sure all participating stakeholders understand the importance of identifying candidates who will contribute to a culture that leads Black students to experience belonging, love, and joy. Listen attentively to the feedback acquired from students, parents, and teachers.

- Provide professional development opportunities that help teachers use a variety of strategies for checking in with students to determine the extent to which instructional approaches are helping them learn. Encourage teacher collaboration teams to consider developing sample questions teachers can use to invite feedback from students. During classroom observations, note when teachers ask students questions about how lesson strategies are helping or not helping them develop strong understandings of concepts. Acknowledge and celebrate teacher efforts to learn how their students of color perceive lesson strategies.

- Dedicate time each week to listen to Black students and their families. Arrange opportunities to visit Black families at their homes and always bring a teacher or other school team member with you. As you visit with families, learn about their concerns, interests, needs, and hopes. Always communicate your appreciation of their openness. Let students and parents know you value them.

- Develop structures and routines that make attending to students' social and emotional well-being a deliberate focus of the school day. Provide professional development to help teachers maximize the benefit of these structures and routines. Regularly observe implementation and provide constructive feedback to help teachers create environments in which students perceive that their social and emotional well-being is a school priority.

- Dedicate regular time to asking Black students and their families the empathy interview questions in the preceding section of this chapter. Engage other school personnel in participating in empathy interviews.

- Involve teachers in 1) monitoring their actions that call attention to student misbehavior and 2) monitoring their actions that acknowledge students' positive behavior/character traits. Help teachers maximize their attention to students' positive behavior as a strategy for minimizing the need to attend to misbehavior. Acknowledge and celebrate teacher progress in increasing their attention to students' positive behavior. Provide assistance and support to teachers who are expending time and energy calling attention to misbehavior without generating improved behavior or improved learning outcomes.

- Engage teachers, counselors, social workers, other support personnel, and other school administrators in tracking incidents that result in exclusionary discipline (including office referrals, in-school suspension, out-of-school suspension, exclusion from curricular or extracurricular activities, or expulsion). Ensure that these data are disaggregated by race, gender, and other groupings, as appropriate. Data collection efforts should include information about where the student behavior issue occurred, when it occurred, and what were the factors precipitating the behavior. Yes, the collection of these data will take time and effort; however, the use of these data will greatly diminish the quantity of time teachers and administrators spend addressing misbehavior and maximize the time available for improving teaching and learning. You will find that some problems can be diminished by rethinking rules and expectations in ways that are more responsive to student needs. Thinking proactively and designing approaches that prevent problems can minimize misbehaviors. As well, giving students opportunities to learn and practice effective responses to difficult situations also mitigates the need for exclusionary discipline practices. Remember, in all six schools featured in this book, the number of exclusionary disciplinary incidents was a small fraction of the number of incidents in schools that served similar populations. By using the data to identify patterns, you and your team will be able to reduce exclusionary discipline substantially.

- Find multiple ways to communicate regularly to every employee (including all teachers, coaches, custodians, secretaries, paraprofessionals, administrators, cafeteria workers, etc.) your expectation that they help create a culture in which Black students experience belonging, love, and joy. This is a nonnegotiable expectation. If you communicate this expectation, you must follow through by looking for evidence of personnel building or eroding this culture. When you see evidence of personnel building the desired culture, your job is to make those individuals know they are heroes who are helping the school improve the lives of children. When you see evidence of personnel eroding this culture, your job is to explain clearly, respectfully, professionally, and unapologetically why such behavior is not acceptable. Always ask personnel what support they need to successfully meet your expectations. Always express a willingness to help personnel improve, but always let personnel know that improvement is expected.

- To the extent possible, provide school personnel opportunities to see and learn from schools that have made substantial progress in creating school cultures where Black students experience belonging, love, and joy. Engage personnel in continuous efforts to evaluate and strengthen the culture of your school in ways that promote outstanding outcomes for Black students.

Implications for Teachers

- Ask school leaders and district leaders how you can participate in processes for selecting new teachers at your school. Encourage school and district leaders to include demonstration lessons into selection processes. As you participate in selection processes, focus upon the ability of candidates to appreciate the beauty, value, and brilliance of Black students. Focus on each candidate's capacity to build relationships with Black students, their families, and with you and your colleagues.

- Volunteer to participate in empathy interviews focused upon improving services to Black students at your school. If school leaders do not know about empathy interviews, refer them to this book.

- Remember, students don't necessarily realize that your goal is to ensure they understand what you endeavor to teach them. Often, students don't realize you want them to enjoy learning. (Sometimes, they may assume the opposite.) So regularly check in with students to determine the extent to which lesson approaches are helping them learn. Ask students questions such as, "What do you think about how this lesson is going?" "What do you think about what we're reading?" "Does this problem-solving approach make sense to you?" Know that students might not always have clear answers, but if they learn you are likely to ask, they will think more deliberately about what might help them learn concepts well. Attend to the answers students provide and try to adapt in ways that help them learn. Students will appreciate that you care enough to ask their opinion, and they will be more likely to engage in learning.

- Try to monitor 1) how often you call attention to student misbehavior and 2) how often you call attention to students' positive behavior / character traits. Consider working with a colleague to help each other monitor these teaching practices. Deliberately try to increase your efforts to call attention to students' positive behavior. If you do so, you will automatically decrease the amount of time you need to spend addressing misbehavior.

- Monitor your use of exclusionary discipline practices (including office referrals, in-school suspension, out-of-school suspension, exclusion from curricular or extracurricular activities, or expulsion). Ensure that these data are disaggregated by race, gender, and other groupings, as appropriate. Decrease your use of exclusionary discipline practices by using the data you collect to help you proactively prevent behavior issues. Also, decrease your use of exclusionary discipline practices by considering strategies for helping students learn more effective ways of handling difficult situations. (Often, school counselors, social workers, or behavior intervention specialists can help you design prevention strategies and/or develop restorative practices).

- Do not hesitate to talk with your school leaders if you become aware of adult behavior that erodes the positive culture you are endeavoring to establish for Black students. You and your colleagues should work to create an environment in which adults know that colleagues (not only administrators) expect them to contribute to school-wide efforts to ensure that Black students experience belonging, love, and joy.

Implications for District Leaders

- Ensure that principals know they have the support they need to implement new teacher selection processes that maximize the likelihood they select teachers who will strengthen their efforts to ensure that Black students experience belonging, love, and joy.

- Work with principals and other school leaders to consider the need for district-wide professional development opportunities that help teachers use a variety of strategies for checking in with students to determine the extent to which lesson approaches are helping them learn. Support principals in considering how they can utilize teacher collaboration teams and classroom observations to strengthen the use of these strategies to help teachers learn how their students of color perceive lesson strategies.

- Expect school leaders to dedicate a small amount of time each week to listening to Black students and their families. As well, expect school leaders to engage other school personnel in such visits so that leaders build positive, caring relationships with Black students and families.

- Expect school leaders to implement empathy interviews with Black students and Black families. Provide the support principals might need to learn how to lead empathy interviews in ways that help school personnel gain a deeper understanding of what Black students need to succeed.

- Support school leaders in developing strategies for helping teachers increase attention to students' positive behavior in a way that is constructive for both teachers and students.

- Support school leaders in developing systems for tracking incidents that result in exclusionary discipline (including office referrals, in-school suspension, out-of-school suspension, exclusion from curricular or extracurricular activities, or expulsion). Help school leaders develop systems that will disaggregate date by race, gender, and other groups, as appropriate. Data collection efforts should include information about where the student behavior issue occurred, when it occurred, and what were the issues precipitating the behavior. Support leaders in using these data to design strategies for preventing misbehavior.

- Ensure that school leaders know how to use district personnel evaluation tools in ways that call attention to the extent to which every employee (including all teachers, coaches, custodians, secretaries, paraprofessionals, administrators, cafeteria workers, etc.) contributes to the creation of a culture in which Black students experience belonging, love, and joy. If this issue is not explicitly addressed in evaluation tools for teachers or other employees, school leaders should know where it is implicit. If it isn't at least implicit, district leaders should make the revision of evaluation tools a top priority. Furthermore, district leaders should help school leaders know how to communicate with employees about the importance of this issue. District leaders should work to make sure that the issue of ensuring that Black students experience belonging, love, and joy at school is not negotiable. It is part of the district's expectation for every employee.

- To the extent possible, provide principals opportunities to see and learn from schools that have made substantial progress in creating school cultures where Black students experience belonging, love, and joy. Engage principals in continuous efforts to evaluate and strengthen the culture of their schools in ways that promote outstanding outcomes for Black students.

- When principals identify teachers or other school personnel who create a toxic culture for Black students, help principals follow district procedures for supporting personnel in improving their performance. If improvement is not forthcoming, support principals in removing those personnel in a professional, respectful, and legal manner.

Implications for Institutions of Higher Education

- Develop screening strategies to avoid admitting candidates into educator preparation programs (including, but not limited to, teacher education, counseling education, and educational leadership) who do not demonstrate dispositions suggesting that they recognize and appreciate the beauty, value, and brilliance of Black students. If your programs disregard this strong advice, know that you risk subjecting hundreds or thousands of students (prekindergarten through postsecondary education) to a quality of education you would not want for your own children. Some programs prefer to try to develop strong exit criteria addressing these essential dispositions; however, often, the exit criteria lack teeth when candidates have passed courses and exit exams. The individuals you admit into your program represent a practical articulation of your programs' commitment to social justice.

- Actively recruit Black students into your educator preparation programs. Help Black students understand how they can positively influence lives and communities through careers as teachers, counselors, school psychologists, social workers, therapists, and administrators. Identify the barriers (academic, procedural, financial, or other) that might prevent Black students from entering, matriculating through, and completing your teacher education programs and systematically develop supports that will help students overcome those barriers.

- Ensure that student teachers and other candidates for positions in schools have abundant opportunities to engage with Black students and Black families. Specifically, ensure that candidates have opportunities to get to know Black students and their families in ways that dispel myths and create opportunities for understanding and growth.

- Create opportunities for candidates to participate in empathy interviews focused upon improving services to Black students. Help candidates understand how they might use the information acquired from empathy interviews to improve how they will relate to and teach Black students.

- Individuals who prepare candidates for roles in schools should model, with their adult learners, the culture they hope their candidates will establish in schools. This means that faculty members who cannot create cultures in which adult students of color are likely to experience belonging, love, and joy are inappropriate faculty members for preparing teachers, counselors, school administrators, and other school professionals, even if they have impressive publication records and outstanding credentials as researchers.

- Ensure that the teachers, counselors, or administrators your candidates observe and shadow model outstanding capacity to create cultures in which Black students experience belonging, love, and joy. This requires deliberate efforts to identify excellent role models. Additionally, this may require creativity in designing opportunities to ensure that your candidates have opportunities to learn from model educators.

- Engage teaching candidates in seeking feedback from Black students about 1) the effectiveness of lessons in increasing their understanding of important concepts and skills and 2) the effectiveness of lessons in leading Black students to find joy and meaning in learning. Help teaching candidates practice simple, sincere ways of checking in with students to determine the extent to which lesson approaches are helping them learn.

- Teacher education programs can substantially influence the capacity of teaching candidates to develop positive classroom cultures if they help candidates develop the habit of frequently acknowledging and celebrating the positive character traits/behaviors of students. Without deliberate and extensive practice, teachers are more likely to recreate the classroom cultures they experienced as students. Often, those cultures focused on punishing "negative" behavior through progressively greater levels of exclusion. While those cultures may have nurtured the academic success of prospective teachers, those cultures are not conducive to the success of many students of color. When teacher education programs do not address this concern deliberately and assertively, they perpetuate a system in which Black students feel that educators are eager to push them out.

- Programs that prepare teachers, school counselors, and administrators should ensure candidates become skillful in developing systems for monitoring the use of exclusionary discipline practices (including office referrals, in-school suspension, out-of-school suspension, exclusion from curricular or extracurricular activities, or expulsion). Programs should help candidates learn how to disaggregate these data by race, gender, and other groupings, as appropriate. Most importantly, programs should help candidates identify strategies to decrease the use of exclusionary discipline practices by 1) using the data collected proactively to prevent behavior issues and 2) considering strategies for helping students learn more effective ways of handling difficult situations.

Implications for Policy Makers

- Often, the best teacher candidates are hired long before the school year begins. Just as often, schools that serve large percentages of students of color experience fiscal and organizational realities that leave them filling vacancies at the last minute. State leaders should guarantee districts that serve large percentages of students of color adequate funding for teaching positions in high-need schools. This support should require that districts make early hiring decisions, affording schools the opportunity to attract outstanding candidates who help them establish strong, positive cultures for students of color.

- State and local policy makers should support the development of programs designed to recruit Black individuals into the teaching profession. As part of these recruitment efforts, policy makers should work with public and private entities to identify the barriers (academic, procedural, financial, or other) that might prevent Black individuals from entering, matriculating through, and completing teacher education programs or securing teaching positions in schools within your district or state and systematically develop supports that will help individuals overcome those barriers.

- Retaining talented teachers of color remains a serious challenge in many districts and states. While financial incentives are important, the quality of a professional work environment also factors high in Black teachers' decisions to remain in, or leave, the profession. Principals and other school administrators play a major role in shaping the professional environment experienced by teachers of color. Policy makers should look closely at the implications described in Chapter 7.

- Policy makers at all levels should ensure that school leaders have evaluation tools that emphasize the importance of contributing to classroom and school cultures that lead students of color to experience belonging, love, and joy. Teachers should never be considered "satisfactory" or "meets expectations" if they create a learning environment that is hostile to Black students. While policy makers should develop systems that give all employees an opportunity to improve and grow, policy should not prioritize the creation of safe places for toxic adults over the creation of safe places for children. School boards should never negotiate away the expectation that school employees will help create cultures in which children feel their presence is valued, their learning is our priority, and their emotional, social, and physical well-being is nonnegotiable.

- School board members should ask to see detailed, disaggregated data regarding exclusionary discipline practices (including office referrals,

171

in-school suspension, out-of-school suspension, exclusion from curricular or extracurricular activities, or expulsion) in schools across their district. School board members should expect district leaders to develop clear, logical plans for supporting school personnel in ways that result in decreases in exclusionary discipline, especially for students of color.

- Policy leaders must create structures that support the time and energy needed for school personnel to engage in regular home visits or visits with families in their communities. This means ensuring funding to support these efforts. Also, this means ensuring educators understand that building relationships with students and families is part of the professional expectation for every teacher, counselor, and school administrator. It is not an "other duty as assigned." It is a fundamental part of being an excellent educator.

- Little is gained if schools hire outstanding new teachers only to lose them after a year because they receive "pink slips" or layoff notices due to possible reductions in district enrollment numbers. These situations often have the greatest impact on schools serving large percentages of students of color. State policy makers should establish funding mechanisms that guarantee new teachers three years of employment if they satisfactorily meet high performance expectations.

References

Aronson, J. (2008). Knowing students as individuals. In M. Pollock (Ed.), *Everyday antiracism: Getting real about race in school* (pp. 67–69). The New Press.

Brown, A. C. (2019). Engaging and embracing Black parents. In L. Delpit (Ed.), *Teaching when the world is on fire* (pp. 119–127). The New Press.

Collaborative for Academic, Social, and Emotional Learning. (2005). *Safe and sound: An educational leader's guide to evidence-based social and emotional learning (SEL) programs*. Author.

Comer, J. P. (1988). *Maggie's American dream: The life and times of a Black family*. Penguin Books.

Ferguson, R. F. (2008). *Toward excellence with equity: An emerging vision for closing the achievement gap*. Harvard Education Press.

Frey, N., Fisher, D., & Smith, D. (2019). *All learning is social and emotional: Helping students develop essential skills for the classroom and beyond*. ASCD.

Hattie, J. (2009). *Visible learning: A synthesis of over 800 meta-analyses relating to achievement*. Routledge.

Howard, T. C. (2001). Powerful pedagogy for African American students: A case of four teachers. *Urban Education, 36*, 179–202.

Johnson, J. F., Uline, C. L., & Perez, L. G. (2019). *Teaching practices from America's best urban schools: A guide for school and classroom leaders*. Routledge.

Jones, S. M., & Kahn, J. (2017). *The evidence base for how we learn: Supporting students' social, emotional, and academic development*. Aspen Institute, National Commission on Social, Emotional, and Academic Development.

Ladson-Billings, G. (2009). *The dreamkeepers: Successful teachers of African American Children* (2nd ed.). Jossey-Bass.

Losen, D. J., & Martinez, P. (2020). *Lost opportunities: How disparate school discipline continues to drive differences in the opportunity to learn*. Learing Policy Institute; Center for Civil Rights Remedies at the Civil Rights Project, UCLA.

MacNeil, A., Prater, D., & Busch, S. (2009). The effects of school culture and climate on student achievement. *International Journal of Leadership in Education, 12*(1), 73–84. https://doi.org/10.1080/13603120701576241. Retrieved September 10, 2021, from www.tandfonline.com/doi/pdf/10.1080/13603120701576241

Muhammad, A. (2009). *Transforming school culture: How to overcome staff division*. Solution Tree Press.

Noddings, N. (2012). The caring relationship in teaching. *Oxford Review of Education, 38*(6), 771–781.

Noguera, P. A. (2008). What discipline is for: Connecting students to the benefits of learning. In M. Pollock (Ed.), *Everyday antiracism: Getting real about race in school* (pp. 132–137). The New Press.

Olivero, J. L. (1980). *The principalship in California: Keeper of the dream*. Association of California School Administrators.

Osher, D., Cantor, P., Berg, J., Steyer, L., & Rose, T. (2020). Drivers of human development: How relationships and context shape learning and development. *Applied Developmental Science, 24*(1), 6–36. https://doi.org/10.1080/10888691.2017.1398650. Retrieved April 18, 2022, from www.tandfonline.com/doi/full/10.1080/10888691.2017.1398650.

Sparks, S. D. (2019, March 12). Why student-teacher relationships matter: New findings shed light on best practices. *Education Week, 38*(25), 8.

Villani, C., 1999. *Community culture and school climate* (pp. 103–105). [online] Adi.org. Retrieved October 26, 2021, from www.adi.org/journal/ss99/VillaniSpring1999.pdf.

Wood, J. L., & Harris, F. (2016). *Teaching boys and young men of color: A guidebook*. Lawndale Hill Publishing.

9 Ensuring Black Students Experience Pathways to Success

At all six schools featured in this book, educators clung to a few key assumptions: 1) their Black students could achieve at high levels; 2) together, their "dream team" had the capacity to lead their students to impressive academic successes; and 3) although multiple frustrations presented formidable challenges (e.g., district bureaucracies, state policies, budget inadequacies, institutional racism), their team possessed sufficient talent and resolve to work through or around those impediments and ensure the success of their students of color. Educators at all six schools recognized they had both the responsibility and the opportunity to pave pathways that would make success likely for their students. They knew each pathway to success started with ensuring that Black students experienced belonging, love, and joy at school (the focus of Chapter 8).

Educators at the featured schools knew each pathway to success would not be found in a scripted program or blind allegiance to the routines and practices they themselves experienced as elementary or secondary students. School leaders understood the wisdom in Delpit's admonition: "We have to cease attempting to build 'teacher-proof' schools with scripted low-level instruction and instead seek to develop (and retain) perceptive, thinking teachers who challenge their students with high-quality, interactive, and thoughtful instruction" (Delpit, 2012, p. 34).

Success depended upon their ability to pave new pathways to success designed through 1) regular and open communication with Black students and families, 2) persistent attention to formative data about the progress of Black students, 3) willingness to adapt routines, practices, programs, and

DOI: 10.4324/9781003277910-11

policies in ways that would work for Black students, and 4) willingness to work together creatively to solve everyday challenges.

Educators at all six schools knew success for their Black students could be achieved, but they also knew that traditional education programs and practices presented poor signage, huge potholes, dangerous road hazards, and dead ends that could confuse, frustrate, and demoralize many Black students. Educators knew they needed to utilize their wisdom, creativity, and determination to pave routes to excellent learning outcomes for each of their students.

Key Attributes of Schools Where Black Students Experience Pathways to Success

In all six schools featured in this book, we found the following attributes:

1. Educators persistently focused on ambitious goals Black students were excited to pursue. Teachers helped Black students monitor their growth toward personally meaningful goals.

2. Schools created early on-ramps to ensure Black students would experience outstanding opportunities to achieve their ambitious academic goals. In other words, educators began early, providing Black students the requisite knowledge and skills to accomplish rigorous learning outcomes. By starting early, schools helped ensure that Black students would succeed through challenging educational transitions.

3. Teachers taught in ways that maximized the likelihood that Black students would remain actively engaged on pathways to success.

4. Teachers and other school personnel developed pathways to success by creating bridges from the "known" experiences of Black students to "unknown" concepts and skills that would empower Black students for success in school and in life.

5. Teachers and other school personnel developed and implemented practices and policies that helped Black students find and sustain hope.

Focusing on Growth toward Meaningful, Ambitious Goals (Destinations)

If students do not perceive a goal as attainable and worthwhile, they are not likely to exert the effort necessary to achieve it. Students are not likely to embark upon a path if they consider the destination unattainable or undesirable. At the featured schools, teachers inspired Black students to consider, adopt, and retain ambitious academic goals. "You will understand this math concept better than many tenth-grade students understand it," a Patrick Henry middle school teacher promised her students. "The state standards are just our starting point, because you will go much further," a Wynnebrook teacher declared. "I know you have the potential to produce a project that is as detailed and sophisticated as this exemplar," a Maplewood Richmond Heights High science teacher told his students. The pursuit of ambitious goals requires commitment to rigorous academic learning.

At one time, rigor in education referred to strictness in teaching and learning. Rigor equated to completing plenty of homework to achieve good grades. A more updated version of the term acknowledges that *rigor* includes the ability to access knowledge and the ability to think critically and solve problems (Wagner, 2008).

Even though goals were teacher-inspired, it was clear that Black students "owned" their goals and were committed to attaining them. Black students were proud to pursue rigorous academic goals that would demonstrate their brilliance to themselves, their families, friends, teachers, and community. Primary-grade students worked eagerly to read and engage in detailed conversations about chapter books. Intermediate- and middle-grade students committed time and energy to complete high-quality writing projects that often resembled the writing of high school students.

At Young Men's Leadership Academy, Maplewood Richmond Heights High, and O'Farrell Charter High School, most Black students adopted the goal of attending college, and many were focused specifically on competitive four-year colleges. Teachers, counselors, administrators, and other support staff persistently provided students the information they needed to embrace the goal of college attendance and college success. Efforts included visits to college campuses, conversations with recent high school graduates who were attending college, step-by-step support with financial aid processes, and various other strategies intended to help Black students decide they were ready to commit the effort needed for college admission and success. At the three high schools, Black students worked deliberately and persistently to complete Advanced Placement courses, dual-enrollment courses, and other courses that generated college credit.

In more typical schools, teachers direct Black students to attend to lower-level academic goals. Often, teachers assume that Black students cannot pursue more challenging goals until basic goals are mastered. This low-rigor/low-level instruction "denies students the opportunity to engage in what neuroscientists call productive struggle that actually grows our brainpower" (Hammond, 2015, pp. 12–13). When teachers postpone teaching more interesting, rigorous, and meaningful concepts and skills until students of color are "ready" to learn, readiness never occurs. "By focusing only on low-level basics, we deprive students of a meaningful or motivating context for learning and practicing higher order thinking processes" (Hammond, 2015, p. 15).

At the featured schools, however, teachers understood that Black students were not likely to exert effort to pursue a goal that students perceived as a pathway to mediocrity. Sixth-grade students were not likely to get excited about pursuing fourth-grade mathematics goals, and high school students were not likely to arrive early to class for extra tutoring, if they perceived the goal was to move from "far below basic" to "below basic" on the state assessment. Often, however, teachers at the six schools knew some of their students did not possess all the skills typically considered prerequisite. To address this potential dilemma, teachers found ways to utilize the knowledge and skills students already possessed to help them advance toward more ambitious skills.

Teachers at the featured schools understood that many Black students have been demoralized by low academic expectations. Teachers recognized they needed to find ways to excite their students about achieving ambitious learning goals; however, teachers also realized student excitement would be short-lived if teachers failed to help students acquire the "basics" necessary to access these exciting academic goals. For example, at Concourse Village Elementary, first-grade students who had learned many real-life lessons about judging character engaged in detailed conversations about the characters in the novels they were reading. They practiced second- and third-grade-level comprehension skills even though they might not yet read fluently. In all six schools, teachers worked collaboratively to find ways to build upon students' prior knowledge and their cultural, social, and personal strengths in ways that helped them advance toward more sophisticated academic skills, while simultaneously giving them a reason to strive to develop foundational skills.

Beyond the six featured schools, other educators have written about their efforts to excite Black students about pursuing challenging academic concepts and skills while simultaneously building their students' proficiency with prerequisite concepts. For example, one educator reflected upon her teaching successes:

> In the end, I realized that I had to do both: I had to embed necessary work on the fundamentals in substantive academic content that would challenge students to grow as analytical and critical thinkers. . . . If I had thought that my students had no realistic chance of attending college so I might as well not teach them these basic skills, that would have reflected a low estimation of my students' potential, both as individuals and as racial group members.
>
> (Taylor, 2008, p. 88)

Similarly, other researchers have noted that the need to develop foundational academic skills should not exclude Black students from opportunities to learn challenging academic content. Howard (2001) found that teachers who made a powerful, positive difference for Black students held consistently high expectations at the same time they created opportunities for students to acquire the foundational knowledge vital for their future academic success. In Ferguson's Tripod Project for School Improvement (2008), he found Black students were more likely to invest effort when teachers created two conditions: high perfectionism (when the teacher continually presses students to strive for both understanding and accuracy) and high help (when the teacher convinces students that she loves to help them when they are confused or when they make errors). Lee et al. (1999) reported Chicago students were most likely to excel when educators provided both academic press (clear and high learning expectations) and social support (the in-school and out-of-school assistance necessary for students to succeed). These studies suggest that the academic successes achieved by Black students in the six featured schools were predictable. Students were excited to pursue ambitious academic outcomes connected to personally meaningful goals. At the same time, teachers increased the likelihood students would make progress toward the ambitious goals by providing high-quality support designed to ensure that students would access the foundational knowledge and skills necessary to achieve more ambitious learning targets.

Students (especially Black students) are more likely to engage when they believe they are on a path toward academic goals they perceive as challenging and meaningful. Students (especially Black students) are more likely to feel empowered when they have the information needed to monitor their own progress toward the attainment of challenging and meaningful goals. At all six schools, educators helped students understand how their immediate actions (in and outside of classes) influenced the attainment of their goals. Black students learned how to monitor their progress toward the goals they embraced. For example, students at YMLA learned how to use the school district's progress monitoring software to ensure their advancement toward the grade point averages they wanted to attain. Similarly, students at Wynnebrook were excited to monitor their improvements in Lexile levels. By knowing specifically what they needed to accomplish and by knowing how to utilize objective tools to keep track of their progress, Black students at all six schools felt empowered to pursue goals that were meaningful to them.

Creating Early On-Ramps to Ambitious Goals

By creating "early on-ramps" to success, educators in the featured schools ensured that Black students would experience outstanding opportunities to achieve their ambitious academic goals. Educators identified the concepts and skills students needed to achieve ambitious academic goals, and they identified appropriate ways to introduce those concepts and skills early. In elementary schools, early on-ramps to academic success were created through preschool and early childhood education programs. In secondary schools, early on-ramps to rigorous academic concepts and courses were established by deliberately introducing essential concepts and skills into middle schools and ninth- and tenth-grade courses. As well, throughout both elementary and secondary schools, educators ensured that Black students have early access to success by creating effective initial (Tier I) instruction.

At Concourse Village Elementary, Patrick Henry Preparatory School, and Wynnebrook Elementary, educators committed to ensuring that all their students would read fluently early in the primary grades. While many schools tout the goal of helping students read by the end of third grade, at these three schools, many Black students were reading fluently at the end of first grade. Young Black students exuded confidence as they read grade-level texts and beyond, discussed important ideas, and demonstrated their ability to draw meaning from print. In each of the three schools, strong preschool programs were important contributors to their literacy successes.

In their analysis of 18 studies, Meloy et al. (2019) found that preschool attendance benefited children's development of early literacy skills in 17 of the 18 studies. Similarly, they found that preschool attendance benefited children's development of early mathematical skills in 14 out of 16 studies. The authors noted that the quality of preschool programs mattered. Children were more likely to benefit from programs that provided sufficient learning time, low student-teacher ratios, and well-prepared teachers who created engaging interactions. Additionally, these high-quality preschool programs provided classroom environments that supported learning, ongoing support for teachers, and meaningful family engagement. The provision of strong preschool programs at Concourse Village, Patrick Henry, and Wynnebrook increased the likelihood that Black children enjoyed an early on-ramp to success in both literacy and numeracy.

At the three featured high schools (Maplewood Richmond Heights High, O'Farrell Charter High, and Young Men's Leadership Academy) many Black students completed higher-level courses, including Advanced Placement courses and dual-enrollment courses that granted college credit. Educators did not passively wait to see which students would "be ready" to take these challenging courses in 11th or 12th grade; instead, they created early on-ramps to ensure Black students in sixth, seventh, eighth, ninth, and tenth grades would learn the concepts and skills (including study skills) required for success in advanced courses. By working with their colleagues who taught middle school or early high school grades, teachers made sure that many more students would have the opportunity to take and succeed in advanced courses.

In many high schools that serve large numbers of students of color, few advanced courses are offered. When advanced courses are offered, often the students enrolled in the advanced courses are White (even when the overall student population is predominantly Black or Brown). In these three high schools, we were excited to see Black students enrolled, and succeeding, in advanced courses. These students knew they were on a trajectory to achieve their academic and professional dreams. They knew they were being empowered to make a difference in their lives and the life of their communities.

Finally, in the six featured schools, teachers provided an early on-ramp to success by ensuring that Black students received high-quality initial instruction. In many schools, initial instruction is referred to as Tier I instruction, universal instruction, or the instruction students receive the first time the concept or skill is introduced. When Tier I instruction is not effective in helping students learn key concepts and skills, students receive Tier II supports (often called intervention or remediation). When intervention or remediation is not successful, students receive Tier III special services, such as referral to special education (Mesmer & Mesmer, 2008). In many typical schools, Black students receive ineffective initial (Tier I) instruction. After students have fallen behind, Tier II services are initiated; however, these services are rarely tailored to address the specific needs or build upon the specific strengths of students. Tier II services are often not timely (sometimes they are provided after the child has been practicing a misconception for months). And in many schools, Tier II services are not provided by the most qualified instructional personnel. Predictably, many Black students fall further behind with Tier II services and are subsequently referred for Tier III services.

At all six featured schools, we found substantially less time and effort focused upon Tier II and III instruction because Tier I instruction was designed in ways to help ensure all students (and all Black students) would learn concepts and skills well. Black students at these schools did not need to fail to access instruction designed to build upon their strengths and address their academic needs. Teachers worked collaboratively to create high-quality lessons that resulted in all students developing deep understanding of important concepts and skills.

Johnson et al. (2017) described a coherent educational improvement system that provided strong first instruction in high-performing urban schools. The system featured five interrelated components: 1) The system was focused upon a specific set of important, challenging concepts and skills all students needed to develop and master. 2) Teachers developed common assessment strategies and tools for determining the extent to which students developed deep understandings of those specific concepts and skills. 3) Educators worked collaboratively to support one another in creating engaging lessons that would maximize the likelihood that all students would demonstrate mastery through the common formative assessments they developed. 4) When common assessments indicated that students had not mastered the concepts and skills, teachers would work collaboratively to better understand why. Teachers identified student misconceptions and strategies to correct those misconceptions through tailored intervention, and teachers worked to deepen students' understanding of the concepts they learned through enrichment activities. 5) All these efforts were grounded in a school culture that made students, teachers, and support personnel feel valued and respected.

At each of the six featured schools, we found rich evidence of a coherent educational improvement system that was systematically improving the initial instruction students received. Instead of trying to "cover" every state standard, teachers specified the most important challenging standards they wanted students to learn. Instead of relying upon end-of-chapter tests or summative assessments that might offer limited information about the extent to which students mastered specific objectives, teachers worked together to create common formative assessments that gave them clear indication of the extent to which individual students were developing deep understandings of essential concepts. Rather than planning instruction independently, teachers frequently worked together in grade-level or subject-matter teams to pool their knowledge and experience in ways that helped them develop engaging, powerful lessons. As well, after common formative assessments were administered, teachers worked together to analyze the data to better understand how they might improve instruction. And perhaps most importantly, in all six schools, these efforts occurred in the spirit of collaboration, never designed to label, blame, stigmatize, or punish anyone. Teachers knew they were working to support one another and, ultimately, to support every student they had the privilege to serve.

At all six schools, Black students benefitted from outstanding instruction that enabled them to learn rigorous academic skills sooner than many students in neighboring schools and districts. Black students accessed pathways to success much earlier than students in many schools because they benefitted from high-quality first instruction. They did not need to fail to acquire the quality instruction they needed.

Ensuring Student Progress through Active Student Engagement

In the featured schools, Black students were actively engaged in learning. Teachers worked collaboratively to design activities that made learning an active endeavor for every student. In contrast to more typical schools, Black students were not allowed to sit passively and fail. Teachers created environments in which Black students knew they were expected to participate, contribute, and add value. In classrooms throughout the featured schools, student voices were more prominent than teachers' voices because teachers wanted to hear how students thought about various concepts and issues. Continuously, teachers checked to determine what Black students understood and adapted their instruction accordingly. In the featured schools, many teachers regularly engaged students in project-based learning activities, providing students multiple opportunities to demonstrate understanding of important concepts and skills.

In too many classrooms across this nation, Black students can be found sitting in the back of the room, with their heads on their desks, with headphones in their ears (listening to music unrelated to the lesson being taught), or with their eyes on a magazine, comic book, or website (unrelated to the lesson being taught). Often, in these classrooms, Black students are physically present but intellectually absent. Parents send their children to be educated, and teachers are paid to teach them; however, the presence of an unwritten contract between teacher and student stipulates, "If you don't bother me, I won't bother you." "If you (student) don't interrupt my class, I won't interfere with your solitude." "If you (teacher) don't mess with me, I won't mess with your lesson." We found no evidence of such unwritten contracts at any of the featured schools. Black students knew they were expected to engage, and they knew their teachers were determined to help them learn. Teachers actively sought specific evidence that Black students were actively learning.

To maximize student engagement, Johnson et al. (2019) found that teachers in high-performing schools frequently checked to determine what students understood, their depth of understanding, and the reasoning behind their understanding. Teachers used many strategies to check levels of understanding frequently, including asking students to work in pairs or in small groups to generate responses, calling upon students randomly, asking students to write answers on dry-erase boards or whiteboards, or asking students to use technology to share their thinking. These strategies were used abundantly in the six featured schools.

Additionally, teachers in high-performing schools engaged students in ways that helped them develop fluency with key lesson vocabulary (Johnson et al., 2019). They created opportunities for students to utilize key vocabulary in conversation with one another. For example, we observed second-grade students at Patrick Henry working together to prepare their entomology report. We listened to intermediate-grade students at Concourse Village discuss inferences about the article they read concerning White flight from Harlem following the recession of 1893. We listened to ninth-grade students at Maplewood Richmond Heights High discuss various hypotheses they were considering related to a science experiment. Teachers promoted high rates of student engagement in ways that helped students develop fluency with important lesson vocabulary.

As well, teachers in high-performing schools maximized student engagement by leading students to love learning (Johnson et al., 2019). In the six featured schools, teachers infused joy into learning as they used project-based learning at Young Men's Leadership Academy and Patrick Henry Preparatory School, as they integrated the arts into the school curricula at Wynnebrook Elementary and Maplewood Richmond Heights High, as teachers maximized student-to-student engagement in highly relevant learning activities at O'Farrell Charter High and Concourse Village Elementary. Teachers worked creatively, collaboratively, and persistently to design lessons through which Black students were likely to experience joy.

It should be noted, however, that the engagement of Black students did not always come easily. Students needed to trust that teachers sincerely wanted to hear their perspectives and ideas. Too often, Black students have come to feel that teachers want to "engage" them only to expose their errors, highlight their "deficits," and take away any sense of academic competence Black students might feel. Too often, Black students wonder, "Is she calling on me to humiliate me in front of the other students?" "Is he trying to show the other kids how much I don't know?"

Feldman (2019) explained that students take risks each time they choose to engage in learning activities. He wrote:

> The student decides whether to trust the teacher, to assume the risk
> of making herself vulnerable to someone who could do her harm.

185

How does a student decide whether to trust or not to trust the teacher with that vulnerability? She evaluates the teacher's behavior when her weaknesses are exposed: "If I make a mistake or reveal that I don't know something, what will I gain or lose? If I disclose a weakness – academic or otherwise – will the teacher respond with understanding, care, and support, or with ridicule, punishment, and indifference?"

(Feldman, 2019, p. 29)

To maximize the likelihood that Black students engaged in learning, teachers at the featured schools responded consistently "with understanding, care, and support." Often, doing so is challenging because students may receive feedback as criticism, especially if the student has endured substantial negative feedback in the past. Cohen (2008) explained that sometimes, students had good reason to wonder about the intent of teachers' critical feedback. Students might wonder if feedback was a critique of their performance or a critique of their ability or intelligence. To address such important student concerns, Cohen recommended framing critical feedback in a way that emphasizes the teacher's belief in the student's ability. As an example, he suggested feedback such as: "Remember, I wouldn't go to the trouble of giving you this critical feedback if I didn't think, based on what I read in your essay, that you are capable of meeting the higher standard I mentioned" (Cohen, 2008, p. 83).

At the featured schools, teachers nurtured very high rates of engagement of Black students. They did so by creating environments in which Black students knew their teachers believed in them and wanted them to succeed. Teachers found ways to make Black students feel safe in sharing what they knew and what they didn't know. Teachers respected the engagement of Black students by acknowledging and celebrating their thinking, helping them correct their misconceptions, and celebrating their successful correction of their misconceptions. By continuously building and sustaining strong trusting relationships with students, teachers at the featured schools helped Black students believe that their teachers wanted them to succeed, almost as much as they wanted to succeed. Black students came to believe that by engaging in learning, their "dream team" teachers could help them succeed along the path to their ambitious dreams.

Building Bridges from the Known to the Unknown

When the stories read are familiar, when the problems posed have already been pondered or experienced, when the language utilized has been heard many times in different contexts, when the required steps have been rehearsed in family vacations, summer camp games, or family rituals around the dinner table, learning proceeds with a sense of ease. Often, however, Black students attend schools where learning is structured around unfamiliar stories, using semantics and syntax that sound foreign, and requiring students to perform in ways that seem alien to everything they have experienced. In contrast, in each of the six featured schools, we found many examples of teaching that utilized students' personal, social, and cultural knowledge and experiences to help students learn new concepts and skills. Teachers, working in collaboration with students, built bridges of understanding that were based solidly in what was familiar to Black students, in ways that made acquiring new knowledge seem manageable.

To build bridges of understanding, educators at the six featured schools taught in ways that exemplified culturally responsive teaching. Culturally responsive teaching includes aspects related to caring, communication, curriculum, and instruction (Gay, 2010). The importance of caring relationships in all six featured schools was emphasized in Chapter 8. When we care about students, we seek to know and understand their backgrounds, interests, concerns, strengths, and needs. Delpit (2005) emphasized the importance of teachers knowing the cultures of the students they serve so they might provide more effective instruction. Gay (2010) argued that students would achieve much more if educators taught to and through their students' personal and cultural strengths, prior accomplishments, and experiences.

Teachers who utilize culturally responsive teaching recognize that their students are more likely to develop deep understandings of concepts if they see how the concepts connect to their lives, experiences, background, and culture. For example, acclaimed educator Baruti Kafele wrote:

After my fourth year as a certified teacher in New Jersey, I was named, school, district, and county Teacher of the Year and was a finalist for New Jersey Teacher of the Year. Many asked, considering that I hadn't taught for very long, what I'd done to deserve such recognition and how my students were achieving at such high levels. I told them that I simply ensured that my students could identify culturally with what I taught. In other words, I put them in the lessons and on the pages. They saw the relevance of the lessons taught because I ensured that everything I taught spoke to them as Black students. I hadn't rewritten the curriculum; I breathed life into it and ensured that it wasn't generic. It was important to me that my students were able to connect culturally to *everything* that I taught.

(Kafele, 2021, pp. 69–70)

In the six featured schools, teachers taught the same rigorous academic standards students in other schools and districts were expected to learn; however, they taught those standards in ways that "spoke to" their Black students. The teachers "breathed life" into curricula that Black students might have considered lifeless if they could not see how the content related to them.

Specifically, in all six featured schools, teachers taught literacy standards using literature about Black children, youth, families, and communities. For example, Black students at Concourse Village, Patrick Henry, and Wynnebrook Elementary learned sophisticated comprehension skills, in part, because those skills seemed logical and easy to understand when they were used in connection with stories about Black children and Black communities. In fact, Black students at all three schools demonstrated higher rates of proficiency on literacy standards (as measured by state assessments) than statewide averages for all students.

Similarly, Black students at the three high schools advanced their literacy skills as they read, wrote about, and discussed both fiction and nonfiction that reflected Black lives and issues important in Black communities. Black students learned important concepts in English language arts, social studies, and science because they saw how the concepts taught related to their lives. For example, students at Maplewood Richmond Heights High eagerly sought to understand how glucose is an example of negative feedback in the body, because their teacher helped them understand how the issue influenced diabetes (a disease that affected several of the students' family members). Teachers at both O'Farrell High and YMLA described how they utilized literature that resonated with the lives of their students in ways that helped them teach their students challenging academic concepts.

When teachers at the featured schools utilized literature that reso-nated with Black students, issues related to race, politics, and social issues emerged. Teachers did not squelch those conversations; instead, they endeavored to create safe places where students could express their opin-ions and voice their concerns. Black students at O'Farrell Charter High were proud to have teachers who were willing to allow them to discuss difficult issues related to race. Black students at Maplewood Richmond Heights High felt honored when their teachers and administrators allowed them to organize responses to police violence against Black individuals. Black students at Concourse Village Elementary were comfortable talking with Principal Sorden about issues related to race within their community.

Teachers at the featured schools focused upon ensuring their Black students would learn the academic concepts and skills they needed to achieve their personal, academic, and professional goals. As well, teach-ers endeavored to build the cultural competence of their Black students so they appreciated and cherished their own culture while they simulta-neously learned to respect and appreciate other cultures. Additionally, teachers helped prepare their Black students to influence change in their lives, in the lives of their communities, and in the world. Ladson-Billings (2014) referred to these as the three major domains of the work of success-ful teachers. Teachers at these schools knew they were preparing students to pursue pathways toward leadership in their community and their world, not simply pathways to the next grade.

Teaching in ways that resonate with the personal, social, and cultural backgrounds of Black students is not easy (Johnson et al., 2019). Most textbooks, workbooks, teacher manuals, word problems, stories in basal readers, software programs, and many other educational tools were not written to reflect the lives of Black children, resonate with the challenges of Black communities, or elevate the spirits of Black youth. Nonetheless, in the featured schools, teachers worked together to create powerful les-sons and powerful learning opportunities for Black students. For example, at both Concourse Village and Patrick Henry, teachers worked together to identify a sequence of novels their students would read at each grade level. In particular, teachers at Patrick Henry used the work of Gholdy Muham-mad (2020) as a framework for developing the literacy of their students. At each school, the selected novels included multiple books written by Black authors and featuring positive Black characters who improved their lives and the lives of others. Teacher collaboration teams or professional learning committees (PLCs) met often to consider how they could identify, modify, or create materials, projects, or problems that would resonate with the cultures, backgrounds, and experiences of Black students. Teacher collaboration was a powerful engine of reform in these schools.

Sustaining Hope

Hope is an essential commodity in teaching and learning; however, typical American schools (especially secondary schools) are not structured to provide hope. Students are expected to bring their own supply from home. In many ways, schools assume responsibility for "managing the expectations" of Black students and their families when educators perceive students' hopes don't match how educators perceive students' abilities. We use special programs, special tracks, report card grades, test scores, behavior records, eligibility criteria for curricular and extracurricular programs, and a multitude of other tools to communicate to students and families when they should and should not be hopeful about the student's chances of success in school and success in life.

Our strategies for denying hope are particularly devastating for many Black children and youth, especially those students whose parents did not find any reason to be hopeful as they matriculated through elementary and secondary education systems. In typical schools, we find Black students who have given up hope at age 18 when they realize, at their current rate of progress, they would be 22 by the time they met all the high school graduation requirements. We find Black students who have given up hope at age 15 when they realize they cannot earn passing grades in key courses because they earned many "zeroes" in the first six weeks of the semester, so their semester average could not possibly reach the level required for a "D." We find Black students who have given up hope at age 12 when they realize they have been assigned to a low-level math track that will never give them access to the knowledge and skills they will need to succeed in either college or the workplace. We find Black students who have given up hope at age 12 when the principal tells them that their suspension will be part of their educational record for the rest of their life. We find Black students who have given up hope at age nine when they recognize that teachers feel no responsibility for trying to teach them to read, because "somebody else should have done that a long time ago." We even find Black students who have given up hope at age six when they conclude their teachers don't like them and prefer when they are absent from school.

Maximizing hope along pathways to success means minimizing the roadblocks and frustrations that can cause Black students to despair. Grading policies that punish students for what they did not know or do well at the beginning of the semester construct roadblocks that deter students from exerting the effort necessary to learn challenging academic skills later in the semester. In contrast, in the featured schools, grading policies acknowledged and celebrated what students demonstrated they knew and accomplished by the semester's end.

Discipline policies that deprive students' opportunities to participate in instruction derail students from pathways to their goals. Instead, in the featured schools, discipline policies helped students learn how to manage difficult situations, provided students a route to restore the relationships they damaged, and kept students engaged in the instruction they needed to pursue and achieve their goals.

Homework policies can create multiple barriers for students who do not have home situations and resources conducive to completing homework assignments. In the featured schools, we found teachers who were sensitive to their students' circumstances, adjusting homework expectations in ways that made assignments meaningful and reasonable for every student.

The school's master schedule articulates a wide array of policy priorities. The master schedule can make it difficult, or even impossible, for students to maintain pursuit of their ambitious goals. For example, when the only section of Advanced Placement calculus is offered at the same time as the only section of Advanced Placement physics, students who hope to pursue admission to competitive university engineering programs may be severely disadvantaged. At the featured schools, administrators, counselors, and teachers creatively developed and refined master schedules that maximized options for students.

In all six featured schools, Black students experienced hope every day. At Concourse Village, Black students heard hopeful messages from their principal and teachers as they sincerely welcomed students to school and asked them about their families. At Wynnebrook Elementary, Black students observed hope as they charted regular improvements in their Lexile levels. At Patrick Henry Preparatory School, Black students built solid foundations of hope as they experienced success in curricula just as rigorous as the curricula provided in suburban schools. At Young Men's Leadership Academy, Black students discovered hope in both their personal and academic accomplishments as they developed and practiced true leadership skills. At Maplewood Richmond Heights High, Black students felt immersed in hope as their teachers specifically described what constituted exemplary academic work and then provided the information and support they needed to accomplish it. At O'Farrell Charter High School, Black students knew their hope was justified because, upon graduation, they would qualify for admission to outstanding four-year public universities.

Empathy Interviews

Students will not pursue a pathway to success if they don't see the path, if they don't believe the path was intended for them, or if they perceive the pathway is more likely to be a dead end that leaves them feeling frustrated and humiliated. It is important for educators to ask Black students about the extent to which they perceive clear pathways for their academic, personal, and professional success. These empathy interview questions are intended to help school teams learn how they can strengthen pathways that will lead Black students to success. Even though several questions are listed, remember that successful empathy interviews usually focus on just one question at a time.

Questions for Black Students or Their Family Members

1. Question for Students: What are some of your goals for your success at school? What are some of your goals for success beyond your school years? In what ways is school helping you achieve your goals? What could we do to better help you achieve your goals?

2. Question for Students: How do you know if you're making progress toward your goals? What could we do at school to help you monitor your pursuit of your goals?

3. Question for Students: Do you believe you are on track to participate and do well in advanced classes when you reach higher grade levels? If so, what makes you believe you are on track for advanced classes? If not, what could we do to better prepare you for advanced classes?

4. Question for Family Members of Black Students: Do you believe your child is on track to participate and do well in advanced classes when he or she reaches higher grade levels? If so, what makes you believe that he or she is on track for advanced classes? If not, what could we do to better prepare your child for advanced classes?

5. Question for Students: Do you recall a recent lesson you found interesting and engaging? What was the lesson about? What made it interesting? What could your teacher(s) do to make more lessons interesting and engaging for you?

6. Question for Students: What was the last book you read in class about someone who was Black? Did you like the book? What did you like about it? Would you like to read more books with Black characters at school? Why?

7. Question for Students: Does your teacher ever return assignments for you to correct? Why do you think the teacher asks you to correct assignments? How does it make you feel?

8. Question for Students and/or Their Family Members: Do you believe you (or your child) have/has a good chance of graduating from high school? What makes you believe so? Do you believe you (or your child) have/has a good chance of attending a college or university? What makes you believe so?

Implications

All stakeholders have a role in ensuring that Black students experience strong, clear pathways to academic success and success in life. The following implications indicate how all of us can play important roles in creating pathways to ensure all Black students excel.

Implications for Parents

- Ask your child what he or she would like to accomplish in school. Ask what he or she would like to accomplish beyond high school. Help your child explore and learn more about what might be required to achieve his or her goals. Never discourage your child.

- If your child qualifies for preschool, look for a preschool with well-qualified staff, low student-teacher ratios, engaging lessons, and a warm, caring environment where Black children feel valued, accepted, and brilliant.

- If your child is in elementary school, ask school leaders what children need to know or be able to do to qualify to participate in advanced classes in middle school. Ask what is being done at your child's elementary school to prepare him or her to acquire the concepts and skills necessary to qualify for advanced classes in middle school.

- If your child is in middle school or high school (below 12th grade), ask school leaders what students need to know or be able to do to qualify to participate in Advanced Placement classes, dual-enrollment classes, career and technical education classes, or other classes/courses of study that might be of interest to your child. Ask what is being done to help prepare your child to acquire the concepts and skills necessary to qualify for these options.

- Ask teachers and school leaders what they are doing to infuse positive literature about Black individuals into the school's curricula.

Implications for School Leaders

- Encourage teachers to engage students in discussing and setting academic, personal, and professional goals for themselves. Similarly, encourage teachers to work with students to identify the factors that could enhance the likelihood they achieve their goals.

- If you lead an elementary school, promote school-wide collaboration among teachers who educate children in early grades (preschool, kindergarten, first, second, and third grades). Ensure that teachers develop a common understanding of the language, preliteracy, and literacy skills students should be able to exhibit before the end of each grade so that students are likely to become proficient readers before the end of third grade. Engage teachers in identifying, selecting, and using literature that positively reflects the lives of Black children, youth, families, and communities. Ensure that teachers know how to use the literature in a manner that builds language, critical thinking, and reading comprehension skills.

- If you lead a secondary school, organize opportunities for teachers to work together to maximize the likelihood that all students (including all Black students) will be well prepared to take advanced courses, if they choose to do so. Promote school-wide collaboration among teachers who educate middle school and high school students in core academic areas (especially English language arts, mathematics, science, and social studies). The collaboration should be designed to create a common understanding of the knowledge and skills (including study skills) students should be able to demonstrate to succeed in the most advanced courses (e.g., Advanced Placement courses, dual-enrollment courses, certain career and technical education courses) in each academic discipline. This information should be shared with students and families to motivate attention to the acquisition of the knowledge and skills specified. Also, support middle school, ninth-, and tenth-grade teachers in ways that help them embed the specified knowledge and skills into their courses. Ensure that criteria for enrollment into advanced courses is minimal, as long as students and parents understand the level of effort required to succeed in the courses. Do not allow enrollment criteria to inappropriately reduce access to advanced courses for Black students.

- If you lead a secondary school, collect and monitor data regarding the availability of advanced courses (e.g., Advanced Placement courses, dual-enrollment courses, certain career and technical education courses) at your school. Also, collect and monitor data regarding the enrollment, course grades, and national test performance (when applicable) for Black students at your school. Work with teachers, parents, and students to increase the number of Black students who are well prepared to take and succeed in advanced courses. Strive to become a school where large percentages of Black students take and succeed in advanced courses.

- To maximize the success of Black students taking advanced courses, create support structures that increase the likelihood that students will succeed in advanced courses. Ensure support structures are accessible to Black students who participate in advanced courses.

- Lead teachers throughout your school in developing coherent educational improvement systems to ensure initial (Tier I) instruction becomes increasingly effective for Black students. Work with teachers to structure collaborative planning time in ways that 1) support teachers in identifying a relatively short list of high-priority, rigorous standards all students will be expected to master by the end of each grade level or by the end of each secondary course; 2) support teachers as they work together to create, adapt, or adopt common formative assessments aligned tightly to the high-priority, rigorous standards they have identified and help teachers design a tentative calendar for administering those assessments; 3) support teachers in working together to design lessons that have a high likelihood of leading Black students to demonstrate mastery on the common formative assessments teachers created or adopted (emphasizing engaging instruction and culturally responsive teaching); 4) after common formative assessments are administered, support teachers in reviewing and learning from the assessment data and help teachers plan effective intervention and enrichment accordingly; and 5) ensure that all these are pursued in a manner that results in teachers feeling supported and valued, keeps families informed and empowered, and keeps students on the path to strong academic, personal, and professional success.

- Dedicate regular time to asking Black students and their families the empathy interview questions in the preceding section of this chapter. Engage other school personnel in participating in empathy interviews.

- Observe classrooms frequently. Persistently attend to the extent to which Black students are actively engaged in learning the lesson objectives. Acknowledge and celebrate teachers who successfully engage Black students. When teachers experience difficulty engaging Black students, provide constructive support emphasizing strategies for checking for understanding, helping students build fluency with lesson vocabulary, project-based learning, and other strategies that might increase the engagement of Black students. Help teachers remember the important role trust plays in influencing the engagement of Black students. Remember that part of your responsibility is to help your teachers feel efficacious in educating Black students. In all likelihood, they did not learn to become efficacious about educating Black students in their teacher preparation programs. To build their sense of efficacy, you must be prepared to model, support, and provide job-embedded professional development.

- Examine how your school's master schedule may positively or negatively influence learning opportunities for Black students. Work with colleagues to consider strategies for minimizing negatives and maximizing the positive impacts of the master schedule.

- Organize time for teachers to identify literature that positively reflects the lives of Black children, youth, families, and communities. Help teachers integrate this literature into their curricula. Encourage the development of a school culture that helps students appreciate and value the culture of all students who attend your school.

- Dedicate ongoing professional development time and resources to building the capacity of educators to provide culturally responsive teaching. Engage teacher collaboration teams in preparing high-quality first instruction based in culturally responsive approaches.

- Critically examine grading, homework, and discipline policies. These may lead Black students to feel hopeless. Work with teachers to modify antiquated grading policies that often lead students to give up. The best grading policies communicate what students have learned by the end of the grading period, because those policies give students a reason to keep trying and keep learning. Help teachers remember that many grading policies were designed to sort students rather than lead all students to academic success. Carefully examine homework policies, discarding those that serve little purpose other than to frustrate students who have home situations not conducive to completing homework. Reconsider discipline policies that punish students but show little success in teaching students how to manage difficult situations and choices.

Implications for Teachers

- Engage your students in discussing and setting academic, personal, and professional goals for themselves. Work with your students to identify the factors that could enhance the likelihood they achieve their goals.

- If you teach an advanced course (e.g., an Advanced Placement course, a dual-enrollment course, or challenging career technical education course) in a secondary school, specify the knowledge and skills (including study skills) students must master to succeed in your course. Share this information with students and families. Support your colleagues who teach middle school, ninth-, or tenth-grade students in embedding the knowledge and skills you have identified into the design of their courses. If you teach a course to middle school, ninth-, or tenth-grade students, encourage your colleagues who teach advanced courses to specify the knowledge and skills students must master to succeed in their courses. Then, refine your course to lead your students to be well prepared to take advanced courses if they choose to do so.

- Work with your grade-level or department colleagues to develop a coherent educational improvement system that ensures initial (Tier I) instruction becomes increasingly effective for Black students. Work with your colleagues to use planning time to 1) identify a relatively short list of high-priority, rigorous standards all students will be expected to master by the end of each grade level or by the end of each second-ary course; 2) create, adapt, or adopt common formative assessments aligned tightly to the high-priority, rigorous standards you have iden-tified and design a tentative calendar for administering those assess-ments; 3) design lessons that have a high likelihood of leading Black students to demonstrate mastery on the common formative assessments you and your colleagues created (emphasizing engaging instruction and culturally responsive teaching); 4) after common formative assess-ments are administered, review and learn from the assessment data and work with your colleagues to plan effective intervention and enrich-ment accordingly; and 5) ensure that all the above are pursued in a manner that results in your colleagues feeling supported and valued, keeps families informed and empowered, and keeps students on the path to strong academic, personal, and professional success.

- Dedicate regular time to asking Black students and their families the empathy interview questions in the preceding section of this chapter.

- Observe other classrooms frequently. Especially observe teachers who successfully engage Black students. Learn from their best practices. If you successfully engage Black students, open your classroom to other teachers. Allow them to learn from your best practices.

- Model the use of literature that positively reflects the lives of Black chil-dren, youth, families, and communities. If your school does not provide you the funds for class sets of books, seek small grants for this purpose.

- Identify one or more colleagues who are committed to enhancing their efforts to provide culturally responsive teaching. Work together to cre-ate lessons that are more likely to engage Black students.

- Critically examine grading, homework, and discipline policies that may lead Black students to feel hopeless. Modify antiquated grading policies that lead students to give up. The best grading policies communicate what students have learned by the end of the grading period, because these policies give students a reason to keep trying and keep learning. Remember that many grading policies were designed to sort students rather than lead all students to academic success. Similarly, critically examine your homework and discipline policies, discarding those that are not helping Black students excel. When we leave our students with no path to redemption, we have failed as educators.

Implications for District Leaders

- Promote district-wide collaboration among teachers who educate children in early grades (preschool, kindergarten, first, second, and third grades). Ensure that teachers develop a common understanding of the language, preliteracy, and literacy skills students should be able to exhibit before the end of each grade so that students are likely to become proficient readers before the end of third grade. Engage teachers in identifying, selecting, and using literature that positively reflects the lives of Black children, youth, families, and communities. Ensure that teachers know how to use the literature in a manner that builds language, critical thinking, and reading comprehension skills.

- Promote district-wide collaboration among teachers who educate middle school and high school students in core academic areas (especially English language arts, mathematics, science, and social studies). The collaboration should be designed to create a common understanding of the knowledge and skills (including study skills) students should master to succeed in the most advanced courses (e.g., Advanced Placement courses, dual-enrollment courses, certain career and technical education courses) in each academic discipline. This information should be shared district-wide with students and families to motivate attention to the acquisition of the knowledge and skills specified. Also, the district should support middle school, ninth-, and tenth-grade teachers in ways that help them embed the specified knowledge and skills into their courses. These efforts should be designed to maximize the number of Black students who are well prepared to succeed in advanced courses.

Ensure that criteria for enrollment into advanced courses is minimal, as long as students and parents understand the level of effort required to succeed in the courses. Do not allow schools to establish enrollment criteria that inappropriately reduce advanced course access for Black students.

- Collect and monitor data regarding the availability of advanced courses (e.g., Advanced Placement courses, dual-enrollment courses, certain career and technical education courses) at each secondary school in your district. Ensure that schools that serve large percentages of Black students offer the full range of advanced courses offered at schools that serve large percentages of White students. Also, collect and monitor data regarding the enrollment, course grades, and national test performance (when applicable) for Black students at each secondary school in your district. Work with principals to increase the number of Black students who are well prepared to take and succeed in advanced courses.

- Ensure that schools offering advanced courses also provide support structures that increase the likelihood students will succeed in advanced courses. Ensure support structures are accessible to Black students who participate in advanced courses.

- If your district has acquired scripted programs or other materials that dictate, step-by-step, what teachers should say and how teachers should teach, know that we have not found any schools generating outstanding results for Black students using such programs or materials. If your district acquired such programs or materials because you have many new or uncertified teachers who do not know how to teach rigorous academic content, understand that your new or uncertified teachers are likely to never learn how to teach rigorous academic skills to Black students as long as they are required to use scripted materials. Black students need caring, thinking teachers who are constantly learning from their practice, continuously responding to the strengths and needs of their students, and always aware of their power as educators to lead Black students to deep levels of understanding. If you place teachers (even new teachers or uncertified teachers) in situations where they do not need to learn from their practice, never need to respond to students' strengths and needs, and never experience their power to make teaching decisions that matter, you construct a huge roadblock to their professional growth and you deny Black students access to pathways to success.

- Support principals in your district in developing coherent educational improvement systems to ensure initial (Tier I) instruction becomes increasingly effective for Black students. Support principals in working with teachers to structure collaborative planning time in ways that 1) support teachers in identifying a relatively short list of high-priority, rigorous standards all students will be expected to master by the end of each grade level or by the end of each secondary course; 2) support teachers as they work together to create, adapt, or adopt common formative assessments aligned tightly to the high-priority, rigorous standards they have identified and help teachers design a tentative calendar for administering those assessments; 3) support teachers in working together to design lessons that have a high likelihood of leading Black students to demonstrate mastery on the common formative assessments teachers created or adopted (emphasizing engaging instruction and culturally responsive teaching); 4) after common formative assessments are administered, support teachers in reviewing and learning from the assessment data and help teachers plan effective intervention and enrichment accordingly; and 5) ensure all these are pursued in a manner that results in teachers feeling supported and valued, keeps families informed and empowered, and keeps students on the path to strong academic, personal, and professional success.

- Create opportunities for principals and other school leaders to work together to identify strategies for improving master schedules in ways that maximize learning opportunities for Black students.

- Eliminate district scope and sequence charts if they "cover" state standards but give teachers insufficient time to teach the standards well. Although these scope and sequence documents may have been developed with good intentions, they often have a negative impact on Black students because teachers feel pressured to rush through content without offering students sufficient opportunity to develop deep understandings. Instead, support principals and teachers in identifying a relatively short list of high-priority, rigorous standards all students will be expected to master by the end of each grade level or by the end of each secondary course.

- Eliminate district benchmark assessments if they "cover" more standards or objectives than teachers have had the opportunity to teach. Often, these assessments have a negative impact on Black students because they consume time that could be spent on teaching and learning. In addition, they do not offer teachers useful information for improving instruction. Instead, support principals and teachers as they work to develop common formative assessments aligned tightly to the high-priority, rigorous standards they have identified to teach.

- Expect principals to dedicate regular time to asking Black students and their families the empathy interview questions in the preceding section of this chapter. Expect principals to engage other school personnel in participating in empathy interviews.

- Support principals in their efforts to observe classrooms frequently. Design strategies to help principals monitor the amount of time they spend observing instruction. Work to protect principals' time so they spend less time in district meetings and less time completing paperwork. Support principals in using their classroom observation time to note the extent to which Black students are actively engaged in learning the lesson objectives. As well, support principals in providing teachers constructive feedback that can help teachers maximize the engagement of Black students. To engage and empower Black students, principals must be skillful at building teachers' sense of efficacy about educating Black students. In all likelihood, principal preparation programs did not build the capacity of your principals to elevate teachers' efficacy concerning the education of Black students. Districts committed to the success of Black students must build the capacity of principals to build this sense of efficacy among their teachers.

- Expect principals to develop a school culture that helps students appreciate and value the culture of all students who attend their school. Dedicate ongoing professional development time and resources to building the capacity of educators to provide culturally responsive teaching.

- Critically examine district grading, homework, and discipline policies that often lead Black students to feel hopeless. Work with principals and teachers to modify antiquated grading policies that lead students to give up. Carefully examine homework policies, discarding those that serve little purpose other than to frustrate students who have home situations not conducive to completing homework. Reconsider discipline policies that punish students but show little success in teaching students how to manage difficult situations and choices.

Implications for Institutions of Higher Education

- Ensure that candidates for credentials/certificates/licensure as teachers, counselors, or school administrators understand their roles in helping students develop ambitious goals for their academic, personal, and professional success. As well, ensure that candidates understand the importance of helping students understand the factors that are likely to influence their success in achieving their goals. Especially, ensure that candidates understand that our responsibility, as educators, is to support all children and youth, including Black children and youth, in achieving their goals.

- Ensure elementary teacher candidates develop a strong understanding of the language, preliteracy, and literacy skills students should be able to exhibit before the end of each grade so that students are likely to become proficient readers before the end of third grade. Engage elementary teacher candidates in identifying, selecting, and using literature that positively reflects the lives of Black children, youth, families, and communities. Ensure teachers know how to use the literature in a manner that builds language, critical thinking, and reading comprehension skills.

- Some educator preparation programs do not prepare teachers to be strong collaborators who are skillful at both learning from and supporting their colleagues. Institutions of higher education should focus upon providing educator candidates opportunities to learn and practice collaboration skills that support ongoing improvement in learning outcomes for Black students, especially as a result of high-quality initial (Tier I) instruction.

- Design preparation programs in ways that help candidates realize that Black students can and will learn challenging academic content when educators teach content with a clear focus on specific learning objectives, in ways that build positive relationships with Black students, and in ways that promote high levels of engagement among Black students. Your preparation program should ensure candidates develop a core belief that Black students will learn rigorous academic content when educators structure learning environments in ways that build upon the strengths and respond to the needs of Black students.

203

- Teacher candidates will not exit your preparation program with a sense of efficacy about educating Black students unless they have opportunities to work with, and learn from, teachers who possess a strong sense of efficacy for educating Black students. Identify teacher role models and provide opportunities for your candidates to learn from them.

- Leadership candidates will not exit your preparation program prepared to lead schools that serve Black students well unless they have opportunities to learn how to build teachers' sense of efficacy about teaching Black students. Identify principal role models and provide opportunities for your candidates to learn from them.

- Design leadership preparation programs in ways that build the capacity of leaders to support teachers in improving teaching and learning for Black students. Support leaders in learning how to work with teams of teachers to develop coherent educational improvement systems that result in Black students excelling.

- Prepare leadership candidates to understand that leadership roles require them to stay attuned to the perspectives and needs of Black students and their families. Ensure that leadership candidates have opportunities to participate in and lead empathy interviews with Black students and their families.

- Prepare leadership candidates to observe classrooms frequently in ways that support teachers in increasing the engagement of Black students. Leadership candidates should learn and practice using classroom observations to note the extent to which Black students are actively engaged in learning the lesson objectives. As well, candidates should learn and practice providing teachers constructive feedback that can help teachers maximize the engagement of Black students.

- Prepare leadership candidates to develop school cultures within which teachers appreciate and value the culture of all students who attend their school. Dedicate specific course time to building aspiring principal's understanding of culturally responsive teaching.

- While many colleges of education help education candidates learn the importance of advocating for social justice, many new teachers, counselors, and school leaders do not realize how policies and practices they experienced as elementary and secondary students are, in fact, barriers to social justice for Black students. Preparation programs should help candidates critically examine grading, homework, and discipline policies, master schedules, teacher assignment practices, and many other policies and practices that may inhibit the success of Black students. Candidates should learn how they can utilize their professional roles in ways that promote constructive change in policies and practices.

Implications for Policy Makers

- Work with superintendents to promote district-wide collaboration among teachers who educate children in early grades (preschool, kindergarten, first, second, and third grades). In many districts, such collaboration may be most effective during summers or intersessions. Work with superintendents to ensure that the collaboration results in teachers developing a common understanding of the language, preliteracy, and literacy skills students should be able to exhibit before the end of each grade so that students are likely to become proficient readers before the end of third grade. The collaboration should be designed to ensure that teachers identify, select, and use literature that positively reflects the lives of Black children, youth, families, and communities. Policy makers should ensure that funding is available to purchase classroom sets of the literature selected.

- Work with superintendents to promote district-wide collaboration among teachers who educate middle school and high school students in core academic areas (especially English language arts, mathematics, science, and social studies). The collaboration should be designed to create a common understanding of the knowledge and skills (including study skills) students should master to succeed in the most advanced courses (e.g., Advanced Placement courses, dual-enrollment courses, certain career and technical education courses) in each academic discipline. This information should be shared district-wide with students and families to motivate attention to the acquisition of the knowledge and skills specified. Also, the collaboration should lead middle school, ninth-, and tenth-grade teachers in ways that help them embed the specified knowledge and skills into their courses. Almost every course, in core academic areas, should be designed to prepare students to take and succeed in advanced courses. These efforts should be designed to

205

maximize the number of Black students who are well prepared to succeed in advanced courses. Policy makers should ensure that schools do
not construct artificial barriers that reduce access to advanced courses
for Black students.

- Policy makers should expect district leaders to collect and monitor data
regarding the availability of advanced courses (e.g., Advanced Placement courses, dual-enrollment courses, certain career and technical
education courses) at secondary schools. Policy makers should expect
superintendents to improve the extent to which schools that serve large
percentages of Black students offer the full range of advanced courses
offered at schools that serve large percentages of White students. As
well, policy makers should expect superintendents to collect and present data regarding the enrollment, course grades, and national test
performance (when applicable) for Black students at each secondary
school in the district. State policy makers should ensure that these data
are available to parents statewide.

- Policy makers, at both the state and the district level, should ensure students who take advanced courses also have the benefit of support structures that increase the likelihood students will succeed in advanced
courses. Policy makers should ensure support structures are accessible
to Black students who participate in advanced courses.

- Support superintendents in eliminating district scope and sequence
charts if they "cover" state standards but give teachers insufficient time
to teach the standards well. Although these scope and sequence documents may have been developed with good intentions, they often have
a negative impact on Black students because teachers feel pressured to
rush through content without offering students sufficient opportunity to
develop deep understandings.

- Eliminate district benchmark assessments if they "cover" more standards
or objectives than teachers have had the opportunity to teach. Often,
these assessments have a negative impact on Black students because
they consume time that could be spent on teaching and learning. In
addition, they do not offer teachers useful information for improving
instruction. Instead, districts should support principals and teachers as
they work to develop common formative assessments aligned tightly to
the high-priority, rigorous standards they have identified to teach.

- Support principals in their efforts to observe classrooms frequently. Design strategies to help principals monitor the amount of time they spend observing instruction. Work to protect principals' time so they spend less time in district meetings and less time completing paperwork. Support principals in using their classroom observation time to note the extent to which Black students are actively engaged in learning the lesson objectives. As well, support principals in providing teachers constructive feedback that can help teachers maximize the engagement of Black students.

- Expect superintendents to develop a district-wide culture that encourages students, teachers, support staff, and administrators to appreciate and value the cultures of all students who attend their school. Dedicate ongoing professional development time and resources to building the capacity of educators to provide culturally responsive teaching and the capacity of school leaders to encourage and support culturally responsive teaching.

- Critically examine district grading, homework, and discipline policies that often lead Black students to feel hopeless. Work with superintendents to modify antiquated grading policies that lead students to give up. Carefully examine homework policies and discard those that serve little purpose other than to frustrate students who have home situations that are not conducive to completing homework. Reconsider discipline policies that punish students but show little success in teaching students how to manage difficult situations and choices.

References

Cohen, G. L. (2008). Providing supportive feedback. In M. Pollock (Ed.), *Everyday antiracism: Getting real about race in school* (pp. 82–84). The New Press.

Delpit, L. (2005). *Other people's children: Cultural conflict in the classroom* (2nd ed.). The New Press.

Delpit, L. (2012). *"Multiplication is for White people": Raising expectations for other people's children*. The New Press.

Feldman, J. (2019). *Grading for equity: What it is, why it matters, and how it can transform schools and classrooms.* Corwin.

Ferguson, R. F. (2008). Helping students of color meet high standards. In M. Pollock (Ed.), *Everyday antiracism: Getting real about race in school* (pp. 78–81). The New Press.

Gay, G. (2010). *Culturally responsive teaching: Theory, research, and practice* (2nd ed.). Teachers College Press.

Hammond, Z. (2015). *Culturally responsive teaching and the brain: Promoting authentic engagement and rigor among culturally and linguistically diverse students.* Corwin.

Howard, T. C. (2001). Powerful pedagogy for African American students: A case of four teachers. *Urban Education, 36,* 179–202.

Johnson, J. F., Uline, C. L., & Perez, L. G. (2017). *Leadership in America's best urban schools.* Routledge.

Johnson, J. F., Uline, C. L., & Perez, L. G. (2019). *Teaching practices from America's best urban schools: A guide for school and classroom leaders* (2nd edition). Routledge.

Kafele, B. K. (2021). *The equity and social just education 50: Critical questions for improving opportunities and outcomes for Black students.* ASCD.

Ladson-Billings, G. (2014). Culturally relevant pedagogy 2.0: a.k.a. the Remix. *Harvard Educational Review, 84*(1), 74–84.

Lee, V. E., Smith, J. B., Perry, T. E., & Smylie, M. A. (1999). *Social support, academic press, and student achievement: A view from the middle grades in Chicago.* Consortium on Chicago School Research.

Meloy, B., Gardner, M., & Darling-Hammond, L. (2019). *Untangling the evidence on preschool effectiveness: Insights for policymakers.* Learning Policy Institute.

Mesmer, E. M., & Mesmer, A. E. (2008). Response to intervention (RTI): What teachers of reading need to know. *The Reading Teacher, 62*(4), 280–290.

Muhammad, G. (2020). *Cultivating genius: An equity framework for culturally and historically responsive literacy.* Scholastic.

Taylor, A. (2008). Teaching and transcending basic skills. In M. Pollock (Ed.), *Everyday antiracism: Getting real about race in school* (pp. 86–89). The New Press.

Wagner, T. (2008). *Rigor redefined*. ASCD. Retrieved November 11, 2021, from www.ascd.org/el/articles/rigor-redefined

Afterword

If this book included profiles of 60, or even 600, schools where Black students achieved outstanding educational outcomes, some individuals would find reason to discount the possibility that Black students could excel in their state, district, school, or classroom. This book was not written for those individuals.

Some individuals will take pains to identify and highlight the imperfections among the schools we featured. This book was not written for those individuals. None of the educators we interviewed claimed perfection. Instead, in every featured school we found educators who urgently sought greater successes for each Black student they served. We are honored to include these schools, not only because of their accomplishments, but also because of their passionate pursuit of *greater* accomplishments on behalf of their students.

This book was written for those who know, deep in their souls, Black children are born brilliant, with impressive intellectual curiosity, creativity, and wisdom, and with tremendous capacity to excel academically. This book was written for those who believe we face a collective challenge to employ all we know and all we believe as we reshape our classrooms, schools, districts, educator preparation programs, and state education agencies in ways that ensure our Black students excel.

Paul Batalden from Dartmouth University is frequently credited with saying, "Every system is perfectly designed to achieve the results it gets" (see www.ihi.org/communities/blogs/origin-of-every-system-is-perfectly-designed-quote). This book was written for those who aim to perfectly design systems (small and large) to achieve outstanding results for Black students. We hope this book supports the ongoing efforts of those who seek to exert their leadership as teachers, school administrators, parents, counselors, school support personnel, university professors, college of education deans, principal supervisors, district administrators, superintendents, local school board members, state education agency administrators, or state policy makers to create schools that engage and empower Black students. In the stories of the six featured schools, we hope you discover practical tools and strategies to assist you in reinventing "school" in a way that is perfectly designed to lead Black students to excel.

We recognize, however, that readers may need additional resources to accelerate progress toward educational equity and excellence. Toward this end, we provide the following suggestions:

1. Visit schools that are achieving outstanding learning results for Black students. Encourage a colleague to join you. If you cannot visit one of the schools identified in this book, work with your district or state leaders to identify schools that do not use selective admissions and still achieve outstanding evidence of educational success for Black students across multiple indicators. If you cannot visit in person, visit virtually by inviting principals, teachers, or other personnel from outstanding schools to meet with you. As you visit, pay close attention to the way leaders are influencing outstanding results for Black students to determine how their practices relate to the practices described in Chapter 7. As well, attend to the way educators are creating environments that cause Black students to experience belonging, love, and joy at school. Note the specific practices that relate to the descriptions in Chapter 8. Finally, attend to the way educators have shaped pathways that make success likely for Black students. See how the practices utilized compare to those described in Chapter 9.

2. As you learn more, do more. In the classroom, school, district, or state where you work, identify a major learning outcome for Black students that needs improvement. Then, identify a small (but important) step toward the attainment of that outcome. Engage a group of stakeholders who can help play a role in achieving the small step you hope to achieve. Work with the stakeholders to identify an evaluation strategy for determining if the small step you hope to achieve is effective in making a difference for Black students. Then, engage stakeholders in determining what might need to change in order to improve both

relational issues and curricular/instructional issues that may impact the attainment of the small step. The empathy interview questions in Chapters 7, 8, and 9 may be helpful.

3. As you do more, keep learning from your practice. Identify thought partners (outside of your stakeholder group) who can help you refine your efforts in ways more likely to achieve results. Keep attuned to changes (or lack of changes) in your data. Always seek input from students, parents, and teachers to help understand the challenges you encounter. As you identify successes, always celebrate the efforts of everyone who contributed.

4. Visit the National Center for Urban School Transformation's website (www.ncust.com) to learn more about the center's programs and supports. Participate in the center's efforts to celebrate and learn from schools around the nation that achieve outstanding results for every demographic group. Reach out with your questions and partner with this organization and other organizations that are committed to helping schools engage and empower Black students.

There is nothing easy about changing the tide of 400 years of history. Fortunately, however, the schools featured in this book help us know it can be done. It *is* being done in some places. Across this nation, we can create schools that are perfectly designed to lead Black students to excel. Today is a perfect day to accelerate our progress accordingly. Our children deserve nothing less.

Index